THE VIETNAM VETERAN REDEFINED

REDEFINED

Fact and Fiction

THE VIETNAM VETERAN REDEFINED

Fact and Fiction

Edited by

Ghislaine Boulanger
Charles Kadushin

Center for Social Research
The Graduate School and University Center
The City University of New York

LEA LAWRENCE ERLBAUM ASSOCIATES, PUBLISHERS
1986 Hillsdale, New Jersey   London

Lawrence Erlbaum Associates, Inc., Publishers
365 Broadway
Hillsdale, New Jersey 07642

Library of Congress Cataloging-in-Publication Data
Main entry under title:

The Vietnam veteran redefined.

Bibliography: p.
Includes index.
1. Veterans—Mental health—United States.
2. Vietnamese Conflict, 1961–1975—Psychological
aspects. 3. Posttraumatic stress disorder.
I. Boulanger, Ghislaine. II. Kadushin, Charles.
RC451.4.V48V54 1986   616.85′212   85-15965
ISBN 0-89859-761-7

Printed in the United States of America
10 9 8 7 6 5 4 3 2 1

For Isaac

"When will they ever learn?"
— *Pete Seeger*

May your generation be the one to learn.

Contents

PART II
Social Support

    — *Charles Kadushin*

10. Effects of Support on Demoralization and Problem Drinking   133
    — *John L. Martin*

11. Women Friends of Men   153
    — *Sheryl Canter*

    Appendices   165

    Afterword — Who Can Take Away the Grief of the Wound?   171
    — *Chaim Shatan*

    References   181

    Author Index   191

    Subject Index   197

Acknowledgments

As we explain in the Introduction, the data on which this book is based were collected with the help of a grant from the National Institute of Mental Health (MH 26832) and a contract from the Veterans Administration. A second grant from NIMH (MH 34580) permitted us to pursue those topics that were of particular interest to each of us. We are grateful to NIMH and to the VA for giving us the opportunity to undertake this work.

It was a call for papers from the Society for the Psychological Study of Social Issues that first prompted us to find a connecting thread between our widely differing interests. In August 1982, the theme for the SPSSI program at the American Psychological Association Meetings was "Redefining Social Issues." It occurred to us that the thrust of our analyses was an attempt to understand and redefine the several myths about Vietnam veterans that had begun to circulate in American society. This book is an expansion of the symposium, "Further Legacies of Vietnam," that we gave at those meetings in 1982.* At that time we profited from the wise comments of Jule Segal, whose emphasis on coping and survival during and after periods of psychic trauma offers an important counterpoint to the current interest in the destructive nature of trauma.

Many friends and colleagues have offered encouragement and criticism over the years since we first became involved in researching the aftermath of Vietnam. Jay Schulman recruited Charles Kadushin to the cause of Vietnam veteran research in 1975. Jack Elinson, David Sills, and Yole Sills offered valuable comparisons to the *American Soldier* data. Jack Ewalt, then at the

---

*Chapters 2, 3, 6, 7 and 8 are adapted from papers delivered at those meetings.

Veterans Administration, offered encouragement. For the last five years, Robert Allen has been a source of support and frequently contributed a new perspective to our work. John Clausen read parts of the final manuscript and offered some helpful comments. Bruce Dohrenwend kindly permitted us to use the PERI scales he and his colleagues had developed and was equally generous with time and advice. Ronald Kessler was an invaluable consultant. Harold Proshansky, President of the Graduate Center at the City University of New York, offered his support and made additional time available. Morton Bard, who was Director of the Center for Social Research at CUNY until his retirement this year, offered both institutional support and insights into victimization.

Obviously, this book could not have been written without our contributors, whom we would also like to thank for their forebearance during the time it has taken to prepare the manuscript for the publisher. Special thanks go to John Martin, who, in addition to his own analyses, undertook several other data processing tasks over the years. The staff of the Computer Facility at the Graduate Center of the City University of New York deserves special mention for their cooperation and efficiency. Sharon Kahn did meticulous work checking and rechecking references. Over the last year, Halina Maslanka has supported us on so many levels — editorial, organizational, and emotional — that we can honestly say we do not know where we or the book in its final form would be without her.

There have been so many late evening talks with so many Vietnam veterans over so many years that we would inevitably leave out names if we tried to recall them all. But three men in particular have contributed to our understanding of veteran issues and our determination to present the facts in all their complexity. They are David Grady, Jack Smith, and Tom Williams. We also wish to express our gratitude to the veterans who consented to be interviewed for this study between 1976 and 1979. At a time when America was less sensitive to the difficulties that Vietnam veterans had in talking about their experiences, our respondents' courage made this book possible. Last of all, we want to thank the Vietnam veterans we did not interview, whom our respondents represent.

Ghislaine Boulanger
Charles Kadushin
Fishers Island, N. Y.
December 31, 1985

Contributors

Ghislaine Boulanger, Ph.D. is a clinical psychologist in private practice and Research Associate at the Center for Social Resarch, CUNY. She is Co-director of the Psychology Externship Program at the New Hope Guild.

Martha Ann Carey, R.N. is a graduate student in the Social/Personality Program of the Graduate Center, CUNY.

Sheryl Canter is a graduate student in the Social/Personality Program of the Graduate Center, CUNY.

Helen Dermatis, R.N. is a graduate student in the Social/Personality Program of the Graduate Center of CUNY.

Charles Kadushin, Ph.D. is Professor, Sociology and Psychology, Graduate Center of CUNY.

Nava Lerer is a graduate student in the Social/Personality Program of the Graduate Center of CUNY.

John L. Martin, Ph.D. MPH is a senior researcher with the School of Public Health, Columbia University.

Randy Martin, Ph.D. is Associate Professor with the department of Anthropology and Sociology at Rhodes College, Memphis.

David M. Rindskopf, Ph.D. is Associate Professor, Education and Psychology, Graduate Center, CUNY.

Laurie Michael Roth, Ph.D. is Research Associate, Columbia University School of Business.

Chaim Shatan, M.D., Clinical Professor, Postdoctoral Psychoanalytic Program, New York University, received the first Annual Holocaust Memorial Award. He has worked on the psychological impact of man-made catastrophes since 1970.

1 Introduction

Charles Kadushin
Ghislaine Boulanger

American involvement in the centuries old struggle between North and South Vietnam officially ended with the American surrender on April 30, 1975. In the twelve years during which the American government backed the various South Vietnamese regimes against encroachments from the Communist North, 45,958 Americans were killed in action; 10,303 more died from other causes in Vietnam; 734 men were reported missing in action; and 303,704 troops were wounded; at least half of them seriously.[1] But the casualties did not end with the ceasefire. For at least a decade, the war has continued to be the subject of political and social turmoil as the causes, nature, and consequences of American involvement in Southeast Asia have been reassessed and the problems of American Vietnam War veterans discussed.

Despite significant gains made by the majority of Vietnam veterans since the war, in many instances, public attitudes toward the veterans have taken up where the enemy's bullets left off. Vietnam veterans have been a continuing source of concern, embarrassment, fear, or distrust to the American public, to politicians, to future employers, to the legal and mental health professions. In addition, the media and the film industry frequently capitalize on the myths, misconceptions, and distortions of fact that surround the veterans and their adjustment to peacetime America. There is an abundance of speculation about the nature, source, and extent of the veterans' problems, but very few studies have been in a position to make definitive statements about these men and women. In this book we examine some of the myths that surround the Vietnam veteran community and, in the light of empirical stud-

---

[1] These figures were extrapolated from a Department of Defense (OASD Comptroller) memorandum dated January 15, 1976.

1

ies, establish to what extent the myths are fact and to what extent, fiction. First, however, it may be important to examine the larger social and political context in which this empirical study was undertaken and to contrast this work with research on the consequences of earlier wars.

There is, in fact, a significant precedent in the American social sciences for studies of the effects of combat on the men and women who participated. The two volumes of the American Soldier (Stouffer, Lumsdaine et al., 1949; Stouffer, Suchman, DeVinney, Star, & Williams, 1949) together with Houland, Lumsdaine, and Sheffield (1949) and Stouffer et al. (1950) are among the most illustrious applied studies of any topic. Thirty-five years after the publication of this work there still seems to be consensus that these studies had a major impact on basic theory and methods in the social sciences. The contrast between studies carried out during World War II and those dealing with the aftermath of Vietnam are instructive. When we understand some of these differences, a discussion of methodological and theoretical outcomes of research on the epidemiology of the war in Vietnam may have greater meaning.

Except for a few pacifists, the social science community was united in opposing the Axis powers through any means. For many social scientists, this meant applying their professional talents to the problem of winning the war. Through a series of events related in some detail elsewhere (Buck, 1985), a research group was formed in the War Department with the belief that public opinion and propaganda studies would materially help in motivating soldiers to perform more effectively. This research group was able to draw on the finest talents then available to social science. The list of participants now reads like an honor roll of leading methodologists and theorists (Clausen 1984a). While some of the participants were, even at the time, known to be giants in the field, many became much better known in the years that followed (Clausen, 1984b).

The political problems of conducting applied research in a setting in which national goals are primary will be addressed shortly. But the bureaucratic problems should not be forgotten. Samuel Stouffer made the following comments in his "Afterthoughts to *The American Soldier*" (1950):

the very fact that the American Soldier has received a certain amount of acclaim may mislead not only students but also their elders, who may be in important positions in universities or foundations, into thinking that the kind of atmosphere in which our work was done is exceptionally favorable for social science. Most of our time was wasted, irretrievably wasted, insofar as any contribution to social science was concerned.... In order to help the Army, or to "sell" research to the Army, I had to be concerned first and foremost with what was immediately wanted or purchasable. When I supported longer range studies, I ran the risk of being suspect of trying to exploit our situation for social science and on several occasions was severely censured by superiors. (pp. 200-201)

Bureaucratic wisdom may not have always served the Army's best interests. The talents of the Research Branch were sometimes devoted to studies of "whether men preferred Coca-Cola to Pepsi Cola or whether they preferred nuts in their candy bars" (Stouffer, 1950). Still, there were some important gains for both policy and social science.

Though it is often difficult to pinpoint the effects of research on policy makers, it seems that the only incontrovertible direct policy application of the Research Branch's extensive work was the "point" system used after the war to demobilize those soldiers who had seen the most combat; had been overseas; had children; and had been in the service for the most time (Buck, 1985). Otherwise, the Research Branch soon discovered that ideology accounted for few measurable differences in motivation among soldiers. When this obvious application of public opinion and propaganda studies was dismissed as inconsequential, the Research Branch concentrated on the effects of "primary groups" on combat effectiveness and attention turned to more micro phenomena. Guttman scaling and latent structure analysis; "reference group" theory (further developed during a reanalysis of the data in Merton and Lazarsfeld, 1950), the concept of "relative deprivation"; the rediscovery of the impact of primary groups; and the development of the first screening scales for mental disorder were all covered first in these four volumes (not too bad a score, considering Stouffer's frustrations). Among the many important analyses undertaken was a classic description of the horrors of war as seen by the participants.

The differences between the war in Vietnam and World War II are obvious. The lack of support of the war in Vietnam in the social science community meant that few major social scientists contributed to the war effort while it was going on. In fact, anthropologists and sociologists who did contribute to studies of "pacification" were severely castigated. A major field work study of the role of primary groups in the military (in the tradition of *The American Soldier*) was conducted by Moskos (1970) but funded by a private foundation. Thus, any studies of the war or its aftermath are after the fact rather than based on contemporary data. Further, the lack of major mobilization meant that the social scientists who work in this field would not have the prestige of the World War II group. The most important difference between World War II and Vietnam War studies, however, is their focus.

Although the Research Branch documented in detail that war is bad for one's health, the patriotic thrust of the work turned most of the research in other directions; the country's need to get on with peace, prosperity, and the Cold War also meant that there was little concern for the long-term impact of war on those who were participating in it. In contrast, then, the major concern of present unclassified applied studies of war (aside from a continuing interest in primary group effectiveness) is the long-run effects of war on former soldiers.

The political context of this research is critical to an understanding of its nature. The genesis of current research on the aftermath of the war in Vietnam grew out of the concerns of many veterans with their own and their peers' adjustment problems and their impression that they were viewed by the public and the government with indifference, or loathing, or both. The impetus for the research reported in this volume began at the First National Conference on the Emotional Problems of Vietnam Era Veterans in St. Louis in April of 1973. The group, composed of one third Vietnam veterans, one third Chaplains, and one third mental health professionals, felt that many veterans had a host of psychosocial problems no one was prepared to acknowledge. Further, they felt they were the victims of circumstance, that they were being blamed for a situation over which they had little or no control. It was difficult to deal with such a situation. The best they could do was to document the true state of Vietnam veterans so that no one could claim to be biased or self-serving. It was hoped that once the government or the public saw what was happening and what had happened to veterans the veterans would be seen in a different light; something would be done for those (believed to be a minority) who were experiencing serious problems in postwar adjustment. Through various networks these veterans enlisted social scientists (most of whom had radical backgrounds and who saw this work simply as another, though different, anti-war activity) who worked as volunteers, designing studies of veterans and raising the funds necessary to carry them out.

The volunteer research group (composed of a mix of Vietnam veterans and social scientists) managed to raise small sums of money from private foundations — in amounts ranging from a few hundred to a few thousand dollars. Eventually, in 1976, a grant was obtained from NIMH to study 450 Vietnam veterans and their nonveteran counterparts in the Northeastern United States and in Toronto, Canada.

Most of the research subsequent to this grant, and all subsequent data collection, was done under contract with the Veterans Administration. The fate of the Canadian sample illustrates one of the differences between grants and contracts. The research team was interested in the situation of draft resisters and military deserters — they, too, were victims of the war. The Veterans Administration, however, had no interest in resisters and deserters, and the Canadian aspects of the study were dropped from further research efforts.

This brings us to a discussion of the way the basic research interests of the social scientists intermeshed with the subject matter and research needs of the Vietnam veterans who were the first "clients" for the research and who remain (three contracts and at least two grants later) the ultimate clients, though various governmental and bureaucratic filters now stand between the researchers and the Vietnam veterans.

The major interests of the clients of this and subsequent studies of Vietnam veterans have always been in the "marginals", which is true of most applied research. In this case, our clients focused on the percentage of Vietnam veterans experiencing psychosocial adjustment difficulties. In 1981, Congress made public the findings of the first federally funded nationwide survey that compared the psychological and social adjustment of Vietnam veterans with that of their peers. (Kadushin, Boulanger, & Martin, 1981). The 1380 respondents in this multisite probability sample were stratified for age, race, and military status. When the sample was weighted, it reflected national norms on several critical dimensions and could be generalized to the population as a whole. The key finding concerned the extent of Posttraumatic Stress Disorder (PTSD) among Vietnam combat veterans, one third of whom experienced a disproportionate number of stress symptoms. The stress reaction was more intense and more likely to persist among men whose position in our society made them less able to cope — blacks and other minorities, the unemployed or irregularly employed, the poor, and men with varying levels of stability in their families when they were children.

Thus the parameters of the problem were established and our clients' needs met. The report's findings were used by Congress as justification for mandating the continuation through 1989 of the Veteran Outreach Centers. These Vet Centers were established by the Veterans Administration to meet the needs of veterans so alienated by the bureaucracy of the traditional Veterans Administration Medical Centers and their failure to treat Vietnam veterans successfully that they avoided such services.

Unlike Stouffer and his associates, the researchers who undertook this study of Vietnam veterans initially did so on a voluntary basis, and, free of contractual constraints, they extended the focus of their work beyond the headcount initially requested by their clients. Many personal intellectual interests were pursued but not reported in depth in the government report. The funds to develop these ideas further came not from the Veterans Administration but from the National Institute of Mental Health and the university, just as the funds to write *The American Soldier* (Stouffer, Lumsdaine, et al., 1949; Stouffer, Suchman, et al., 1949) came from the Social Science Research Council and the Carnegie Foundation, not from the Department of the Army. Although this is an interesting footnote to this account of the similarities and differences encountered during the process of researching the effects of the World War II and the war in Vietnam, we do not imply that the outcomes are comparable.

In the present book the authors of Volume IV of *The Legacies of Vietnam: Comparative Adjustment of Veterans and Their Peers,* a study prepared for the Veterans Administration, further explore their own intellectual interests, addressing themselves to the public stereotypes of Vietnam veterans and asking how such stereotypes should be redefined in light of current findings. For example, many believe that the men who went to Vietnam represent a self-selected sample of misfits and dropouts who would never have fitted into society under any circumstances. Others hold that the experiences in Vietnam turned men into junkies or alienated them from the political mainstream. What about the media view of the physically violent veterans — is this a just representation? The notion of Vietnam veterans healing themselves and each other through informal "rap" groups has become legend in psychotherapy circles. Under what conditions, and to what extent, does this informal therapy work? What other informal resources exist in the community to alleviate the stresses veterans experience?

The chapters in this volume address each of these questions (and several more) from a common data base, described in detail in the Appendix A to this volume. They do not simply prove or disprove the stereotypical views, but show under what conditions the stereotype might hold true; where it is false; and where, if it is true, it is true not only of veterans of Vietnam but of veterans of other wars.

Because the psychological and social consequences of war are so dependent on the characteristics of the men who went to war, the first stereotype with which we must deal is that, unlike other American wars, the Vietnam conflict was a class war. It has been claimed that men from working class backgrounds were much more likely to enter the military during the Vietnam era, to serve in combat, and to suffer casualties than were men from higher classes. Similar claims have been made about racial inequities. It was thought that blacks were more likely to serve in Vietnam, to enter combat, and to die. In Chapter 2, we show that the class part of the myth is, in part, true. Lower class men were more likely to enter the military, but this has been true in America at least since the Civil War; Vietnam was no exception. However, except for officers, who tended to come from the ranks of the better educated and who were more likely to serve in combat, the military was largely blind to prior social class. Race is a more complex issue. In fact, there are few differences between blacks and whites overall in the proportion likely to serve in the military, though there are considerable local differences in this respect. Blacks were slightly more likely to serve in combat, although in our samples, the differences do not hold up statistically. But rank favored whites, even among enlisted men. Furthermore there were at least twice as many disciplinary actions against blacks as against whites. In many qualitative ways, blacks experienced inequality in Vietnam. These inequities may be responsible for the myth that the war in Vietnam was a white man's war.

Although this analysis occurs after the fact and there is little opportunity to redress whatever racial and social class imbalances may have occurred, in dispelling or supporting popular beliefs about the types of men who went to war, Chapter 2 provides a background against which the other chapters in this volume may be considered.

Related to the notion that men who served in Vietnam were more likely to be black or lower class is the assumption that those men who were not able to avoid the draft, or who actually enlisted for service in Vietnam, were psychologically vulnerable. Thus, because a significant minority of Vietnam veterans developed severe psychological problems since the war, their problems are attributed not to the war but to earlier vulnerability. There is a cherished myth in America that "war makes a man of you." This myth is important politically; it supports war as a worthwhile activity. If combat has long lasting and debilitating psychological consequences, even among those who were not physically wounded, then there are good reasons to oppose war as a national policy. Moreover, if it is shown that war produces psychological problems, then there are serious fiscal implications for a country with a large Veterans Administration dedicated to the care of wounded veterans.

Chapters 3 and 4 explore the etiology and the form of psychological problems to which many Vietnam veterans have fallen prey. Chapter 3 shows that this syndrome is exhibited not only by some Vietnam veterans, but also by veterans of earlier wars and by victims of violent crimes, natural disasters, flash fires, and other life threatening disasters. In this chapter, it is demonstrated that the symptoms experienced by survivors form a comprehensive syndrome distinct from depression, other forms of anxiety reactions and psychosis — all categories that in the past have been applied to these survivors. Chapter 3 also shows that men exposed to heavy combat are substantially more likely than other veterans to exhibit the special set of symptoms now called Posttraumatic Stress Disorder.

Chapter 3 having established the coherence of the diagnosis and its relation to combat exposure, Chapter 4 raises the question of predisposition as the latent cause of reactions to trauma. A measure of predisposition is developed that is not dependent on retrospective psychological diagnosis, but on the stability of the family of origin. The stereotype of the Vietnam draftee or enlistee as a man who was likely to be psychologically impaired is at least partly dispelled. Men who were predisposed to serious psychopathology were less likely than others to find their way into the military, but those who did get to Vietnam were more likely to see heavy combat. The findings in this chapter, while complex, demonstrate that under extreme conditions even men from the most stable families are at risk.

It has been demonstrated, then, that combat is a significant source of psychological distress. In Chapter 5, we ask whether there are ways in which the psychological distress of combat might be mitigated during the battle itself. Since the days of Homer, we have been led to believe that comradeship helps soldiers carry on in the face of terror. Translated into more modern terms, this becomes the ideal of primary group cohesion explored in *The American Soldier*. According to this view, solidarity among the troops is based not on some ideological cause such as freedom or justice but, rather, on comradeship fostered by unit traditions and long time association begun during basic training. It has been argued that solidarity (primary group cohesion) prevents men from running away and thereby letting down their colleagues. Primary group cohesion makes for a more effective fighting unit less likely to break down in battle. In Vietnam, so the myth goes, primary group cohesion was undermined by the practice of rotating troops individually, rather than in units, and by racial conflict. After the Tet offensive in 1968, primary group cohesion was alleged to have decreased, and the American army experienced the symptoms of "disintegration." Our data suggest that although the myths that combat units have higher cohesion, and that the Marines in particular enjoy high cohesion, are true, there was no evidence after 1968 of a decline in the proportion of men who experienced this cohesion. Though we have no direct measures of combat effectiveness, our data suggest that group cohesion leads to higher rates of posttraumatic stress in the short run among men exposed to heavy combat. Men who are personally attached to one another are affected by the loss of their comrades—a commonsense conclusion, but one neglected by myths that emphasize the heroism of combat and the effectiveness of group cohesion.

For the first time in American history, drug use by combat troops became a *cause célèbre*. There was not only a high level of alcohol consumption among American troops in Vietnam—common enough in war—but a high level of heroin use, abuse of other hard drugs, and widely prevalent marijuana smoking. There was great public concern, reflected in Congress, that drug use in Vietnam not only undermined our fighting effectiveness but would lead to continued addiction problems among Vietnam veterans. In one sense, the Vietnam war was a "critical experiment": give high quality drugs to men with no prior history of involvement with drugs and see if they become physically addicted so that they cannot "shake the habit." If physiological addiction is not involved in continuing drug use, then we might expect that when the social situation leading to drug use in the first place is changed (that is, when the men return home to their previous social situations, which did not feature heavy drug use) the use of drugs would decline; hence men who served in Vietnam would be statistically indistinguishable from comparable other men who had never entered the military. The newspapers and Congress were both firmly of the first opinion—the commonly held myth that drug addiction has a strong physiological component. They were concerned about a wave of substance abuse attributable to Vietnam veterans.

In fact, careful multivariate research as shown in Chapter 6 should firmly lay to rest the myth of physiological addiction to drugs, since there is absolutely no evidence that men exposed to either "hard" or "soft" drugs in Vietnam, men who would not otherwise have even tried these substances, are any more prone to their use today than are other comparable men. Drug addiction appears to be more a psychological than a physiological problem. The stereotype of the alcoholic veteran is also called into question.

If serving in combat or even serving in a support position in Vietnam did not contribute to long-term effects on substance use or abuse, it is still possible that substance abuse leads to psychological problems — and the converse, as has been frequently alleged. Indeed, in Chapter 6 we report a correlation between psychological symptoms and high levels of both drug use and alcohol use. Further, there is a somewhat higher association (though only marginally statistically significant) for combat veterans. However, contrary to some claims, there is no evidence that substance use is a functional alternative for Posttraumatic Stress Disorder. Rather, the evidence suggests that combat veterans medicate themselves with drugs or alcohol when they are suffering from PTSD.

Perhaps the most popular and most damaging stereotype to emerge from the war — one that is perpetuated in movies, TV series, news bulletins, and newspapers — is that Vietnam veterans are violent and lawless, that they are time bombs programmed to explode at the slightest provocation. A further complication is the argument that men with a greater predisposition towards violence are more likely to enter combat in the first place. The findings in Chapter 7 do not unequivocally dispel this stereotype. Combat veterans are more likely than comparable others to exhibit violent behavior today. Antisocial behavior in adolescence and disciplinary problems within the military are related to current violent behavior. On the other hand, those prone to violence were no more likely to enter combat. Further, it is sobering to observe that combat has the greatest effect in producing current violent behavior among those men who were not otherwise predisposed to violence. Finally, PTSD is associated with greater tendencies toward violent behavior. Combat veterans with no PTSD symptoms are no more violent than comparable other men.

In Chapter 8, we address the question of whether Vietnam veterans are more likely to be politically alienated than their peers who did not serve. Several myths are involved. First, observers of many wars have predicted that men who were involved in the horrors of war would tend to reject war as a solution to political problems. Many classic novels about combat seem to carry an antiwar message. Notable examples are *The Red Badge of Courage, All Quiet on the Western Front, Johnny Get Your Gun, The Naked and the Dead, Catch 22,* and now a spate of novels about Vietnam. Careful analysis of our data, with a complex set of controls and comparisons with both nonveterans in our sample and with comparable national samples, shows few marked differences in political point of view between Vietnam Era veterans and comparable men who did not serve. Combat itself leads to few appreciable differences in political point of view. If anything, veterans are more accepting of war than nonveterans, though they may have been so prior to their military service.

The second myth about political alienation, and one that is particular to defeated armies, is the "stab in the back theory" (Dorpalen, 1964, pp. 49–53) which was originally touted by Adolf Hitler to explain the German defeat in World War I—the troops at the front did not lose the war; instead, the war was lost by the civilians. Applied to Vietnam veterans, this myth means that the men were not emotionally supported while in Vietnam and, most particularly, were not welcomed on their return. Rather than being given ticker-tape parades, they were shunned, ignored, even castigated. Our data suggest that indeed this part of the myth is true: veterans and nonveterans alike felt that veterans were unwelcome when they returned. The most widely held corollary of this myth is only partially true. Careful analysis reveals that the main cause for the current psychological problems of Vietnam veterans is past psychological problems, which, in turn, were caused by exposure to combat. If a man did come home from the war with problems, he was more likely to have problems in readjusting to civilian life, to believe that he was unwelcome, and to be politically and economically alienated. Consequently, the sense of being unwelcome and the feelings of alienation contributed in a minor degree to a veteran's current psychological problems. In short, to blame the public for its lack of support of Vietnam veterans is to vastly oversimplify the conundrum facing the Vietnam veteran. Donald Knox (1984), citing the homecoming experience of veterans from Bataan, Corregidor, and Korea, maintains that the Vietnam veteran "sits snugly on a continuum of American attitudes that first ignores, then forgets the warriors who come home without a victory."

Chapters 9, 10, and 11 analyze social support by other Vietnam veterans, by friends and families, and by wives and women friends. In addition, the effects of professional help are compared with the effects of lay social support. Healing and social support are the subject of many myths and stereotypes. One of the more fashionable current concepts in psychology, social support is held to be "good for whatever ails you"—from the effects of cancer to depression. The preface to these three final chapters lays the foundation for understanding the concepts of networks and networking and introduces the notion of the "interpersonal environment"—the set of others known to the veteran who affect his life. We show that whether or not the interpersonal environment is benign, helpful, or even harmful depends on a number of conditions and circumstances. An interpersonal environment that approximates the mythic village life of 19th century America—a town in which "everybody knows everybody else"—is in fact helpful to Vietnam veterans only in nonmetropolitan locations in which these "communities" may have some meaning. In big cities, an interpersonal environment in which everyone knows everyone else is not helpful. In small cities, hanging out with other Vietnam veteran friends may simply be people with problems seeking out others with problems. In either case, the interpersonal environment affects the current prevalance of Posttraumatic Stress Disorder only for men exposed to combat, what the literature calls the "buffering effect" of social support. Finally, male veteran friends are much more likely to be helpful than medical and mental health professionals — or at least those professionals who were available to our respondents during the years prior to large scale outreach programs. In fact, even when we control for the presence of PTSD during or right after the war, men who have seen professionals for help with their problems are more likely currently to have PTSD symptoms.

Chapter 10 deals with the relative effects of wives and friends on symptoms of everyday life stress. The construct is called demoralization—which includes, among other symptoms, poor self-esteem, feelings of helplessness and hopelessness, sadness, anxiety, and psychophysiological problems. Another dependent variable used in this analysis is problem drinking. Demoralization and problem drinking are also related to combat stress, but not as strongly as Posttraumatic Stress Disorder. Again, contrary to most of the reported literature, there is no simple relationship between social support and mental health. For men who have partners, that is, who are living with a spouse or other companion, the partner's support is associated with lower levels of demoralization. Though this is true for everyone, the effect is marked among combat veterans. On the other hand, having a friend available is associated with lower levels of demoralization among only those combat veterans who have little or no partner support. For about half the nonpartnered men—those who are single, divorced, widowed, or separated—having a confidante, that is, someone whose help is sought if the respondent has a serious problem, is a functional alternative to having a partner. As we shall see in the next chapter, somewhat more than one fourth of the confidantes for single or nonpartnered men are women. The effect of having a confidante, however, is the opposite of what might be expected: among combat veterans, higher levels of demoralization are associated with turning to a confidante. Again, this may be an instance of men with problems seeking out help. Further, merely having a friend available does not help nonpartnered men.

Problem drinking seems to work in a different way from demoralization. First, partners are not much help to partnered men. Second, there are no buffer effects with combat. That is, among combat veterans partner support or having a friend available does not reduce the probability of problem drinking. But *all* men who have *low* partner support and friends available tend to have *more* problem drinking. It appears that the myth of the misunderstood husband going off to drink with his buddies has some truth to it. In any case, the kind of social support we are measuring here does not seem to help with problem drinking, something Alcoholics Anonymous found years ago.

The last chapter on social support, Chapter 11, deals with a topic that to our best knowledge has never been previously investigated — the women friends of men: what kinds of men have women friends, and what effect, if any, do these friends have on psychological adjustment? By friends, we mean just that. We do not know whether the men have sexual relations with these women. In the context of this study and the questions asked, the presumption is probably not. In any event, the issue is irrelevant to the analysis pursued. Several factors, taken independently of one another, affect the probability that men will have women friends: higher social class, metropolitan residence, and, most important, a liberal or "modern" attitude toward women. As one might expect, married men have proportionately fewer women friends than single men, if wives are not counted. For married men of the Vietnam generation, wives are most often named as best friend, and the confidante for a married man is almost always his wife. However, if a single man has women friends, one of them is much more likely than one of his male friends to be his confidante, that is, the person he turns to for help with a serious problem. There are also obvious differences in the nature of the relationship between men and women if the men are married. The women friends of married men are met through the regular social circle of the men – through relatives and friends. Single men meet women more often on the job and in social situations not linked to an existing social network. Of course, all these findings are from the perspective of the men. No women were interviewed.

It has already been demonstrated that supportive wives seem to alleviate the stress of combat. This does not seem to be the case either for the women friends of married men or for the women confidantes or the other women friends of single men. Given the present data set, we do not know whether this lack of an effect is caused by the paucity of information about the relationship between the men and their women friends or because, as was previously demonstrated, Vietnam veterans, who are almost always male, are best able to help other Vietnam veterans.

The three chapters on social support systems show that the effects of friends, wives, relatives, and the rest of the interpersonal environment on combat veterans is complex: sometimes it is helpful; sometimes it makes matters worse; and in other situations it has no effect at all. On the other hand, the record for professional assistance appears, on the average, to be negative regardless of context. This part of the study was designed in 1974 and 1975, when the field of social support was just beginning to develop. Though our understanding of social support has advanced considerably since those days, the issues highlighted by the present study remain problematic. Further investigation is needed concerning the situations and conditions under which both lay and professional assistance can be given to the victims of traumatic stress in general and combat related stress reaction in particular. Simple answers are not correct.

I STEREOTYPES AND MYTHS

2 Who Went to War

Randy Martin

In the aftermath of the Vietnam Era, many questions remain about the impact of that conflict on American society. Scarcely enough time has elapsed since American forces were withdrawn from Vietnam to place the era in an historical perspective, but in that time the Vietnam "conflict," as it was called, and the Americans who fought it have assumed almost mythical significance in our society. The legacy of the Vietnam war to the men who served there — who they are today, how they have found postwar society — is addressed in later chapters. The focus here is on those who actually went to war.

We shall reconstruct the demographic aspects of who went to war and capture some sense of what happened to these soldiers once they were there; the images of Vietnam veterans are shaped as much by their experience in the war as before it. Specifically, this chapter considers whether there were any disparities before the war between Vietnam veterans, particularly among Vietnam veterans who fought in combat; Era veterans (men who were in the Armed Forces but served elsewhere than Vietnam during the Vietnam Era); and men who did not serve at all. We shall examine race and class to see whether popular beliefs that Vietnam was a war fought predominantly by blacks and by the lower classes are true. We shall find that in the case of class, the popular myth is borne out by our data, although we introduce a new twist. But our findings apparently dispel the myth about racial inequities in the selection process.

At the conclusion of this chapter however, We present evidence to show how this statistical misconception arose; for, while our figures do show that blacks and whites went to Vietnam in equal proportion, analysis of the qualitative material in the 1,401 interviews with the men in our sample shows that the statistics reveal only part of the story. It is our impression that the way this problem has been conceptualized in the past has not captured all potential sites of inequality. In the end, we suggest that much of the confusion about the nature of the men who fought in Vietnam is a consequence of collapsing three distinct processes, each a potential site of inequity. The first of these is procurement of military personnel; the second, assignment to military occupation; and the third, actual experience in the field.

In order to make sense of these three distributive processes and the more generic question of who went to war, we shall review briefly the military selection process since colonial times. The contention that the selection process was biased did not originate with Vietnam, though in no other American conflict did it have the same political impact. Nor is Vietnam the first war where the poor, the working class, and racial minorities encountered a different fate from others in their cohort. Yet in no previous conflict do these differences appear to have had the same effect on military organization as in Vietnam.

From the first universal manpower law of Plymouth colony in 1663 to the present, procurement of military personnel has demonstrated a fundamental conflict between civilian and military ideals. On one hand is the idea of universal conscription, which implies that every citizen is responsible for the defense of the country; on the other hand, certain segments of the population — and this has been defined differently at different times — have had a social value that exempts them from military service. In the colonial period:

> Despite the large number and diversity of local ordinances, twin themes emerge. First the rich could get out: by paying cash (commutation), buying munitions, and/or providing a paid substitute (substitution). Second the poor had little choice; they could not afford the options available to the rich, and their financial conditions often forced them to accept cash bounties for service. (Surrey, 1982, p. 10)

Buying one's way out of military service reduced the available labor reservoir. A system of bounties emerged as an incentive to enlist, but this system generated its own set of problems. In The War of 1812, bounties had to be raised continuously to meet the demand for troops. (Murdock, 1967)

During the Civil War, the problems of military procurement mushroomed, as did resistance to going to war. The procurement system divided the population not only along class lines but racially as well. This was reflected in the bounty system, under which whites received $100 for three years' service while blacks received $10.00. Individual resistance was manifest in the practice of "bounty jumping," moving from one country or state or side to the other, deserting, reenlisting, and collecting on the way (Murdock, 1971, pp. 218ff.). In response to the failure of the bounty system, the federal Enrollment Act of 1863 was passed as a form of limited draft. The draft only regularized the inequities; after the first call-up, a national wave of protest erupted in the form of draft riots. In New York City, estimates ran to 3,903 dead. The rioters protested against class inequities but seemed blind to racial ones; blacks, doubly discriminated against by the procurement system, were included among the targets of violence (Surrey, 1982). Wars throughout the 19th century were fought, primarily hand to hand, by large numbers of troops. Assignment to military occupation and experience in combat were relatively homogeneous. It is not surprising that systematic bias and conflict focused on the procurement system per se.

In the 20th century, as the division of labor and capital intensity of the military changed, occupational assignment and experience in combat became loci of discriminatory practices along the lines of class and race. During World War I, the Selective Service Act of 1917 sustained biased procurement practices. Labor was "assessed" as contributing least to the war effort; laborers were the first ones drafted and deferments could be obtained on occupational grounds (Gates, 1970). As in the past, resistance was not uncommon. An estimated 250,000 men evaded the draft, and the stealing of draft lists was extensive.

In World War II, greater procurement needs tended to erode class differences, though units were still racially segregated. However, exemptions persisted in smaller numbers along class lines, and discrimination in assigning military occupation status multiplied (Surrey, 1982). World War I is considered the first fully modern war, in effect a war where noncombat roles were as numerous as men in arms. Between the Civil War and World War II, noncombat assignments, mainly technical and clerical positions, jumped from .98% to 49.6% respectively. Securing a noncombat position substantially behind the frontline diminished the risk in going to war; these positions were assigned on a class biased, educationally based system (U.S. Bureau of the Census, 1975). Despite the fact that this was considered a popular war, 348,217 evaded the draft (Wittner, 1969).

With Korea, discrimination in assignment rose and the system of procurement again became the terrain for class manipulation as overall demand for draftees dropped. Those with resources for a lawyer could appeal their 1A status. The number of appeals rose from 3 in 1,000 in World War II to 47 in 1,000 in Korea (Smith, 1971). At the other end of the scale, draft violation prosecutions increased. Once in the war, the poorest soldiers were almost four times as likely as the wealthiest to become casualties.

With Vietnam, each of the three axes of discrimination — who serves, in what capacity, and the actual experience of service — took on a life of its own. Class bias in procurement blossomed as some 483,000 received occupation deferments and virtually millions got student deferments (Surrey, 1982). Racial distinctions were also sharpened. Whites received twice the medical deferments of blacks, and in 1969-70 only 1% of the National Guard was black (Baskir & Strauss, 1978). When General Hershey's Selective Service policies came under increasing attack during the 60s, reforms corrected some of the glaring inequities in the system of assignment (Baskir & Strauss, 1978). But this attempt to correct differences in assignment did not alter the differential experience of soldiers from the lower classes or racial minorities.) The disparities emerge when a demographic analysis of rank or punishment for military offenses is undertaken, as we demonstrate later. (The other indicator that race and class made a difference irrespective of assignment can be seen in the casualty rates. The casualty rate of the poor was three times that of the most affluent sectors of the population (Badillo & Curry, 1976). While the percentage of black combat personnel declined during the course of Vietnam (though it was still higher than the percentage of whites), their casualty rates remained over a third higher than those of white soldiers (Moskos, 1970). At the end of this chapter, we take up the roots of this differential experience in detail. Suffice it for now to say that in Vietnam, a war with fewer combat soldiers than any previous war and with no clear cut front lines, experience in the field offers evidence of discriminatory practices distinct from assignment to military occupational status.

During the Vietnam era, from 1964 to 1973, nearly 27 million men came of draft age. Roughly 11 million served in the military; some 2,150,000 (approximately one fifth) were sent to Vietnam. In Vietnam, 51,000 American men died — 8,000 from nonhostile causes, 350 from suicide. Two hundred seventy thousand were wounded (Baskir & Strauss, 1978). On these broad demographics there can be general agreement, but studies of the Vietnam era tend to diverge regarding who bore the brunt of the effects of the war. It is useful to take a glance at some of these studies before turning to our own data.

We have seen that historically those who went to war have been divided along racial and class lines. In a war like Vietnam, where more stayed out of the war through legal or illegal means, what happens to those who stayed home is an important extension of the procurement process. Baskir and Strauss (1977) cite this as the other side of discriminatory selection processes as evidenced by who could not elude the war through legal means:

> The overwhelming majority of Vietnam era offenders were from underprivileged backgrounds. Almost half of all "draft evaders" were members of minority groups who never registered for the draft. Three quarters of the deserters were high school drop-outs, and less than 1% ever graduated college. Most offenses were motivated by family problems. (p. 2)

According to the authors, the groups penalized most heavily for not going to war also paid the highest tolls for going: "The burdens of Vietnam were very unevenly imposed. (The economically and socially disadvantaged did most of the fighting.)They also paid most of the penalties for not fighting" (p. 4). For Baskir and Strauss, class, race, and family background form a triangle of discrimination. In other studies, with more multivariate analysis, these factors are not so evenly emphasized.

Lou Harris (1980), finds no significant differences in exposure to heavy combat along racial lines and argues for the centrality of class based differences:

> Our sense of the data however, is that while minority Americans may have suffered a disproportionate share of the exposure to combat and combat fatalities, their suffering was the product not of racial discrimination, but of discrimination against the poor, the uneducated, and the young, regardless of their racial or ethnic heritage. To summarize, it appears the military induction and combat assignment processes did not create a system of discrimination against minority Americans, but rather, merely served to mirror the underlying class discrimination of the society itself. (p. 7)

Harris' conclusions are justified as long as he considers only procurement and assignment processes. However, he does not examine experience in the field, where differences between black and white soldiers from the same class background become evident. Hence, his contention that racial differences are an artifact of class is not fully justified.

John Helmer's study (1974) is an example:

> Here we must emphasize that the Vietnam War was planned by college educated and relatively affluent Americans in Washington, and fought in the field by the less educated, the economically disadvantaged and the poor. For no other war in our history can it be said that the American Army was a poor man's army and that this was by design. (pp. 9-10).

Although Helmer's study goes further than others in analyzing experience on the field of battle, he takes class discrimination as a point of departure and focuses on working class veterans. Hence, although his study can give rich insights into the way the war was fought, he does not follow the fate of an entire cohort from selection to experience and lacks many of the comparisons needed to ascertain systematic bias.

It is clear from this glance at other studies of who went to war that some, but not all, of the three potential axes of discrimination are addressed in each study. In the following analysis of our sample, which is described in detail in the Appendix 2-A, each axis is considered in turn. Our sample was drawn to reflect the entire Vietnam era cohort. All the data presented here have been weighted. The weights adjust for the oversampling of certain cells in our population, particularly veterans and minority members; thus the data as they are presented here accurately reflect the population from which the sample was drawn. The two variables on which we focus in the quantitative analysis that follows are race and class. The move from the quantitative data to the qualitative adds the third dimension to the discriminatory process: procurement, assignment, and experience. Hence, we do not just present figures for who went to war and who actually fought in combat, but we analyse the qualitative experience of the men who fought.

The index used to measure class is found in detail in Appendix 2.A. Briefly, it was based on on the class of the respondent's father, his level of education, his profession, and his income. For the purposes of this analysis, respondents have been assigned to one of four classes: lower class, lower middle, higher middle, and higher class.

It is generally assumed that more men from lower classes went to Vietnam than did higher class men. And, indeed, our data, as they are presented in Fig. 2.1, show that while an average of approximately two fifths of the men from the three lower classes served in the military, only one fifth of men from higher class families served. However, at the next stage of the analysis, we discover that among the men in the military higher class men went to Vietnam as frequently as, and sometimes more frequently than, the two middle classes, and only slightly less frequently than lower class men. Furthermore,

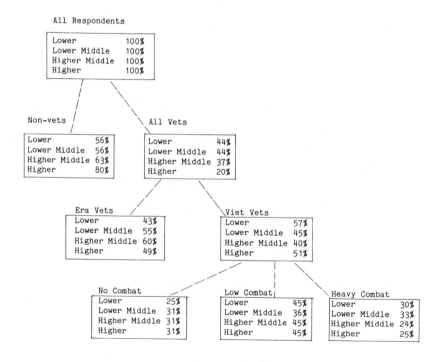

FIG. 2.1   Breakdown of Military Experience Across Class Lines (weighted data)

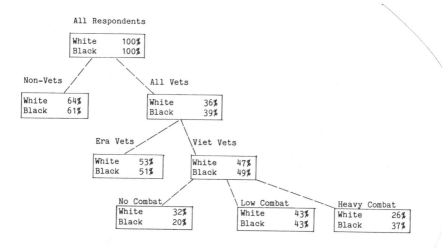

FIG. 2.2   Black–White Differences Across Vietnam Era Experience (weighted data)

there are slight differences between the amounts of combat to which higher class men and lower class men were exposed, but the differences are not significant. Thus, the argument that combat status is assigned on class lines is not supported by our data.

Turning to the racial differences, we ask: were proportionately more black respondents sent to Vietnam? As Fig. 2.2 shows, 64% of the white respondents and 61% of black respondents in our weighted sample did not go into the military, an insignificant difference of 3%. The difference is even smaller at the next level: 47% of all our white military respondents and 49% of our black military respondents went to Vietnam. In Vietnam, larger differences exist. There is a 12% difference between blacks and white who engaged in no combat and in heavy combat. Thirty-two percent of the whites and 20% of the blacks who were sent to Vietnam claim not to have been involved in any combat at all. This relationship is reversed for heavy combat; 12% more blacks than whites were involved in heavy combat, but, given the size of our sample, the difference is not statistically significant.

We could end the story here were it not for the troubling statistics on differential casualty rates between rich and poor, black and white that we cited earlier. Either there is a discrepancy in lower class or black soldiers' ability to avoid dangerous contact, or there is a divergent exposure to risk that has not been accounted for.

Rank is an obvious place to look for discriminating practices because in military society rank assigns power, prestige, and mobility. When rank as opposed to occupational assignment, is considered, the casualty rates just cited are are more easily understood. That officers (at least those above the rank of platoon commander) were relatively safer than enlisted men in Vietnam becomes clear when we remember that the primary ground tactic was the search and destroy mission. The purpose of the search and destroy mission was to lure the enemy out of hiding in order to subject him to aerial and ground bombardment. Within units committed to search and destroy operations, the advance and peripheral positions of the lower ranks were more susceptible to ambush and ran greater risks (Helmer, 1974). As we shall see when we look at the qualitative data, rank rather than occupation emerges as central to the soldiers' experience of the war. The focus on rank also indicates that the military has its own means of organizing a class structure which is quite distinct from the occupational basis that informs many sociological notions of class (Martin, 1983). Military occupational status may be related to civilian class structure and exposure to combat, but, in combat engagements, rank is a more potent measure of military class structure. Where there is an indication of discrimination along racial lines in the field, as we indicate by looking at incidence of formal punishment, rank as the measure of class becomes all the more important.

If rank were assigned without deference to race, we would expect to find proportionately equal numbers of black and white officers and enlisted men. This is not the case in our sample, as Table 2.1 demonstrates. Approximately 70% of the whites in our weighted sample were privates, as opposed to 13% of the minority members. Corporals and sergeants were approximately proportionate to their representation in the population. However, although 9% of the whites were officers, there were no black officers in our sample.

If rank can be considered the insignia of class within military society, then clearly class is assigned along racial lines, and racial conflicts become the idiom for class conflicts — struggles not only for racial equality but also for the reordering of an entire system of power. The implications of this inequality are described in the men's own words later, but first an analysis of the differ-

TABLE 2.1

Racial Differences in Rank and Punishment Received Among Vietnam Veterans (a)

	% Minorities (n = 65)	% Whites (n = 167)	χ² Significance
Privates	13.0	6.8	.001
Officers	0	9.0	.000
1 Article 15	24.7	14.3	.001
2+ Articles 15	17.9	4.7	.001
Court Martialled	19.6	5.3	.001

(a) weighted data

ential rate with which officers punished their subordinates contributes to a demonstration of racial inequality.

At a general level, incidence of punishment reflects both the difficulty a particular racial group has in adapting to the rigors of military life and the way in which the military accommodates or fails to accommodate a racial group. Since recommendation for and assignment of punishment are made by officers, punishment levels across race are also an expression of the relation between officers and enlisted men. The two formal instruments of punishment in the military are the articles 15 and the court martial. Articles 15 are formal reprimands for any kind of misconduct ranging from untidy uniform to assault on a officer. Table 2.1 shows that 14.3% of the whites received one article 15, and nearly a quarter of the minorities did. These differences become more marked when broken down by number of articles 15 received. Only 4.7% of the whites received more than one article 15, as opposed to 17.9% of the blacks. Receiving two or more articles 15 is particularly significant because according to Army sources, one article 15 would have little effect on a soldier's career whereas two or three would severely dampen any possibility for advancement and would likely lead to a court martial.

It is not surprising that with more severe punishment, the disparity between white and minority Vietnam veterans increases still further: 5.3% of the whites and nearly four times that number of minorities were court martialed.

Although at first our findings did not reveal racial differences in procurement or assignment to military status, in the analysis of what we have called the "experience" axis we have now discovered possible discriminatory practices in the assignment of rank and the official meting out of punishment. The verbatim accounts below from three black Vietnam veterans and one white officer provide first-hand evidence of how these inequalities were played out in the field.

[When] someone [would] say something racially derogatory towards me..we looked towards our commander to take care of this and he didn't say nothing. Then finally one day, one of the blacks had gotten into a fight with two whites over the soda machine and that started a whole big thing and like the whole barracks just turned out. I think it was like maybe two to three hundred people in there and everybody was fighting each other. And then they sent troops, they sent the security police down to the barracks and the security police were white and they attacked the blacks first rather than go to the central point and separate people period. We [the blacks] were the ones who had gotten hit with the nightclubs and the sticks and things and pulled off and put into jail. And I think there was only one white that went in, 10 blacks, one to ten you know. Most of the people who were involved in that had gotten court-martialed or had gotten discharged or sent to the other bases. [We met with the base commander about the incident] but I didn't see any change.

In this case, white officers and security forces commanded by them ignored racial tensions until they exploded. The blacks who had complained of a potentially volatile situation in the first place bore the punitive consequences alone.

At times racial tensions were not the product of benign neglect by white officers but were precipitated by them:

> [My lieutenant] built this boxing ring and he wanted me to get in the ring with him and he's six foot seven you know and I told him — I said — man I can't box you — you a officer I'm the private.

For some white officers, relations with individual black soldiers were friendly, yet blacks were resented as a group. This suggests that discriminatory behavior may have been a consequence of blacks' organization and struggle for power. The following account by a white officer makes this clear:

> I worked with a couple of blacks in Vietnam that I respected and liked, but when you got them in a group they were just worthless. I just got tired of hearing all this crap about how they were discriminated against and this and that.... I just had a real dislike for them ..all their black bands they wore on their wrists with their hairdos and soul slapping and all that crap.

Blacks attempting to organize against a white power structure were rebuked by the formal punitive system. This in turn led to greater conflicts. A black veteran reports:

> A couple guys went to jail. They was like leaders — guys that had been there a little while. It almost turned into a race riot...it was bad...three hundred black dudes facing a couple of hundred white dudes and they all had their guns pointed at each other.

The demand for black leadership was acute enough to promulgate such serious confrontations. Deprived of access to power and apparently ignored when they demanded change, blacks invoked the only resources immediately available to them. But these were not the only means by which black soldiers organized to get their demands met. In the next account, a black veteran relates how a strike was organized to render the meting out of punishment for blacks and whites more equitable:

> The conflict was started because a black marine had got stabbed in a joint — one of the local watering holes, and he had got stabbed by two white marines that wasn't taken into custody — they just returned — you know — to their unit. The other marines saw that — they refused at least 300 black marines refused to

cooperate with the battalion at all until those two white marines were brought up on charges and finally they were brought up on charges and the black marines who had been sitting out for 12 hours all returned to duty — returned to their duties. A lot of changes came about. More black officers were brought in to handle the heavy load of black soldiers that was coming in at the time. They stressed the point that they wanted minorities to control, because the white officers kind of lost control over the whole unit - that kind of disappointed the commander in chief so he started cracking down and getting more black officers in there to relate to the problems and the needs of the blacks.

Unlike those in U.S. civilian society, military lines of power are not formally divided, and the arbiters of justice are not separated from the administrators of daily life. The roles of manager, judge, and politician are all embodied in the officer. Without the conflict-diffusing mechanisms available in civilian society, minority soldiers were forced to bond together and take serious action to achieve tolerable conditions in military life. It is perhaps in this respect above all others that the experience of blacks and Mexican Americans in Vietnam was unique.

There is evidence suggesting that the experiences just recounted are not unique to our sample. Vietnam appears unique among American wars in the intensity and extent of enlisted men's opposition to officers' rule. Officers who were deemed to be threatening the safety of the unit with excess bravura or productivity were singled out through the practice of fragging, a form of assassination by fragmentation grenade. Official estimates put these deaths at 300–400 (Moskos, 1975). Further, although none of our respondents claimed membership, there were soldiers' unions that responded formally to the conditions suggested in our interviews. Totaling perhaps 20,000 members, the organizations called for collective bargaining, an end to racism, federal minimum wage standards, and constitutional rights for enlisted personnel (Hayes, 1975). These formal organizations (though predominantly underground) are some indication of the magnitude and importance of the experiences related earlier. Experience in the field can help to explain reports of discriminatory practice despite apparent improvement in the formal processes for procurement and assignment.

In this paper I have addressed some of the popular mythology about the men who were sent to fight in Vietnam. Myths themselves sometimes reflect a partial reality. And we have borne this out. From a general point of view, myths, such as blacks' going to war in larger numbers than whites, have fallen. Yet if the intention of the myth was to capture some of the inequality that blacks and the lower classes experienced in Vietnam, our data on specific experiences of blacks exceed the expectations of the myth. Hence, it is only through the variegated methods of social research that the complexity of reality can be fully portrayed.

APPENDIX 2.A
THE CLASS VARIABLES[1]

The respondent's social class was assigned on the basis of the following three variables: his father's education at the time he came of draft age, occupation and income. In each of the three cases, the respondent's parent (father, unless his data were missing, in which case the mother's data were substituted) was given a possible score ranging from one to five and the scores were then added up. The class variables, then, ranged from a possible low of three to a possible high of fifteen. Individual scores were based on the following criteria:

Parent's Social Class Index

Parent's Education
Graduated college, graduate school, graduate degree	5
Attended vocational or other training school or college	4
Completed high school or high school equivalency	3
Some high school	2
8th grade or less	1

Parent's Occupation[2]
Professionals, technicians, official managers in corporations, schools, stores, self-employed persons owning their own business	5
Retail and wholesale salespersons and other representatives, office clerical staff, clerical staff not in offices such as bank tellers, postal clerks, mailman, telephone operator	4
Craftsmen and repairmen	3
Operators of machinery, transportation, service workers in restaurants, homes, stores	2
Protective servicemen such as policemen, laborers, farmers, students, military, unemployed	1

Parents Income
Over $15,000 p.a.	5
$10,000 to $14,999 p.a.	4
$7,000 to $9,999 p.a.	3
$5,000 to $6,999 p.a.	2
Under $5,000 p.a.	1

---

[1] These indices were designed by John Martin (Kadushin, Boulanger, & Martin, 1981).

[2] These divisions are based on the Edward Occupational Index.

3 Posttraumatic Stress Disorder: A Valid Diagnosis?

Ghislaine Boulanger
Charles Kadushin
David M. Rindskopf
Martha Ann Carey

For at least 30 years the American mental health profession has been singularly ambivalent about posttraumàtic stress[1] reactions. On one hand have been the groups of researchers and practitioners who have noted a discrete set of symptoms that often occur among people who have recently, or not so recently, lived through a traumatic event (Grinker & Spiegel, 1945; Horowitz, 1976; Kardiner, 1969; Krystal, 1968; Shatan, 1973). The characteristic symptoms include autonomic arousal, which is often manifest in panic attacks or startle reactions; a preoccupation with the traumatic event in the form of nightmares, flashbacks, or persistent thoughts about the trauma that intrude into everyday affairs; and a general dysphoria, a numbness that takes the meaning out of life and makes it hard to relate to other people. Researchers have documented cases of traumatic stress reactions lasting 5 years (Futterman & Pumpian-Midlin, 1951), 10 years (Brill & Beebe, 1955), 15 years (Archibald, Long, Miller, & Tuddenham, 1962), 20 years (Archibald & Tuddenham, 1965) and, in one study of World War II veterans, even 30 years (Klonoff, McDougall, Clark, Kramer, & Horgan, 1976) after the trauma ended. In other cases, observers have noted that the symptoms manifest themselves after a latency period of several years or that they alternate with apparently asymptomatic periods that, on closer inspection, turned out to be periods of denial.

---

[1]For a fuller discussion of the history and recent research on Posttraumatic Stress Disorder, see Boulanger (in preparation).

Until 1980, these observations were met with skepticism by many mental health professionals (among them Borus, 1973, 1974; Fairbairn, 1952; and Worthington, 1978), who found their most influential expression in the first two editions of the Diagnostic and Statistical Manual (DSM) of the American Psychiatric Association (APA, 1954, 1968). It is true that the editors paid lip service to the fact that in some cases individuals, "without any apparent underlying mental disorders" (APA, 1968, p. 49) could develop acute reactions to overwhelming environmental stress, but they failed to define the form that these reactions might take. In 1954, in the first DSM, the diagnosis was called Gross Stress Reaction, and the editors pointed out that such a reaction "differs from neurosis or psychosis chiefly with respect to clinical history, reversibility of reactions, and its transient character. If the reaction persists," the editors warned, "this term is to be regarded as a temporary diagnosis to be used only until a more definitive diagnosis is established" (p. 40). In 1968, with the advent of the second edition of DSM, the word stress was dropped altogether, and the diagnosis was subsumed under the category of Transient Situational Disturbances. The editors reiterated that if the "symptoms persist after the stress is removed, the diagnosis of another mental disorder is indicated" (p. 49).

With the publication of DSM III in 1980, the mental health establishment appears to have finally caught up with the researchers and observers. Posttraumatic Stress Disorder is described as the development of characteristic symptoms following a psychologically traumatic event that is "generally outside the range of usual human experience" (APA, 1980 p. 236). The editors of DSM III go on to define an acute phase of the disorder, where the onset of symptoms occurs within 6 months of the trauma and lasts less than 6 months, and a chronic or delayed phase, where symptoms either last 6 months or more or manifest themselves at least 6 months after the trauma. It is this chronic phase of the disorder and the description of a discrete diagnostic entity, as opposed to a diffuse set of anxiety related symptoms, that distinguishes Posttraumatic Stress Disorder from Gross Stress Reactions and Transient Situational Disorders.

The validity of the diagnosis continues to be called into question (Frazier & Borgida, 1985; LaGuardia, Smith, Francois, & Bachman, 1983). Debates about whether it is most aptly categorized as an anxiety disorder, an affective disorder, or a dissociative disorder have sprung up (Dohrenwend, 1979; Sierles, Chen, McFarland, & Taylor, 1983). Some question whether PTSD occurs alone or concurrently with other diagnoses (Green, Grace, Lindy, & Titchener, 1983). Others question whether the diagnosis should not be broken down still further (Horowitz, Wilner, & Alvarez, 1979; Horowitz, Wilner, Kaltreider, & Alvarez, 1980). Still others question whether the symptoms selected by the editors of DSM III do, in fact, reflect the symptoms of the disorder (Atkinson, Sparr, Sheff, White & Fitzsimmons, 1984; Baraga, Van

Kampen, & Watson, 1983; Weisaeth, 1983). All in all, the apparent official acceptance of this diagnosis by the American Psychiatric Association appears to have generated considerable controversy.

The publication of DSM IIIR (APA, in preparation) in 1986, with slightly altered criteria for the diagnosis of PTSD reflects some of these questions, but the fundamental symptom picture is not greatly different from that published in 1980. The data that follow are concerned with the original 1980 DSM III definition of PTSD.

In this chapter, a statistical procedure to which the diagnosis of PTSD has been subjected is described. This procedure, called Latent Class Analysis (LCA), in effect rigorously tests the coherence of the diverse set of symptoms that the editors of DSM III have selected as representative of the diagnosis by determining whether a set of items, in this case symptoms similar to those listed in DSM III, form characteristic patterns, and whether the empirically observed patterning of these items can be accounted for by postulating a specific underlying construct, which in this case is the diagnosis of Posttraumatic Stress Disorder.[2]

We could look at Latent Class Analysis as a new diagnostic tool that confirms statistically, rather than relying on the clinician's judgment, whether symptoms in a set are related to one another and that determines the patterning of the symptoms. In effect, Latent Class Analysis works like the editors of DSM III, taking symptoms and determining how many must be present and in what combination in order to justify a given diagnosis. In this case, however, the relationship between the symptoms is determined on the basis of a statistical program rather than on the clinician's observations.[3]

We are, then, treating the criteria, or a list of symptoms very similar to those suggested by the editors of DSM III, as an hypothesis. If respondents can be assigned to different classes on the basis of the distinctive patterns of symptoms they manifest, there is justification for the diagnosis of PTSD; if the items turn out to be random symptoms that disintegrate under the rigors of the statistical program, we could conclude that in the long run stressors merely exacerbate existing pathology, as the previous editions of DSM suggested. Or we could argue that the symptoms selected by the editors of DSM III do not accurately reflect the symptoms of a posttraumatic disorder.

---

[2]For a more technical discussion of the use of LCA as a tool in psychiatric diagnoses, see Rindskopf, Kadushin, and Boulanger (1984).

[3]For those familiar with factor analysis the difference between Latent Class Analysis and factor analysis is noted. Latent Class Analysis assumes the presence or absence of symptoms, unlike factor analysis, which is based on the degree to which any symptom is present. Further, unlike factor analysis, which is based on the correlations only between pairs of symptoms, latent class analysis examines the full patterning of all the symptoms. Finally, factor scores derived from a factor analysis are continuous variables, and additional criteria must be involved to establish "caseness." Latent structure analysis gives the cut points or the caseness as part of its procedure.

In the analysis that follows, the 1,001 respondents interviewed during the second wave of data collection represent the sample. The combat scale is divided in the ways described in Appendix B at the conclusion of this volume.

During each 4- to 5-hour, face-to-face interview, respondents were asked about a series of symptoms that they might have experienced in their lifetime. We inquired into the intensity of the symptoms and considered to have said "yes" only those who said they had experienced the symptom often or fairly often. We asked when they first noticed the symptom, whether it was before they entered the military or before the draft period for nonveterans, while they were in the military, (or, in the case of nonveterans, during the period they were most concerned about the war), within the first year after they left the military, or more than a year after they left the military. And we asked whether they had experienced the symptom in the 12 months immediately preceding our interview. Thus, in terms of DSM III criteria, we had an opportunity to gauge whether the symptoms were of acute onset — during or within a year of active duty — and whether they had become chronic — those who claimed to have experienced or continued to experience the symptoms in the 12 months preceding the interview.

The selection of items for the stress scale was based on a review of the literature of traumatically stressed populations. Although the questionnaire was designed before DSM III was published, we did have access to the working papers of DSM III, and they were used in the selection process. Any symptom that had been mentioned 75% of the time was included on the symptom checklist. Table 3.1 presents these 22 symptoms in the left hand column.[4] From the ways in which the symptoms are grouped, it is apparent that many of them are, in effect, functional clinical alternatives of one another. For example, someone who claimed to have lost interest in usual activities and someone who felt that life was not meaningful could be argued to represent a similar construct. The notion of functional clinical alternatives is implicitly followed by the editors of DSM III, where several alternative symptoms are noted under each of the three or four criteria for a particular diagnosis. For example, Criterion B for the diagnosis of PTSD is given as "Reexperiencing the traumatic event"; and three possible symptoms, "Recurrent and intrusive recollections of the event, recurrent dreams of the event or suddenly acting or feeling as if the traumatic event occurred..." are listed as alternative ways of reexperiencing the event. Therefore, the items that in our clinical judgment represented functional equivalents of one another were collapsed into the seven major categories or symptom constructs listed in the right hand column of Table 3.2.

---

[4]The authors are grateful to Jack Smith, who made the preliminary selection of these items.

TABLE 3.1
Original Stress Items Grouped According to Symptom Construct

1. Have you had troubling thoughts about your experience in the military?	) INTRUSIVENESS
2. Have you had frightening dreams or nightmares?	)
3. Have you had trouble staying asleep?	)
1. Have you had a loss of interest in usual activities?	) DIMINISHED INTEREST
2. Have you felt that life is not meaningful?	)
1. Have you felt that what others care about does not make sense?	) DETACHMENT
2. Have you had trouble trusting others?	)
1. Have you felt numb?	) CONSTRICTION
2. Have you felt sad, depressed or blue?	)
1. Have you felt like lashing out?	) HYPERALERT
2. Have you felt you were getting out of control?	)
3. Have you felt jumpy or easily startled?	)
4. Have you had attacks of sudden fear or panic?	)
1. Have you had trouble concentrating?	) COGNITIVE DYSFUNCTION
2. Have you felt confused or had trouble thinking?	)
3. Have you had trouble remembering things?	)
1. Have you felt dizzy?	) GENERALIZED ANXIETY
2. Do you have headaches or pains in the head?	)
3. Do you have stomach troubles?	)
4. Do you feel easily tired?	)
5. Do you feel anxious or tense?	)
6. Do you feel irritable?	)

Table 3.2 presents the new list of seven composite symptoms in the right hand column and constrasts them with DSM III criteria for the diagnosis of Posttraumatic Stress Disorder. There is considerable overlap between the symptoms; to put this another way, the list of items that we used has face validity with DSM III. Note that a recognizable stressor is DSM III's prerequisite for the diagnosis of PTSD. We will avoid the temptation to discuss this tautology, but it should be noted that DSM III includes military combat in the list of possible traumatic stressors. The measure used for combat is described in the Appendix B to this book.

Latent Class Analysis is now used to test the diagnosis of both acute and chronic PTSD. The program takes the seven symptoms and examines all their possible combinations (128 possible combinations in all) to see if they can be said in their patterning to represent two or more underlying classes and, if this is the case, which combinations of symptoms are most likely to represent the different classes.

TABLE 3.2

Comparison Between Stress Constructs and Criteria for DSM III Posttraumatic Stress Disorder Diagnosis

DSM III Criteria	Stress Scale Constructs
A. Recognizable Stressor	
B. Reexperiencing the traumatic event either by:	
1. Recurrent and intrusive recollections of the event, or	INTRUSIVENESS
2. Recurrent dreams of the event, or	
3. Suddenly acting or feeling as if the traumatic event occurred because of an association with an environmental or ideational stimulus.	
C. Numbing of responsiveness or involvement with external world beginning sometime after the traumatic event as shown by either:	DIMINISHED INTEREST
1. Markedly diminished interest in one or more significant activities.	DETACHMENT
2. Feeling detachment or estrangement from others.	
3. Marked constriction of affective responses.	CONSTRICTION
D. At least two of the following symptoms that were not present before the trauma	
1. Hyperalertness or exaggerated startle response.	HYPERALERT
2. Sleep disturbance.	
3. Guilt about surviving when others have not, or about behavior required to achieve survival.	
4. Memory impairment or trouble concentrating.	COGNITIVE DYSFUNCTION
5. Avoidance of activities that arouse recollections of the traumatic event.	
6. Intensification of symptoms by exposure to events that resemble the traumatic event.	
Associated Features — among those mentioned are: Autonomic Lability Headaches Vertigo	GENERALIZED ANXIETY

The program can attempt any number of solutions to this problem, depending on the clinician's hypotheses about the symptoms and the number of classes. Beyond the initial selection of symptoms, the clinician must hypothesize how many classes will fit the data and must also have some idea about what the clustering of items in the different classes might look like. The clinician might ask, is there more than one kind of stress reaction? Influenced by Horowitz's (1976) pioneering work in this field, one might hypothesize two phases to the stress reaction: an intrusive phase and a denial phase. Or, again, one might hypothesize that the sample can be divided simply into those who are stressed and those who are not. The program announces the success or failure of these hypotheses by means of a chi square test of goodness of fit between the patterns of symptoms in the actual data and the data generated by the program in response to the hypotheses given to it.

A two-class solution did not fit the data. If it had, the two-class solution could have been interpreted to support any number of hypotheses, depending on the items and patterning of the items in the two classes. It could have suggested that there are two fairly separate phases to the stress syndrome, one in which the balance of symptoms weighs heavily in favor of intrusiveness and one in which a denial phase emerges more strongly; alternatively, a two-class solution could have suggested that the population can be divided into those who are stressed and those who are not. The program rejected this categorical reasoning but accepted a three-class model.

The program reports that three class models for both acute and chronic stress have chi squares of 103.65 and 103.59 respectively, suggesting an excellent fit between the hypothesis and the model.

Table 3.3 makes it clear what the three classes represent. When the frequency and clustering of symptoms in each of the classes are examined, it is obvious that there is one stress syndrome only; that it is characterized by a distinct patterning of symptoms, although these patterns do change somewhat depending on whether the stress reaction is acute or chronic; and that the three classes suggest that the population is divided into those who are stressed, those who are not stressed, and many who have a number of stress symptoms, but not sufficient and not in the right combination to be considered PTSD. This third category is referred to as "possibly stressed." The program also reports its success in assigning each of the 128 patterns of symptoms in the data to one of the three classes. Ninety-one percent of the cases had been correctly allotted in the case of acute stress; 87% in the case of chronic stress. The latent class probability indicates the percentage of the population that falls into each of the three classes, and the percentage of those in each class who endorse each of the symptoms is also given. Table 3.3 demonstrates that 17% of the sample suffer from chronic stress reactions, with 39% and 42% respectively falling into the possibly or not stressed classes. Further, Table 3.3 shows that those who fall in the stressed class will always experience generalized anxiety. This is hardly surprising and hardly discriminates the diagnosis of PTSD from other diagnoses. However, we learn that 90% of those who are stressed are expected to show symptoms of hyperalertness, to feel like lashing out, as if they are getting out of control, or to have startle reactions; 89% of them complain of feeling depressed or numb; 84% have intrusive thoughts; 75% experience some interference with their thought processes, either difficulty concentrating or trouble remembering things; 70% complain that they cannot understand what other people

TABLE 3.3
Percentage of Respondents with Positive Score on Stress Items According to
Diagnostic Class

	Acute Stress Reactions		
Stress Item	Stressed	Possibly Stressed	Not Stressed
Generalized anxiety	97	87	19
Diminished interest	85	21	1
Constriction	85	32	1
Hyperalert	81	40	1
Detachment	78	46	10
Intrusiveness	75	35	3
Cognitive dysfunction	70	23	1
Latent Class prob.	.072	.270	.657 = 1.0
chi square = 103.65	DF = 104		
Percent correctly allocated 91.25			

	Chronic Stress Reactions		
	Stressed	Possibly Stressed	Not Stressed
Generalized anxiety	100	77	12
Hyperalert	90	38	4
Constriction	89	22	1
Intrusiveness	84	39	2
Cognitive dysfunction	75	16	10
Detachment	70	28	2
Diminished interest	70	18	1
Latent class prob.	.177	.397	.424 = 1.0
chi square = 103.59	DF = 104		
Percent correctly allocated 87.99			

care about or that they distrust others; and 70% of them claim to have lost interest in life. Those in the "possibly stressed" class endorse all these symptoms less frequently, and the cluster of symptoms from which they suffer differ from those in the stressed class.

There is a slight difference in the patterning of symptoms between the acute and chronic stress reactions. The immediate or acute reaction to a traumatic stressor appears to be one in which the more subdued symptoms, such as loss of interest and depression, have the upper hand. As time goes by, a chronic reaction emerges in which irritability, startle reactions, and intrusive recollections of the event become more pressing.

DSM IIIR will drop the distinction between acute and chronic or delayed stress reactions, arguing that at least some of the symptoms of PTSD present themselves very shortly after the termination of the stressor. Thus, the idea of a latent stress reaction is no longer viable. While the decision not to address the issue of latency is a controversial one, the findings presented here offer some clues about why it has been difficult to detect stress reactions immediately after the event: it appears that the initial symptoms are those that are less likely to call attention to themselves. It is only over the course of time that the more florid symptoms emerge.

Let us compare these statistical findings with the diagnostic criteria established by DSM III: DSM III asserts that everyone who has PTSD should experience intrusive thoughts of some kind whereas we find that 84% of the chronically stressed have such thoughts. According to DSM III, those with PTSD should have either diminished interest in the world, detachment, or constriction of affect; we find that chronically stressed respondents are more likely to have the constricted affect and are less likely to claim detachment or diminished interest. DSM III claims that at least some of the people who are stressed should be hyperalert or have some cognitive dysfunction; we find that 90% of our respondents who fit into the stressed class have symptoms of hyperalertness, and 75% complain of trouble remembering things or trouble concentrating. We can quibble about percentages here and there, but the fit is generally a good one.

Thus far, however, the presence or absence of a traumatic stressor has not been reckoned with, and such a stressor is necessary to the accurate diagnosis of PTSD. The analysis continues by dividing the respondents into four categories according to their military status and degree of combat exposure to discover whether there is a significant relationship between the amount of combat experienced and the percentage of respondents who fall into the stressed class. Table 3.4 presents these findings.

Within 12 months of being in combat, at least 25% of heavy combat veterans and 17% of veterans who had seen average combat were acutely stressed, compared with an average of 4% or 5% of those who had not seen combat. Today more respondents generally fall into the stressed class, but combat veterans continue to be significantly more stressed. We might hypothesize that 10% more combat veterans are stressed today as compared with the period immediately after the war because they went through a latent or asymptomatic period after they had returned to the United States, and developed chronic stress reactions a year or more later.

Two hypotheses offer themselves for the surprising finding that approximately 16% of the noncombat veterans and nonveterans fall in the chronically stressed class. In the following chapter we find that men whose backgrounds might predispose them to mental disorder appear to suffer from stress-like symptoms independent of a traumatic stressor. It could be argued that such men are highly reactive: they respond to life event stressors with the same intensity as they respond to traumatic stressors. Boulanger (1981) has

TABLE 3.4
Respondents in Three Diagnostic Classes According to Veteran Status

	Acute Stress Reactions*			
	Heavy Combat Veterans	Average Combat Veterans	Noncombat Veterans	Nonveterans
n =	80	118	348	452
Stressed	26.3	16.9	6.6	2.4
Possibly stressed	40.0	38.1	22.4	14.4
Not stressed	33.8	44.9	71.0	83.2
	100%	100%	100%	100%

*Somers' D with Stress Dependent .257, Significance .00001.

	Chronic Stress Reactions**			
	Heavy Combat Veterans	Average Combat Veterans	Noncombat Veterans	Nonveterans
n =	80	118	348	452
Stressed	36.3	23.7	17.2	15.9
Possibly stressed	36.3	44.9	31.6	37.6
Not stressed	27.5	31.4	51.1	46.6
	100%	100%	100%	100%

**Somers' D with Stress Dependent .09, Significance .0003.

found that these men are more likely to come from lower class homes where they are continually exposed to an undue number of life event stressors. As the Dohrenwends (1965) argue, "The high level of symptomatology in the lowest social economic strata represents, at least in part, transient responses to stressors" (p. 64). Alternatively, it could be argued that since we did not inquire into the occurrence of traumatic stressors other than combat, we have no way of gauging whether these respondents were involved in some other disasters. No epidemiological study to date has established the prevalence of the survivors of traumatic stressors in the general population, but it seems unlikely that such a large percentage of the general population would have met with such experiences.[5] Therefore, we must conclude that there are a number of false positives in the stressed class.

Clinical validation would be necessary to judge the scales' ability to measure accurately the incidence of posttraumatic stress disorder. However, the purpose of this particular analysis is not to establish incidence rates, but

---

[5]Recent unpublished estimates by Robins and her colleagues in the Ecological Catchment Area studies place the incidence of PTSD in the general population considerably lower. However, the Diagnostic Interview Schedule used by Robins and her team seems destined to yield false negative responses. (See Boulanger, in preparation for a detailed discussion of this matter)

rather to determine whether the symptoms described in DSM III do in fact form a single diagnostic entity. Our data suggest that traumatic experiences in adult life can produce long lasting psychological consequences in a significant minority of those who were exposed to the trauma, that these reactions are similar in that the form they take appears to be independent of prior pathology, and that these findings represent some empirical proof that the symptoms listed by the editors of DSM III are necessary to identifying this disorder.

ACKNOWLEDGMENT

The authors are grateful to Hilary Liberty, who did some of the preliminary analyses for this chapter.

4 Predisposition to Post-Traumatic Stress Disorder

Ghislaine Boulanger

The last chapter offered data to dispel a myth that is not particular to Vietnam veterans but pervades the mental health profession as a whole: that the effects of trauma in adult life do not have long lasting psychological consequences. We demonstrated the existence of a clear-cut clinical syndrome than occurs significantly more often in those who have been subjected to the trauma of combat. This syndrome has also been found among World War II veterans (e.g., Grinker & Spiegel, 1945; Kardiner,1969), among concentration camp survivors (e.g., Eitinger 1980), among the survivors of natural and manmade disasters such as the Buffalo Creek Dam collapse (Erikson, 1976) and industrial disasters (Weisaeth, 1983), and among those who have been raped (Burgess, & Holmstrom, 1974).

One of the arguments frequently advanced to challenge the diagnosis of PTSD is that those who become symptomatic after exposure to a stressor have in some way already been predisposed to mental disorders. For example, one of the stereotypes of Vietnam veterans is that those who served in Vietnam, men who were unable to avoid the draft or alternatively men who actually enlisted, were more susceptible to developing psychological disorders or were already experiencing more psychological problems than were men who chose to avoid the bloodshed. This point has been raised time after time in other contexts when those who had physically survived a trauma in adult life subsequently sought help with or compensation for their psychological symptoms.

The psychoanalytic imperative that informs the work of so many mental health professionals today insists that the roots of stress-related symptoms lie not in the recently, or not so recently, experienced trauma but in childhood.

Fairbairn (1952) puts this most succinctly: "The chief predisposing factor in determining the breakdown of a soldier...is infantile dependence on his objects" (p. 79). In the matter of compensation, the Germans frequently took a similar position in denying the claims of Jews who had survived the concentration camps only to find themselves continuing to relive the experience in their minds (Krystal, 1968). After the Buffalo Creek Dam collapse, the mining company's attorneys argued that survivors who complained of stress symptoms at the time of the postflood interview were suffering from lifelong psychopathology.

Is trauma itself pathogenic, or does it merely exacerbate previously existing pathology? In establishing the criteria for the diagnosis of PTSD, the editors of the third edition of the Diagnostic and Statistical Manual (APA, 1980) suggested that "prior history of another mental disorder such as Personality Disorder" (p. 235) may be involved. But the research to date has been confusing. Before reviewing a representative selection of this literature, let us make a distinction between two potentially confusing concepts. To argue that PTSD is an exacerbation of prior pathology is a different matter from claiming that there is a predisposition to such reactions. If PTSD is the manifestation or exacerbation of an ongoing neurosis or character disorder, then the symptoms would have been present to some degree before the stressor was encountered, and we should expect the symptoms to be different across character types. In the previous chapter we established that PTSD is a syndrome that appears to be independent of personality traits; however, this is not to say that concurrent personality diagnoses are not present. On the other hand, to argue that predisposition is the "cause" of PTSD must be fallacious since the cause of the reaction is the stressor. If predisposition does play a role in the incidence of PTSD, we should expect it to interact with the stressor to produce a stress reaction while others who are similarly predisposed but not exposed to the stressor would continue to be asymptomatic. A third possibility is that pathogenesis depends not on predisposing factors but on the stressor itself, with symptom emergence dependent on the magnitude of the stressor.

The two former concepts — the exacerbation of existing pathology and the existence of predisposing factors — obviously require somewhat different research strategies. After World War II, researchers tended to focus on preexisting pathology. Brill and Beebe (1955) found that men with preexisting overt neuroses had seven or eight times the chance of developing manifest psychological disorders than previously well-integrated men. Further, they found that 5 years after the war, the only groups showing significant change from preservice personality difficulties were composed of individuals with personality disorders or acting out characters. On the other hand, Ford and Spaulding (1973) made a study of men who had survived a year's imprisonment in North Korea after having been taken captive on the U.S.S. Pueblo.

Although those in the group who had handled the stressor poorly frequently were diagnosed as passive dependent and were more limited in the number of ego defense mechanisms utilized, men with a personality diagnosis of "schizoid" handled the stresses the North Koreans imposed on them as well as did those with "normal" personalities. Wolf and Ripley (1947), studying the survivors of Japanese prisoner of war camps, reached conclusions similar to those of Ford and Spaulding. "Among the survivors two personality types seemed to predominate: First those with features of a psychopathic personality, and second, personalities of the highest order of adjustment" (p. 186). In other words, men with preservice history of impaired object relations were able to survive stressful conditions as well as — and sometimes better than — "normals." Early in their exhaustive analysis of the ways in which different personality types break down under stressful conditions, Grinker and Spiegel (1945) state: "Normal and strong individuals may develop a neurosis if crucial stress is sufficiently severe, but combat soldiers with lifelong anxiety neuroses are able to withstand considerable stress" (p. 11).

Perhaps the lack of conclusive findings here can best be attributed to the difficulty frequently encountered when mental health professionals attempt to arrive at a consensus about a diagnosis (Ricks & Berry, 1970). This difficulty is compounded when the diagnosis is established retrospectively, in this case, after the respondent's exposure to the stressor. A more defensible method and one that is more readily operationalized is to search for factors in the respondent's childhood that might increase vulnerability to stress reactions. Allerton (1969), concluding a review of the literature on predisposition, noted: "The consensus of World War II studies is that men with histories of severe emotional deprivation and frustration during childhood and of prior maladjustment in family, schoolwork, or the community are more likely to be vulnerable to hazardous and privation conditions" (p. 21).

In some of the early studies of Vietnam veteran adjustment, we find equally unequivocal statements. Worthington (1978), for example, reported, "The results of research available today present substantial evidence that veteran adjustment complications are related to a lifelong pattern of coping" (p. 182). In a study he undertook with Salt Lake County Vietnam veterans, Worthington found that differences between veteran groups existed on measures of adjustment based on an earlier evaluation of whether or not they had enjoyed their tours of duty regardless of whether they had served: "Poor adjustment was related to no religious affiliation, being a high school drop out, being unemployed, having served as an enlisted man, not being promoted or being demoted during the service tour, having received some type of disciplinary action while in the army" (p. 177). Borus (1974) found that a group of adjusting post-Vietnam soldiers were older, better educated, and of higher rank, whereas among two representative poorly adjusting groups, 35% to 65% of the men had faced severe family disruptions on their return home.

It is important to note that among the independent variables or "predisposing factors" selected by Borus and Worthington, unemployment or severe disruptions in the family at homecoming could be a result of a stress reaction rather than an indication of poor lifelong coping. Recently researchers have selected independent variables with more caution. In one of the only nonretrospective studies of Vietnam veterans, Card (1983) found that of 14 background characteristics only "low self confidence" at age 15 was associated with chronic PTSD. Other sociodemographic variables, measures of academic ability, and personality traits failed to have any impact on whether or not the veteran developed PTSD.

It is not my intention to offer a comprehensive review of the research on this topic here; that has been done elsewhere (Boulanger, in preparation). But these contradictory findings are representative of the general problem that researchers have faced. Is the issue of predisposition really as cut and dried as Worthington, on the one hand, or Card, on the other, would suggest? Dohrenwend (1979) and Tischler (1969), among others, have constructed stressor-stress reaction paradigms that weigh each of these forces. Tischler describes his paradigm as follows:

> Each man has a particular stressor tolerance and specific resource requirements. The balance between the two is determined by the personality structure of the individual and reflected in his stressor-stimuli threshold. It is an idiosyncratic balance. As long as the balance is maintained, however, that person will be able to come to terms with the situation at hand. If the balance is disturbed, either through an increase in stressor intensity or a decrease of available resources, the sense of overt and covert psychological illness will begin to emerge. (p. 23)

The interaction effect between the level of the stressor and the level of predisposition that Tischler postulates is implicit in the conclusions drawn by many researchers, among them Hocking (1970) and Merbaum and Hefez (1976). They suggested that such a solution is the most plausible explanation for the contradictory findings they obtained, but few went on to test this hypothesis. Helzer (1983) did test the hypothesis. His respondents were Vietnam veterans, but he used depression rather than PTSD as the dependent variable. He postulated that antecedents would have a lesser predictive effect under conditions of extreme stress. He found the reverse to be true; low level stressors did not produce a significant difference in the prevalence of depressive syndromes between those with and without antecedent factors; whereas at high levels of combat stress, a number of the antecedent variables he selected did predict depression. Helzer remarked that an index of the separate antecedent variables would yield even more definitive results, stating, "It is not difficult to speculate that men who had none of the predisposition might show very few later effects of stress at all" (p. 21). Helzer speculated that men from the most stable families were the least likely to experience traumatic stress reactions. Although he did not test this particular hypothesis, he did find "a synergistic effect rather than an attenuation of predisposition under conditions of extreme stress" (p. 20). That is to say, at low levels of the stressor, the predisposing factors did not predict depression, but at higher levels they did.

FAMILY STABILITY

The research described in this chapter tests Helzer's hypothesis on the nationwide sample of 1,001 Vietnam veterans and nonveterans described in the Appendix. As Helzer suggests, the analytic strategy depends on the construction of a scale that measures factors in childhood and adolescence that might render a respondent more susceptible to break down after exposure to a traumatic stressor. We identified variables that would contribute toward a possibly unstable and unsupportive atmosphere in the family of origin, such as poverty, the separation from or death of the parents, the number of times the family moved during a given period (high school), and whether the father was frequently unemployed. In addition, four adolescent behaviors that are known to be associated with poor adult adjustment were added to the list: knowing other children who get in trouble with the school authorities; getting in trouble with the authorities; failing to graduate from high school; and playing hooky frequently (Robins, 1970). Parenthetically, it should be noted that these symptoms do not necessarily indicate the "emotional" climate in the family home, which Robins suggests might be a more relevant predictor of later psychopathy. While we agree with this point of view, such data require a subjective judgment by the respondent and fall prey to the retrospective dangers of distortion.

Given our hypothesis, it is reasonable to assume that the veterans in the present sample — and particularly those exposed to combat — would be more likely to show stress reactions when certain predisposing factors are present. Therefore, the first stage in the construction of the Family Stability Index was to divide the sample into veterans and nonveterans and to cross-tabulate all of those premilitary or pre-draft-age variables that appeared to be likely predictors of later psychopathology, with the a scale consisting of the PTSD items described in the previous chapter. In this case, however, rather than focusing on acute symptoms or chronic symptoms (those that had arisen during or immediately after the war or those that arose subsequently), we asked respondents more generally whether they had ever experienced each of the symptoms. Those who claimed to have experienced a symptom sometimes or often were scored as positive for that symptom, and all others were scored negative. The respondents falling in the top fifth of the scale's distribution were considered to meet the criterion for PTSD.

TABLE 4.1
Percentage of Respondents with Stress Reactions According to Score on
Family Stability Items and to Veteran Status

| | Percentage of Respondents Stressed | | | |
| | Nonveterans | | Veterans | |
Family Stability Item	No	Yes	No	Yes
Was one or both your parents missing from home before you were 18?	13% (351)	21% (101)	20% (415)	27% (130)
Did your parents separate or did either die before you were 18?	13% (383)	25% (69)	29% (495)	31% (70)
Were you raised in a foster home or residential treatment center?	14% (445)	29% (7)	21% (540)	40% (5)
Did your family move more than twice when you were in high school?	15% (366)	14% (86)	20% (445)	28% (100)
Were there more than seven children in your family?	15% (305)	14% (107)	20% (385)	27% (150)
Was your father out of work more than one quarter of the time?	14% (421)	19% (31)	21% (506)	33% (39)
Was your family income less than $5,000 a year?	15% (389)	13% (63)	19% (474)	38% (71)
Did you fail to graduate from high school before entering the military or reaching the age of 18?	14% (491)	22% (51)	22% (470)	21% (75)
Did you have friends who got in trouble with the authorities?	11% (238)	18% (214)	18% (294)	25% (251)
Did you get in trouble with the authorities?	13% (349)	18% (103)	19% (425)	29% (120)
Did you play hooky often?	14% (410)	21% (42)	20% (493)	37% (52)

Note: The *(n)* represents the number on which each percentage is based. Thus, of the 351 nonveteran respondents who answered "no" to the first item, 13% are stressed. Only half the distribution is shown here; the 87% nonveterans who answered "no" to the first item and are not stressed are not shown.

Table 4.1 shows that whereas 13% of the nonveterans who had both parents present at home during their formative years developed stress reactions during the course of their lifetime, 21% of those who come from single parent homes or had neither parent at home did so. However, 20% is the expected figure in this cell, since the Traumatic Stress Reaction Scales were divided at the 20% mark. Therefore, if a disproportionate number of men are suffering from the stress reaction, one would expect to find more than 20% of the respondents falling in that cell. This is true of the item under discussion: 27% of the veterans who come from single parent homes are stressed. In each case but one (failure to graduate from high school), those veterans who answered in the affirmative to a given item scored higher than those who answered in the negative, and higher than all nonveterans, and fall above the 20% baseline. Significance is not reported here because a cumulative trend is sought, which will later be tested with the index.

Although this table does not control for combat, the figures lend credibility to the argument that there is an interaction effect between the traumatic stress reaction and the stressor, which, for the purposes of argument, in this table is considered to be military service.

An index of these items was constructed in a simple additive fashion. It is obvious that a number of the items selected for the Family Stability Index are functional alternatives. For example, a man without a father is probably unable to say whether his father was out of work frequently. Therefore, the Family Stability Index cannot be expected to have very high internal consistency. In fact, the Alpha reliability is .50, an acceptable but not impressive level of reliability.

The Family Stability Index has a mean of 1.6 (and a standard deviation of 1.4) thus the "average" respondent in the sample comes from a family with between one and two problems. To facilitate the analysis, the index was divided into three categories ranging from the level of greatest family stability, (with no problems at all) to the least stable family, (with three or more problems). Consistent with Helzer's and associates (1980) hypothesis, it is assumed that those men who come from the most stable families will be the least likely to develop a stress reaction.

Before testing the hypothesis, we ascertain whether men who were more likely to be predisposed to stress reactions followed different pathways through the Vietnam era than did men from more stable backgrounds.

Figure 4.1 shows that at the first crossroads in the pathway through the Vietnam era, men who were of an age to serve in the Armed Forces were proportionately more likely to serve if they came from the most stable families. Forty-three percent of men from the most stable families entered the military, compared with 38% of men from the least stable families. Thus, men who were predisposed to serious psychopathology were less likely to find their way into the military. At the next crossroads, however, we find that once in the Armed Forces, men from the most stable families were considerably less likely to be assigned to a duty station in Vietnam and subsequently were even less likely to be in heavy combat. Only 17% of the men from the most stable families who were in Vietnam saw heavy combat, as opposed to 27% of men from average families and 34% of the men from the least stable families.

It is clear, then, that any analysis of the incidence of PTSD among Vietnam veterans must control for family stability as well as level of combat

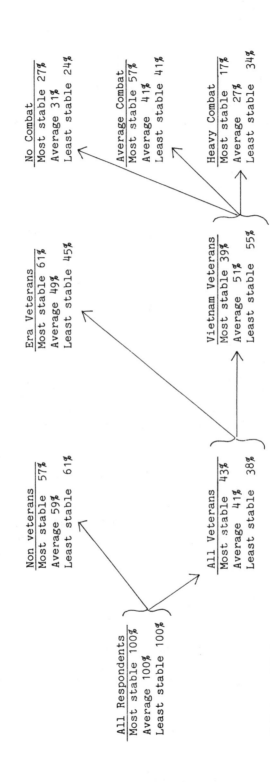

All Respondents
Most stable 100%
Average 100%
Least stable 100%

Non veterans
Most stable 57%
Average 59%
Least stable 61%

All Veterans
Most stable 43%
Average 41%
Least stable 38%

Era Veterans
Most stable 61%
Average 49%
Least stable 45%

Vietnam Veterans
Most stable 39%
Average 51%
Least stable 55%

No Combat
Most stable 27%
Average 31%
Least stable 24%

Average Combat
Most stable 57%
Average 41%
Least stable 41%

Heavy Combat
Most stable 17%
Average 27%
Least stable 34%

* Weighted Data

FIG. 4.1   Distribution of Respondents across Vietnam Era Experience According to Levels of Family Stability (weighted data)

44

exposure; our findings suggest that men from unstable families who were most susceptible to stress reactions were also most likely to be sent into heavy combat once they reached Vietnam.

Family Stability and Postwar Stress Reactions

Table 4.2 presents the percentage of men who developed acute stress reactions immediately after the war according to their Vietnam era experience and according to the level of stability in their families of origin. There are no differences of note between the various levels of family stability and the development of postwar stress reactions among nonveterans. For era veterans and for Vietnam veterans who did not see any combat, Table 4.2 shows that as the level of family instability increases, so does the percentage of men who developed PTSD symptoms. Among low combat Vietnam veterans, there is a large increase in the amount of stress reactions experienced by men from average families and those from the least stable families. At this point, the hypothesis that men from the most stable families do not develop stress reac-

TABLE 4.2
Percentages of Respondents Experiencing Postwar Stress Reactions
by Vietnam Experience and Family Stability

	Level of Family Stability		
	Most Stable Family	Average Family	Least Stable Family
Nonveterans	7% (105)	6% (201)	4% (146) (a)
Era Veterans	3% (69)	15% (116)	22% (87) (b)
No Combat	0% (11)	9% (43)	24% (21) (c)
Low Combat	9% (22)	40% (52)	42% (41) (d)
Heavy Combat	60% (10)	32% (37)	39% (33) (e)

Note: Only half of this table is shown. For example, the 93% of nonveterans from the most stable families who are not stressed do not appear. The *(n)* represents the total number of nonveterans from the most stable families.

(a) Tau c = .02, not significant.
(b) Tau c = .15, significance .0004.
(c) Tau c = .16, significance .01.
(d) Tau c = .20, significance .01.
(e) Tau c = .05, not significant.

tions appears to be correct. But we find that under heavy combat conditions approximately two thirds of the men from the most stable families developed stress reactions. Furthermore, the insignificant Tau C of .05 shows that among men who were exposed to heavy fighting, predisposition had no effect on the development of acute stress reactions in the immediate postwar period. Every man had his breaking point, that point being contingent both the intensity of the stressor and the level of stability in his family of origin.

Figure 4.2 presents these findings graphically, revealing that although a greater percentage of men from the most stable families developed stress reactions under heavy combat conditions than did men from less stable backgrounds, men from the most stable families have a higher threshold for the development of stress reactions. Put another way, it takes a more traumatic stressor to elicit stress reactions in such men. In Fig. 4.2 the sharp rise in the bar graph under different conditions of family stability and different levels of combat exposure graphically illustrates the interaction effect, or acute stress reaction threshold. The Chi Square test of significance in Fig. 4.2 reveals that men from the least stable families are more or less equally stressed no matter what level of combat they were exposed to, whereas men from more stable families are affected by combat. Before drawing any conclusions about these findings, let us consider the current or chronic level of stress reactions under the different conditions of family stability.

Family Stability and Current Stress Reactions

Table 4.3 presents a breakdown of chronic stress reactions across Vietnam Era experience including combat exposure according to the three levels of family stability. A comparison of Table 4.2 with Table 4.3, it will disclose that some shifts have occurred in the percentage of stress reactions over time, but the overall patterns are similar. Once again, for all but the combat conditions, the percentage of stress reactions rises with the level of instability in the family of origin. Nonveterans and era veterans from the least stable families now exceed the stress reaction baseline by 8 and 15 percentage points respectively. Once again, there is a large rise in the percentage of stress reactions currently experienced by men from average and the least stable families who saw low combat, whereas men from the most stable families who saw low combat remain relatively free of current stress reactions.

Table 4.2 reveals that men from the most stable families had a higher threshold for the development of stress reactions in the immediate postwar period, and this continues to be the case now. As many men from the most stable families who were in heavy combat continue to be as seriously stressed as men from less stable families. In other words, there continues to be no significant difference between the levels of family stability and the current prevalence of stress reactions among men who saw heavy combat in Vietnam.

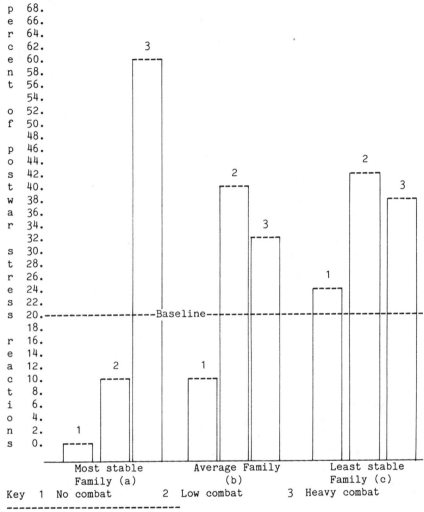

FIG. 4.2   Bar Graph Showing Postwar Incidence of Stress Reactions According to Different Levels of Combat Exposure and Family Stability

TABLE 4.3
Percentages of Respondents Experiencing Current Stress Reactions
by Vietnam Era Experience and Family Stability

	Level of Family Stability		
	Most Stable Family	Average Family	Least Stable Family
Nonveterans	14% (105)	15% (201)	28% (146) (a)
Era Veterans	10% (69)	16% (116)	35% (87) (b)
No Combat	0% (11)	7% (43)	19% (41) (c)
Low Combat	9% (22)	35% (52)	39% (41) (d)
Heavy Combat	40% (10)	30% (37)	39% (33) (e)

Note: See note on Table 4.2.

(a) Tau c = .11, significance .001.
(b) Tau c = .20, significance .0001.
(c) Tau c = .13, significance .02.
(d) Tau c = .19, significance .01.
(e) Tau c = .04, not significant.

Figure 4.3 graphically portrays these findings, giving significance tests within each level of family stability for the level of combat involvement. As in the immediate postwar periods, respondents from the least stable families do not differ significantly in the amount of stress experienced according to the levels of combat in which they were involved. Just being in Vietnam appears to have been and to have remained a stressful experience for such men. (Indeed Table 4.3 shows that the differences between nonveterans and veterans from the least stable families is negligible.) Simply coming from an unusually unstable background appears to produce stress symptoms among such men whether or not they are exposed to a traumatic stressor. This finding could be explained by arguing that the residual effect of the unstable upbringing to which these men were subjected results in a personality type whose features resemble the symptoms of PTSD. Or, it could be hypothesized that men from the most unstable backgrounds are highly reactive; they respond to life event stressors with the same intensity as when they respond to traumatic stressors. Their stressor threshold is significantly lower than others'.

For men from the average family, being involved in even a low degree of combat results in a significant level of chronic stress reactions; and for men

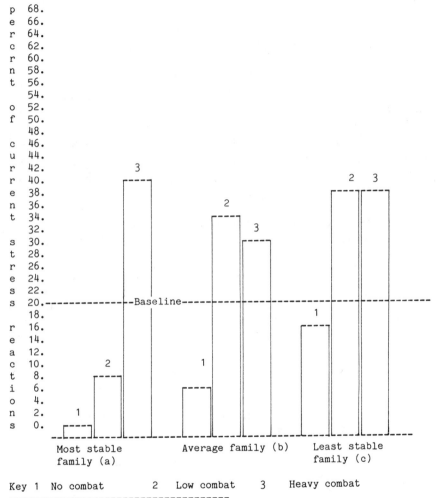

FIG. 4.3 Bar Graph Showing Current Prevalence of Stress Reactions According to Different Levels of Combat Exposure and Family Stability

49

from the most stable families, high combat continues to represent the interaction point between the stressor and the development of significant levels of PTSD.

SUMMARY AND DISCUSSION.

Before conclusions are drawn from these findings, a word of caution should be introduced. The number of men from the most stable families in the heavy combat cell is very low, and therefore these findings maybe somewhat unstable. Nonetheless, the following trends emerge. First, the hypothesis that men from the most stable families would not develop stress reactions has been disproved. Under the most stressful conditions, that is, exposure to high levels of combat, predisposition appears to have no bearing on the development of traumatic stress reactions. We find that in extreme circumstances, men who are least likely to be susceptible to mental disorder are as likely to develop subsequent stress reactions as men who are most vulnerable to psychological problems. At less stressful levels, such as exposure to low levels of combat, men from the most stable families remain relatively free of stress reactions, whereas men from average families with one or two predisposing factors do develop stress reactions. During the war years, military service appears to have produced a disproportionate level of stress reactions in men from the least stable families. Currently, however, such men are experiencing more symptoms of the traumatic stress reaction independently of exposure to a stressor.

We conclude that although the synergistic effect to which Helzer (1983), refers appears to exist for men from very stable families and for those from average families when exposed to varying degrees of combat, it does not occur in men from the least stable families among whom stress-like symptoms can exist independently of a traumatic stressor.

At the beginning of this chapter, we cited a number of ways in which the psychoanalytic imperative has been invoked to argue against the development of a traumatic stress syndrome in previously "normal" individuals. These arguments have been countered by the findings presented in the last two chapters. First, it was established that PTSD does not present as the exacerbation of a preexisting pathological condition. Second, it has been shown that predisposing factors alone do not cause PTSD. Under low or moderately stressful conditions, such factors interact with the stressor to produce stress reactions. However, in the most extreme conditions everyone, even the least susceptible, is at risk to develop PTSD.

5 Effects of Group Cohesion on Posttraumatic Stress Disorder

Nava Lerer
Charles Kadushin

INTRODUCTION

This chapter is an update of the classic literature relating primary group cohesion to the prevention of psychological disorder and group panic among combat troops. While the relation between social structure and combat effectiveness is of great practical interest to post-Vietnam armies throughout the world, the theoretical importance of this relationship to the social science community is of equal or greater importance. Two generations of sociologists and social psychologists have come to believe in the theoretical importance of primary groups and group cohesion as a motivational factor, as compared with abstract ideology. In part, this view is a result of classic analyses of World War II data (Shils, 1950; Shils & Janowitz 1948; Stouffer, Suchman et al., 1949), which have been cited and recited ever since. This literature asserted that primary group integration or cohesion is critical for soldiers' motivation to fight and for their effective performance in combat. Later work building on this foundation claimed that in the Korean conflict men fought not for abstract causes, but because they did not want to let their buddies down (Little, 1964). Most recently, qualitative observations in Vietnam confirmed the importance of group cohesion for combat effectiveness but suggested that primary group ties were based on self-interest rather than identification and solidarity with the group. It has also been argued that unless soldiers at least implicitly support the aims of a war and its underlying legitimacy, group cohesion can actually be counterproductive (Brown & Moskos, 1976; Moskos, 1970, 1975).

Surprisingly, although there is almost unified agreement on the positive influence of group cohesiveness in combat on individual and group perform-

51

ance, there are very few methodologically sophisticated quantitative studies demonstrating these effects. None seems available for the war in Vietnam. The only recent quantitative study we have been able to locate on troops actually exposed to enemy fire is that of Shirom (1976), who in 1974 studied Israeli troops on the front line in the Golan Heights who were subject to "sporadic artillery and mortar barrages and infrequent exchange of small-arms fire" (p. 422). Findings are mixed. Help given to other soldiers was associated with better combat performance, but help received was not. The other available quantitative studies investigated the effects of group cohesion among soldiers who were trainees (Nelson & Berry, 1968; Tziner & Vardi, 1982). Findings obtained in these studies are not necessarily relevant to actual combat conditions, and we are skeptical. We do not rule out the possibility that cohesiveness is a critical variable. Rather, we argue that a better case for it needs to be made and that much further research is required. Merely because propositions are hallowed does not mean that they should not be carefully reexamined.

To begin with, there is no clear operational definition of group cohesiveness in the literature, and each of the studies we reviewed uses a different measure. Several variables have been mentioned as sources of group cohesion: common background, leadership, professional attitude, unit prestige, and time spent together (George, 1971; Johns, 1983; Lang, 1980). Among these variables, leadership has frequently been emphasized as a very important source of combat effectiveness and group cohesiveness (George, 1971; Lang, 1980; Shils, 1950; Shils & Janowitz, 1948; Stouffer, Lumsdaine et al., 1949; Stouffer, Suchman et al., 1949). More recently, macro indicators of cohesion have been introduced in a complex causal chain. Low cohesion in the post-Vietnam war American Armed Forces is said to result from a secular trend in Western society towards rationality and bureaucracy, which is antithetical to a sense of community based on moral commitment and to sanctions based on esteem, affection, prestige, and ritualistic symbols. It has been argued that only when officers endorse these latter values can they be effective leaders. The lack of effective leadership thus results in a decrease in unit cohesion and a corresponding lack of combat effectiveness (Johns, 1983; Savage & Gabriel, 1976).

This chapter introduces some quantitative evidence on the effect of group cohesion among combat troops in Vietnam and its consequences for psychological functioning in combat and thereafter. With admittedly imperfect measures, we first attempt to verify some claimed correlates of group or unit cohesion in an effort to establish some criterion validity for the measures. Then we address the issue of disintegration or lack of disintegration of American troops over the years in Vietnam. Finally, we investigate the immediate as well as the long-term psychological consequences of group cohesiveness. Although psychological functioning is not the same as combat effectiveness, the two are obviously related since men who suffer psychological breakdown in combat are not effective soldiers. Moreover, they cause difficulties not only for themselves but for others, and like all casualties they are a serious drain on military resources.

The psychological consequence on which we focus in this chapter is the development of symptoms of Posttraumatic Stress Disorder, discussed in detail in Chapter 3 of this volume. Here, it is important to note that psychiatric breakdown in combat is often only the tip of the iceberg – PTSD symptoms may appear long after the termination of combat among individuals who did not break down in the field (Boulanger, in press; see also Chapter 3, this volume).

The consensus in the literature is that primary group ties serve as a support system that defends the soldiers against psychiatric breakdown in the field. This literature is based mainly on the World War II studies previously cited and on qualitative psychiatric observations in combat (e.g Grinker & Spiegel, 1963; Marshall, 1947; for a complete review see Marlowe, 1982). No quantitative studies were located that directly relate psychiatric breakdown in the field to group cohesion. However, a study of men admitted to hospitals after the Yom Kippur War with "clinical evidence of acute or late onset of posttraumatic combat reactions" compared with men from elite units with no clinical evidence of "war neurosis" suggests that men in the latter units received more social support from their comrades and had greater trust in their officers (Steiner & Neumann, 1978). Thus there is some evidence that the long-term psychiatric effects may be mitigated by unit cohesiveness at the time of combat.

There is, however, some suggestion in the literature that group cohesion in combat produces, after combat, a counterreaction that results in a sense of loneliness and a feeling of being cut off from one's buddies. This sense of being apart and socially disconnected in turn exacerbates PTSD symptoms (Archibald, Long, Miller & Tuddenham, 1962; Archibald & Tuddenham, 1965; Dasberg, 1982). Archibald and his colleagues suggest that because symptoms now identified as PTSD originated in a group situation, they also can be alleviated in a group. This is indeed a favored approach in the treatment of Vietnam veterans with PTSD symptoms (Smith, 1985). Data from a major study of Vietnam veterans (Kadushin, 1983; Kadushin, Boulanger & Martin, 1981) suggest that association with and support from friends, wives, and especially other Vietnam veterans under some conditions is associated with lower levels of PTSD. But these data refer to cohesion experienced upon the return home after combat, not during combat itself.

We now turn to the only quantitative material we could locate on the war in Vietnam. The available measures of cohesion are not as thorough as the combat scale or the PTSD scale we use, since primary group cohesion in the military was not the focus of the study. Nonetheless, two items seem to capture some of the multidimensional aspects of group cohesion as it is generally used and as it applies to the military (George, 1971). One indicator of group cohesiveness is the degree to which members of a group feel mutually supported. In the present study this was measured by responses to the following question: "How many men you served with were the kind who looked out for the other guy's welfare — none, a few, about half, most, or all?" The confidence that men have in their officers and the degree to which men feel the officers care about them is one of the major sources of both combat effectiveness and group cohesion among the men themselves (George, 1971; Johns, 1983; Savage & Gabriel, 1976). Again, this question was asked very directly: "How many of your officers were the kind who tried to look out for the welfare of the enlisted men?" The same alternatives were offered as in the question about men looking out for one another. When the question about officers is used in the following analysis, only enlisted men are included so as to preclude any possible self-justification on the part of the officers in our sample.

ANALYSIS

Validity of the Indicators of Cohesiveness

Our first step is to establish that the items have external or cross-validity. This is a step notable for its omission from prior research where the validity of the various indicators of group cohesion was taken as self-evident. Other things being equal, combat experiences should increase the sense of group cohesion. "It is indeed ancient wisdom that groups often become integrated more closely when faced by external threat. And it is also true that over the ages military leaders have attempted to incorporate this theorem into military practice" (George, 1971, p. 293–319). In the present study, 54% of veterans not in heavy combat or not in Vietnam ($n = 467$) said most or all of the men looked out for each other; 67% of heavy combat veterans ($n = 79$) affirmed this (significance greater than .05). All tests reported in this section are Chi sq, corrected for 1 degree of freedom. The relationship is even stronger for the item asking about whether officers looked out for the enlisted man. Considering only enlisted men, 30% not in heavy combat ($n = 441$) said most or all of the officers looked out for the men, compared with 50% ($n = 74$) of those who had been in heavy combat (sig .001). The Marine Corps is said to have more unit cohesion than the Army (Blake, 1978; Brown & Moskos, 1976). Forty percent of Army veteran enlisted men who were in heavy combat ($n = 52$) said most or all of the officers looked out for them; 72% of Marine heavy combat veterans ($n = 18$) affirmed this, a difference significant at the .04 level. Among veterans who were in heavy combat, 63% who served in the Army ($n = 56$) said that most or all of the men looked out for each other as compared with 79% of the Marines ($n = 19$). Although this difference is in the predicted direction, it is not significant.

Finally, cohesiveness is said to be related to morale and to a general sense of support for the war, although the literature is of two minds about this latter consequence (George, 1971). In our case, both indicators of cohesiveness were related to support for the war in Vietnam, as judged by the coding of an open-ended item asking respondents how they felt about the war during their period of service in Vietnam. Among our sample of heavy combat veterans, 48% of enlisted men who said the officers looked out for them ($n = 31$) favored the war as compared with 21% of the others ($n = 33$), a difference significant at the .04 level. While 40% of veterans who reported that most or all of the men looked out for one another favored the war ($n = 47$) as compared with 23% of the others ($n = 22$), this difference is not significant. Thus, of the six predictions in testing the external validity of these two indicators of cohesiveness, all are in the expected direction and four are significant.

There is no direct measure of combat effectiveness in the present study and hence no direct test of the proposition that cohesiveness leads to combat effectiveness is possible with these data. The best indicator available is whether or not a veteran thought he had killed someone. Perhaps those who thought they killed someone were more effective. Although over 83% of the men who were in heavy combat ($n = 78$) thought they had killed someone as compared with 36% of other Vietnam veterans ($n = 191$), with combat controlled there is no relation between this thought and the two indicators of group cohesion.

No Evidence of Less Cohesiveness After 1968.

Having established that the indicators of group cohesion in this study are related to most of the variables which the literature associates with group cohesion, let us investigate some of the allegations about the collapse of the Armed Forces in Vietnam (Faris, 1977; Gregory, 1977; Savage & Gabriel, 1976). The year of the Tet Offensive, 1968, is a well-documented, if somewhat controversial, watershed. For a variety of reasons the character of the war changed after 1968, as did the nature of the men serving in Vietnam. Our data show no evidence of a decrease in cohesiveness after 1968 — in fact the opposite! Fifty-five percent of men who came to Vietnam before 1968 said most or all of the men looked out for one another as compared with 67% after 1968, a difference significant at the .05 level. The difference between pre- and post-1968 is due mainly to men who were in heavy combat. For those who were not, there is no difference in the proportion who say the men looked out for one another. For those who did engage in heavy combat, the difference is 20 percentage points in favor of those who were in Vietnam in 1968 and afterward. This increase in cohesiveness after 1968 is not apparent when the item asking whether officers looked out for their men is considered. On the other hand, there is also no evidence that after 1968 men were more likely to feel less support from their officers. In short, our data produce no evidence that there was any decline in cohesiveness in the Armed Forces in Vietnam after 1968.

Cohesiveness May Lead to Greater Short Term Stress.

We now examine the relation between veterans' recall of symptoms of stress during and right after the war and indicators of primary group cohesion. As mentioned in Chapter 3, the stress symptoms break down into three latent classes: those who have all the symptoms of PTSD and who are called "stressed"; those who have some of them and are called "possibly stressed"; and those who appear to have none or very few symptoms. Table 5.1 shows the distribution of these classes for men who said that most or all of the men looked out for one another, and for those who said that half or fewer did so. The associations between the indicator of cohesion and stress reaction are displayed for Vietnam veterans only, divided into categories of various amounts of combat experienced. Table 5.1 displays some of the findings we have already reported. The greater the degree of combat, the higher the stress reaction and the higher the group cohesion. Overall, there is little or no association (Somers' D = .05) between group cohesion and stress reaction, however.

The relation between group cohesion and stress reaction is not "explained" by combat experience. Rather, there is a specification: the higher the level of combat, the higher the negative relationship between group cohesion and stress reaction. That is, the greater the group cohesion, the greater the stress reaction — exactly the opposite of the findings one might expect from a review of the literature. We do not report significance findings for the table since our n's are small and the data analysis is clearly exploratory. If one uses the statistical significance levels given by the statistical package (SPSS) as a rule of thumb guide, then the highest level of combat in the table does have a statistically significant level of Somers' D (at .025 level) and the combined total of heavy and very heavy combat ($n = 79$, the group we had been reporting about above) shows a Somers' D of .295, significant at the .01 level.

The overall level of symptoms is considerably higher than that reported by military psychiatrists, but is in keeping with most investigations of the phenomenon by others. The differences that cohesion makes are not affected by the pre/post-1968 watershed, though absolute levels of PTSD are higher post 1968. (This may well be due to memory factors; the increase in symptoms is almost linear with the recency of the experience. There is no sharp jump in any one year as has been alleged by Lauffer, Yager, Frey-Wouters, and Donnellan, 1981). When we look at the effects of the feeling that officers

TABLE 5.1
Percent of Vietnam Veterans with Varying Degrees of Stress During or 1 Year After Service in Vietnam, According to Combat Experience and Their Degree of Cohesiveness

Extent of Combat	Cohesiveness: Men Looked Out For One Another	Stress Class				
		Stressed	Possibly Stressed	Not Stressed	Total	n
No Combat	half	3	20	78	101%	(32)
	most	9	9	81	99%	(42)
Low Combat	half	20	33	47	100%	(45)
	most	15	41	44	100%	(73)
High Combat	half	10	53	37	100%	(19)
	most	26	44	29	100%	(34)
Very High Combat	half	14	14	71	99%	(7)
	most	47	32	21	100%	(19)

Extent of Combat	Score on the Combat Scale	Asymmetrical Somers' D Cohesion Independent, Stress Dependent
No Combat	0 – 2.99	.045
Low Combat	3.0–16.99	.004
High Combat	17.0–24.99	– .167
Very High Combat	25.0–33.00	– .526

looked out for their men, there are no differences in levels of PTSD. An additional analysis was performed in which the same independent variables were used, but the dependent variable was current (i.e. 10–16 years postcombat) level of PTSD. No differences for either indicator of group cohesiveness in current levels of PTSD symptoms were found.

DISCUSSION

At the very least, these data offer no support for the positive effects of group cohesion on psychological functioning during or after combat among American troops in Vietnam. On the contrary, we suggest that cohesiveness is a double-edged sword. Although a group may be supportive, members of a tightly knit group may also suffer from feelings of loss when other members are killed or wounded. Further, there are a number of different ways the relation between combat, group cohesion, and psychological consequences can be modeled. For example, it is logically possible that the relation between measures of cohesion and symptoms of stress reaction is spurious, because both cohesion and stress reaction can increase with an increase in exposure to combat. This situation does not hold true, however, for the present data, since controlling for the level of combat does not make the association between cohesion and stress reaction disappear; rather, the higher the level of combat, the higher the association between believing that men looked out for one another and symptoms of posttraumatic stress disorder.

A possible explanation for the finding of no differences in PTSD between soldiers who felt that most officers looked after their men and those who did not feel so is that the sense of personal loss among the enlisted men may be less when officers are killed or wounded, for the men may not feel as close to officers as they do to other enlisted men. Another interesting finding is that when the relations between current PTSD symptoms and the measures of group cohesion are analyzed, no differences are found. The feelings of personal loss may disappear over time and may not have long-term consequences. At the very least, the short term consequences of strong group cohesion in heavy combat may not necessarily be positive.

Despite the importance attached to the topic of group cohesion in the military, since *The American Soldier* (Stouffer, Suchman, et al., 1949) there have been few quantitative studies of the effect of group cohesion on men in combat. The present study suffers from a number of obvious weaknesses: the data are retrospective and the indicators of cohesiveness are limited. Furthermore, the dependent variable, psychological stress, although very important, may not be an indicator of combat effectiveness. Nonetheless, unlike most literature in this field, the present study systematically checks the validity of its group cohesion indicators; the analysis provided on the effects of group cohesion in combat is one of the few currently available. The conclusions of the present study are at some variance with the existing literature. In extrapolating from these findings we suggest that units with high short term military effectiveness may also produce members with severe symptoms of PTSD, a presumably undesirable long run consequence both from the point of view of continued military effectiveness and from the point of view of an Armed Force which is an extension of the citizenry.

By calling present stereotypes about the nature and consequences of group cohesion among men in combat into question, the present study raises a number of issues:

1. What do we mean by group cohesion, and how should it be measured?
2. If various dimensions of group cohesion, such as interpersonal attraction, interdependency, morale, sense of belonging, or the perceived success of the unit were investigated, would the results be different for each dimension?
3. Similarly, according to our evidence, the American Armed Forces did not "collapse" in Vietnam. On the contrary, group cohesion might even have

increased after 1968. If the reports on decrease in "morale" after 1968 are accurate, is it possible that contrary to most of the literature (for review, see Hare, 1976; Marlowe, 1982) group morale and group cohesion are not equivalent?

4. In our study, group cohesion had an effect only on recalled stress symptoms during and right after the war, but not on current stress symptoms. Are there differences between short term and long term consequences of group cohesion in the military? What models of the relation between combat, cohesion, and psychological consequences are appropriate to what kinds of situations? Further, what are the appropriate dependent variables consequent in group cohesion?

5. Since group cohesion is a group, not an individual property, how can the relation between individual psychological attributes or outcomes and group cohesion best be measured and understood?

One thing is clear. Much more study and attention to this problem is necessary. However intuitively appealing is the proposition that group cohesion has positive effects in the military setting, the concepts involved must be clarified, the theory developed, and any resulting statements given more empirical support than is now available.

6 Substance Use and Mental Health Among Vietnam Veterans

Laurie Michael Roth

Although the Vietnam War ended over a decade ago, the substance use behavior of Vietnam veterans has remained a *cause célèbre*. During the middle and late 1960s, as U.S. involvement in the war grew, reports of widespread use of marijuana among American servicemen in Vietnam drifted back to the United States, and by the spring of 1971, heroin use had purportedly reached epidemic proportions (Robins, 1974; Stanton, 1976; Wilbur, 1974). Heavy drug outbreaks among U.S. servicemen stationed at other overseas posts were also reported during this period. In Vietnam and in other foreign countries where Americans served, heroin and other hard drugs were widely available and inexpensive (Wilbur, 1974). Norms against use were lax. For many, illicit drug use and drinking provided much needed relief from "the awareness of danger, the hardships of battle, and the regimentation of military life" (Robins, 1978, p. 181).

The American public's concern about the drug epidemic among U.S. servicemen in Vietnam grew largely out of fear that the returning veteran would bring his newly acquired drug habits home. Traditional theories of physical addiction hold that even the occasional use of heroin or any other narcotic is bound to lead to drug dependence and that drug dependence in one social setting will necessarily persist in another. It was also expected that as a result of exposure to and experimentation with drugs in the military, the young veteran would turn to drugs, alcohol, or both to deal with personal stress and to express dissatisfaction with life as he attempted to reintegrate into civilian society. Thus, it was feared that substance abuse would be the major disability of the Vietnam War casualty, who was unable to cope with either the traumas of combat or the stresses of readjusting to civilian life.

As the Vietnam Era came to a close, images of the poorly adjusted Vietnam veteran "addict" and "alcoholic" pervaded the media, despite little evidence suggesting that the postwar substance use patterns of Vietnam veterans differed considerably from those of their nonveteran peers. Throughout the decade following the war, researchers continued to debate whether the worst fears of the American public concerning the substance use behavior of Vietnam veterans have come true.

DRINKING AND DRUG USE IN VIETNAM

Robins and associates (e.g. Goodwin, Davis, & Robins, 1975; Robins, 1974; Robins, Helzer & Davis, 1975) conducted the most comprehensive epidemiological study of the drinking and drug use patterns of U.S. Army men who served in Vietnam in 1971 during the height of the heroin epidemic and of Vietnam returnees within one year after service in that combat zone. They studied both a random sample of Army men released from Vietnam in September, 1971, and a sample of men detected as drug users in urine screenings at time of departure from Vietnam. Based on retrospective data, Robins (1974) estimates that 69% of Army men in Vietnam used marijuana at least once; 34% used heroin at least once; 38% used opium at least once (nearly five times the rate of preservice use); 25% used amphetamines at least once; and 23% used barbiturates at least once (twice the rate of preservice use). They also report that 19% of Army enlisted men felt themselves to be dependent on heroin at some time during their year of Vietnam service.

There has been considerable speculation about the causes of the heroin epidemic among U.S. soldiers in Vietnam. Some have attributed the epidemic to the military crackdown on marijuana, which peaked in 1969 (Zinberg, 1972); to the availability of "pure" heroin at low cost (McCoy, 1972; Stanton, 1976); to G.I. disenchantment with the war and deterioration in unit morale after the Tet Offensive in 1968; to boredom, depression, and fear of combat; as well as to curiosity and rebellion (e.g. Bentel & Smith, 1971; Robins, 1974; Sanders, 1973).

It is likely that, for at least some U.S. soldiers in Vietnam, illicit drugs served as a combat zone coping device, a role played by alcohol in previous military conflicts (Stanton, 1976). Researchers have reported a variety of contradictory findings concerning the association between exposure to combat and drug use in Vietnam. These differences may be partially a function of different sampling procedures, definitions of combat exposure in a guerrilla war, and patterns of substance use among Vietnam soldiers during various periods of the war.

Postel (1968) found a higher incidence of marijuana use in forward combat areas than in base camps and support areas, whereas Stanton (1976) reported that most illicit drug use occurred in the rear areas away from actual combat areas. In a similar vein, Figley and Eisenhart (1975) found that noncombatant soldiers in their sample used drugs and alcohol less frequently than others. Based on interviews with heroin addicted Vietnam returnees, Ingraham (1974) concluded that for most soldiers combat stress was not a major factor in contributing to use in Vietnam, and Robins (1974) found no relationship between combat experiences and drug use in Vietnam.

POSTWAR SUBSTANCE USE BY VIETNAM RETURNEES

Despite media coverage to the contrary, research findings concerning the early postwar substance use behavior of Vietnam returnees are rather consistent. Robins' (1974) work is generally considered the definitive follow-up study of Vietnam returnees during their first year after Vietnam service. She found, to everyone's surprise, that Vietnam drug users did not carry their patterns of substance use back to the States after discharge. Eight to twelve months after Vietnam service, Army veterans' drug use returned to pre-Vietnam levels. On the other hand, regular and problem drinking, when merged into one category, declined in Vietnam but increased after Vietnam even beyond their preservice levels. These findings concerning post-Vietnam drug use challenged scientific theories of physical addiction, which claim that drug dependence is persistent and intractible until the individual undergoes the withdrawal syndrome.

Robins' (1974) study also mitigated fears that Vietnam veterans exposed to combat might be particularly prone to use drugs after military service as a means of coping with the memories of wartime trauma and the stresses of readjusting to civilian life. Robins found no relationship between combat experiences and later drug use in her sample of Vietnam returnees. A year later, however, DeFazio, Rustin, and Diamond (1975) reported that in their study of approximately 200 Vietnam veterans who were attending a community college 3 to 6 years after military service, men who had seen combat in Vietnam were more likely than other veterans to use marijuana.

Nace, O'Brien, Mintz, Ream, and Meyers (1978) addressed many of the issues studied by Robins (1974), but with a much smaller and nonrandom sample of Vietnam veterans in the metropolitan Philadelphia area. Their sample consisted of veterans who had been admitted to drug treatment centers in Vietnam in 1971 or 1972 and a control group of veterans who had been admitted to Army hospitals in Vietnam for other medical reasons. The average time since discharge from the Army — 28 months — was longer than in Robins' sample. Postservice illicit drug use rates in Nace et al.'s drug positive sample corresponded closely to those of Robins' drug positive veterans. Nace and colleagues concluded, as did Robins, that continuing narcotic addiction among Vietnam veterans was "considerably less than had been anticipated" (p. 80) although alcohol-related problems were extensive, with 16% of the sample categorized as problem drinkers.

The findings reported by Rohrbaugh, Eads, and Press (1974) were only modestly discrepant from those just reviewed. Those investigators compared the incidence of recent drug use in three samples of Vietnam returnees serving at stateside military installations in 1971 with a sample of active duty "controls" who had not been sent to Southeast Asia. The Vietnam returnees in these samples had been discharged from Vietnam for varying lengths of time, ranging from less than 6 months to over a year. After introducing statistical controls for preservice differences in the samples, they report that current opiate use was marginally higher among Vietnam returnees in only one sample. The researchers caution readers that their samples were not representative of the general Vietnam veteran population. Veterans discharged from the military soon after their return to the States were not represented, nor were "casualties" of Vietnam drug use — men discharged from the military because of drug problems and veterans who entered residential drug treatment programs.

Research comparing the substance use behavior of Vietnam veterans and civilian "controls" is scant. In a 1974–75 follow-up study of the Vietnam returnees surveyed in 1971, Robins (1978) compared the drug initiation behaviors of Vietnam veterans and a matched cohort of nonveterans across three time periods. The objective was to determine whether exposure to the Vietnam setting during the height of the heroin epidemic had increased the number of veterans who had any illicit drug experience either during Vietnam service or after. She concludes that exposure to Vietnam had a large net effect on the number of veterans who ever used narcotics or marijuana but only a negligible net effect on the number of veterans who ever used amphetamines or barbiturates.

Card (1983) compared the postwar substance use patterns of a generational cohort of Vietnam veterans, non-Vietnam veterans (men who served in the military during the Vietnam Era but not in Vietnam), and nonveterans who were 36 years old in 1981. The three groups were matched on 51 preservice characteristics so that any effects of military service and war experiences on veteran behavior could be isolated. Consistent with Robins' (1974) findings, she reported that military service during the Vietnam Era was marked by heavy drug and alcohol consumption but these substance use patterns generally were abandoned after military service. Although the veterans continued to report slightly heavier substance use than nonveterans when surveyed at age 36, none of the differences in usage rates was statistically significant.

THE VIETNAM ERA RESEARCH PROJECT STUDY OF
SUBSTANCE USE BEHAVIOR

The Vietnam Era Research Project (Egendorf, 1981; Egendorf, Kadushin, Laufer, Rothbart, & Sloan, 1981; Kadushin, Boulanger, & Martin, 1981; Laufer, Yager, Frey-Wouters, & Donnellan, 1981; Rothbart, Sloan, & Joyce, 1981) published a probability sample of veterans and nonveterans matched on key sociodemographic variables to investigate some of the same issues examined in the studies reviewed as well as some additional ones. As in Card's (1983) study, the drinking and drug use patterns of veterans and their nonveteran peers were compared to determine whether specific military events of the Vietnam Era had long-term effects on the behavior of veterans. Both studies benefit greatly from their sample design. Nationally representative groups of Vietnam Era veterans — those who had served in Vietnam and those who had served elsewhere during the same historical period — were compared with a group of nonveterans, who were matched on pre-service characteristics. With this sample design, the researchers could isolate the current issues or problems critical to the general veteran population of that era, as well as those that apply only to veterans who served in Vietnam or those who served at other military posts. Both studies also share a time frame: they aimed to isolate the long-term effects of military service on substance use behavior. Although one might suspect that a time lag of 10 to 15 years would have washed out any effects of military service on substance use behavior, it is also possible that differences obscured by a "sleeper" effect during the first years might emerge as a function of later success or failure in employment as well as in the family and social domains.

The study described in this chapter also investigated whether drinking or drug use is currently linked to poor psychological health among the general population of Vietnam Era veterans who were exposed to different war experiences and who, 10 to 15 years later, are not institutionalized. Drug researchers often examine prevalence rates within a given population without investigating whether such usage is associated with problems in psychological functioning. Guided by a "deviance" model, they may assume that all drug use, even of marijuana, is symptomatic of illness or maladjustment. On the other hand, research on the psychopathological disorders associated with illicit drug use often study samples of "known" drug users, for example, hospitalized or incarcerated addicts, for whom drug use has directly or indirectly led to unfavorable consequences. Sample representativeness in these studies is questionable.

In the Vietnam Era Research Project study (Egendorf, 1981; Egendorf et al., 1981; Kadushin et al., 1981; Laufer et al., 1981; Rothbart et al., 1981) the association between current drinking and drug use and two measures of poor psychological functioning was measured among nonveterans and veterans with different war experiences. Robins (1974) reported in her original study of Vietnam returnees that drug use and alcoholism after Vietnam were associated with postwar depression. Card (1983) looked specifically at the association between substance use and posttraumatic stress disorder (PTSD) among Vietnam returnees and reported that relatively heavy drinking but not drug use was associated with PTSD. However, several researchers who have investigated the adjustment problems associated with substance use among Vietnam veterans have focused on special samples. Nace et al. (1978) examined veterans who were treated in Vietnam for drug abuse. Penk et al. (1981) looked at Vietnam veterans admitted to drug or alcohol treatment centers, and Robins, Helzer, Hesselbrock, and Wish (1977) studied Vietnam veterans identified as currently addicted to heroin.

An additional research question concerning the relationship between substance use patterns and stress disorder among Vietnam veterans exposed to combat was also investigated. Some mental health professionals (e.g., Nace et al., 1978; Lacoursiere, Godfrey, & Ruby, 1980) have speculated that heavy drug use and problem drinking behave like functional alternatives for the combat veteran: he is likely to exhibit symptoms of either stress disorder or problem drinking but tends not to show signs of both syndromes. According to this theory, it is not that the combat veteran who becomes alcohol or drug dependent was immune to stress disorder; rather, the individual originally turned to heavy substance use to dull the symptoms associated with that disorder, which he was experiencing. But the continued use of alcohol or drugs over time has masked the original stress disorder symptoms, and he no longer exhibits most of them. Lacoursiere et al. (1980) describe a cyclical relationship between stress disorder and problem drinking among Vietnam veterans exposed to combat:

> Repetitive (stress disorder) symptom reduction by means of alcohol leads to tolerance and an increase in alcohol consumption to maintain symptom reduction which leads to problems from the alcohol use itself (e.g. hangovers, gastritis, marital difficulties) and attempts to reduce or abstain from alcohol consumption. This leads to the alcohol withdrawal syndrome, with an exacerbation of... traumatic neurosis symptoms; this stimulates further drinking, closing the vicious cycle. (p. 966)

SUMMARY OF RESEARCH OBJECTIVES

1. To determine whether military service during the Vietnam Era, exposure to Vietnam, and combat had any lasting effects on the current drinking and drug use patterns of veterans
2. To determine whether current drinking and drug use is more strongly associated with poor psychological health among veterans, and combat veterans in particular, than among their nonveteran peers

3. To test the hypothesis that heavy alcohol and/or drug use serves as a functional alternative to posttraumatic stress disorder among Vietnam veterans who were exposed to combat

METHOD

Measuring Drinking and Drug Use Behavior

Two typologies were developed to measure current drinking and drug use behavior. The drinking typology classifies respondents as "heavy," "moderate," or "light" drinkers based on two dimensions of their self-reported drinking behavior — the amount and frequency of reported alcohol use during the last two years and their reports of problems associated with problem drinking.[1]

The drug use typology classifies respondents according to the presumed danger of the illicit drugs they have used during the last two years and the frequency with which they use some of those drugs. It distinguishes between nonusers and six categories of current users. The first three categories refer to users of "marijuana only" who differ in their frequency of use.[2] Next are those who use only marijuana and cocaine; then those who use amphetamines or barbiturates, but not heroin; and in the last category, those who report using heroin. This drug typology conforms closely to a Guttman scale and thus can be viewed as a measure of the extent of drug activity engaged in. As one systematically moves from the "marijuana only" categories to the "cocaine" category, and so on up the scale, respondents are more likely to be multiple drug users, as well as users of the less dangerous drugs in the preceding categories.[3]

---

[1]Respondents were asked whether they felt they were drinking too much, whether they judged themselves to be "dependent on alcohol," and whether they had felt "high" from alcohol 5 or more times during the past 2 years. As measured by the typology, a "heavy" drinker reported that he drank as much as a six-pack of beer, or bottle of wine, or several drinks of liquor almost every day for a period in the last 2 years, or that he drank those quantities at least one evening a week for a period in the last two years and had at least two symptoms associated with problem drinking. "Moderate" drinkers either reported drinking those quantities at least once a week and had only one symptom, or reported drinking less than that amount but had one or more symptoms. "Light" drinkers said they did not drink those quantities once a week and reported no symptoms.

[2]"Marijuana-only" users in the sample include: (a) those who use marijuana only but use it hardly ever, that is, less than once a month; (b) "light" users, who use only marijuana and use it once or twice a month or up to once a week; and (c) "moderate to heavy" users who use only marijuana and use it 3 or more times a week.

[3]See Michael (1980) for a detailed description of the drinking and drug use typologies constructed for the Wave One analyses and used in the analyses to be reported.

Measures of Psychological Functioning

Two measures of current psychological functioning were used in the analyses. General psychological malaise was measured by a scale developed by Dohrenwend and associates (1977). Their scale measures the construct of "demoralization," which some mental health professionals consider to be the chief problem of persons seeking psychological help. Characteristic feelings of demoralization include impotence, isolation, and despair as well as anxiety and depression (Frank, 1974). The demoralization scale used in the study is described in Martin (Chapter 10 in this volume).

Current psychological functioning among Vietnam veterans was also measured by the post-traumatic stress disorder scale (PTSD) developed by Boulanger et al. (Chapter 3, this volume). This scale measures the specific psychological syndrome of stress disorder exhibited in response to traumatic experiences such as combat.

Measuring Social Deviance in Childhood or Adolescence

Deviant behavior in childhood or adolescence was measured by an index composed of three items: (a) Until the time you were about 18, did any of the kids you went around with get into any kind of trouble? (b) Did you get into trouble up to the time you were about 18? (c) How often did you skip school or play hooky—would you say often, sometimes, almost never, or never?

These items are intercorrelated at the .001 level of significance. After their variances were equalized and scaled in the direction of "deviance," the items were added together to form an index.

The Marlowe-Crowne Social Desirability Scale as a Control for Response Set

The Marlowe-Crowne social desirability scale was used in some analyses as a control for response set in the reporting of substance use behavior. Crowne and Marlowe (1964) claim the scale measures the personality construct of need for approval, but an examination of the scale's items suggests the more general explanation that it measures the extent to which respondents try to present themselves favorably—either to themselves or to others. Those who score high on the scale admit to very few common human frailties, such as occasionally getting irritated by people who ask for favors, sometimes feeling jealous of the good fortune of others, gossiping at times, or deliberately saying something that might hurt someone's feelings.

The drinking and drug use typologies are very modestly associated with the social desirability scale (Pearson $r = -.11, -.15$, respectively), such that high social desirability scores are associated with somewhat lower rates of reported substance use. These associations suggest that respondents who were more concerned about "looking good" in the interview situation may have slightly underreported their substance use. As a safeguard against possible underreporting of substance use behavior, the social desirability scale is introduced as a control variable in several analyses. See Appendix 6.A for a description of the social desirability scale used in the study.

FINDINGS

Did Military Service in Vietnam or Elsewhere Have Lasting Effects on Veterans' Drinking and Drug Use Patterns?

The current drinking and drug use patterns of veterans and nonveterans were compared to determine whether exposure to illicit drugs and alcohol during military service and exposure to the Vietnam drug scene in particular had any long-term impact on the current substance use patterns of veterans. Table 6.1 compares the current drinking and drug use behavior of Vietnam veterans, Era veterans, and nonveterans in the general population from which the probability sample was selected. The data have been weighted to yield population estimates; and to ensure the most accurate picture of current prevalence rates, only respondents who scored relatively low on the social desirability scale (the 50th percentile or lower) are included in the analysis. There is most likely little distortion of self-reports among this subsample.

The weighted data show only extremely modest variations in the drinking patterns of the veterans and the nonveterans in the study population. The drug use patterns of veterans and nonveterans are somewhat more varied. Contrary to popular belief, the nonveterans are more likely than the veterans to be drug users, although these differences appear to be due primarily to the larger percentage of nonveterans who use marijuana or cocaine but no other hard drug. Table 6.1 shows that fewer Vietnam veterans are drug users than are veterans who served elsewhere during this time period, although this difference appears to be due entirely to the lower number of Vietnam veterans who very infrequently use marijuana and no other drugs.

Although Table 6.1 suggests that veterans are less likely than nonveterans to be drug users, it is premature to conclude that military service during the Vietnam Era may have exerted some kind of buffering effect so that veterans are currently less likely than their nonveteran peers to be drug users. It is far more likely that the differences in current drug use patterns are due to variations in these two groups' predispositions to use drugs in the first place and not to their experiences during the Vietnam War.

Regression analyses were conducted to test whether there are significant differences in the drug use and drinking patterns of veterans and nonveterans

TABLE 6.1
Percentages of Types of Drinkers and Drug Users in the Study Population
By Veteran Status (a)
(Low Social Desirability Group Only)

A.

		Veteran Status		
Types of Drinkers		Vietnam Veterans	Vietnam Era Veterans	Nonveterans
None–light		33	29	34
Moderate		35	38	37
Heavy		33	34	30
	Total (b)	101%	101%	101%

B.

		Veteran Status		
Types of Drug Users		Vietnam Veterans	Vietnam Era Veterans	Nonveterans
No drug use		57	47	34
Marijuana only – hardly ever use		11	25	23
Marijuana only – light use		11	8	11
Moderate to heavy marijuana use only		4	3	6
Marijuana or cocaine use only		5	6	10
Amphetamines or barbiturates, but no heroin use		11	11	15
Heroin use		2	1	2
	Total (b)	101%	101%	101%

(a) Weighted data are presented.
(b) Percentage does not total 100 because of rounding error.

after social background factors related to substance use are controlled. This procedure would isolate the effect, if any, that military service may have had on the substance use patterns of veterans. Table 6.2 shows the summary statistics for the regression equation predicting drug use patterns. After controls are introduced for social desirability and the major predictors of drug use in the sample — race, social deviance in childhood or adolescence, and age — military service in Vietnam or elsewhere does not contribute significantly to the variance in current drug use.[4]

On the other hand, Table 6.3 shows that when social desirability and the major social background predictors of drinking — religion and past social deviance — are controlled, military service specifically in Vietnam contributes slightly to the variance in drinking patterns.[5] Although the effect due to

---

[4]Race is defined in this regression equat˙ɔn as black versus other.
[5]Religion is defined in this regression equation as Jewish versus other.

TABLE 6.2
Multiple Regression of Drug Use on Age, Social Desirability, Past Social Deviance, Race, Vietnam Veteran Status, and Vietnam Era Veteran Status (a)

DV: Drug Use Typology Independent Variables	B	Beta	F
Age	−.49	−.22	74.11***
Social Desirability	−.27	−.15	32.41***
Social Deviance in Childhood	.11	.20	62.00***
Race	−.44	−.11	18.59***
Vietnam Veteran Status	−.11	−.03	1.04
Vietnam Era Veteran Status	−.07	−.02	.29
(Constant)	5.55		

Analysis of Variance		df	SS	MS	F
Multiple r .37 r2 .14	Regression	6	623.87	103.98	36.33***
	Residual	1352	3869.52	2.86	

(a) Drug use measured by the seven-category drug use typology. Race defined as black vs. other.

***$p < .001$.

TABLE 6.3
Multiple Regression of Drinking on Social Desirability, Past Social Deviance, Religion, Vietnam Veteran Status, and Vietnam Era Veteran Status (a)

DV: Drinking Typology Independent Variables	B	Beta	F
Social Desirability	−.09	−.11	18.00***
Social Deviance in Childhood	.06	.23	80.33***
Religion	−.37	−.11	16.36***
Vietnam Veteran Status	.11	.07	4.61*
Vietnam Era Veteran Status	−.008	−.004	0.02
(Constant)	2.32		

Analysis of Variance		df	SS	MS	F
Multiple r .30 r2 .09	Regression	5	74.23	14.85	26.04***
	Residual	1352	770.70	0.57	

(a) Drinking measured by the 3-category drinking typology. Religion defined as Jewish vs. other.

***$p < .001$.

*$p = .05$.

Vietnam service is statistically significant, it is of only minor practical significance. The beta value for Vietnam veteran status (.07) is the smallest of all of those that are statistically significant. Being a Vietnam veteran as compared to being a nonveteran is associated with only one-tenth of a step increase on the 3-category drinking typology.

Did Exposure to Combat in Vietnam Have Any Lasting Effect on Veterans' Drinking and Drug Use Patterns?

The relationship between combat experience in Vietnam and current substance use patterns was also examined. When nondrinkers and moderate drinkers are combined into one category, combat veterans are slightly more likely to be heavy drinkers than are Vietnam veterans with no exposure to combat (Somers' D = .09, p = .05). Combat exposure also weakly predicts current drug use behavior (Somers' D = .12, p < .05). Combat veterans are just somewhat more likely to be drug users, but they are not more likely than the other Vietnam veterans to use hard drugs such as amphetamines, barbiturates, or heroin.[6]

However, the finding of weak associations between exposure to combat and later substance use does not prove a causal relationship. The same background variables could predict both combat assignment and current substance use, leading to a false impression that combat stress contributes to later drinking and drug use patterns.

Regression equations were computed to test for the independent effect of combat as a predictor of current drug use and heavy drinking after major background factors were controlled.[7] Past combat exposure did not contribute significantly to the variance in either drug use behavior or heavy drinking when appropriate background factors were controlled, suggesting that exposure to combat has not had any lasting effect on the current substance use patterns of the Vietnam veterans in the sample.

Substance Use and General Psychological Malaise

The strength of the association between substance use and a measure of general psychological malaise is one indicator of the extent to which drinking or drug use constitutes "problem" behavior. The advantage of examining statistical associations is that no assumptions need to be made about the direction

---

[6]See Appendix B to this volume for a description of the combat scale used in these analyses.

[7]In the drug use equation, social desirability, past social deviance, age, and race were controlled. In the drinking equation, social desirability, past social deviance, and religion were controlled.

of causation. Although psychopathology may predispose individuals to use drugs, alcohol, or both, it may also be an outcome of drug or alcohol use. Considering the relatively low rates of substance use in the sample generally,[8] one would expect that drug use behavior and heavy drinking would be only modestly associated with general psychological malaise, as measured by the demoralization scale. In fact, heavy drinking, drug use in general, and hard drug use in particular are associated with somewhat higher levels of demoralization in the sample. The Kendall's tau association between the drug use typology and the demoralization scale trichotomized is .16 ($p < .001$). With the drinking typology collapsed to distinguish between heavy drinking and all other levels, it's tau association with demoralization is .19 ($p < .0001$).[9]

But is the association between substance use and demoralization stronger among veterans, and combat veterans in particular, than among nonveterans, suggesting an increased vulnerability resulting from war experiences?

The Kendall's tau association between heavy drinking and demoralization is .32 ($p < .0001$) among combat veterans, as compared to .16 ($p < .001$) among all other veterans and .17 ($p < .0001$) among nonveterans.[10] This heightened effect for combat veterans suggests that these men may be more likely than others to turn to heavy drinking when they feel anxious or depressed. Log linear analysis using the Multiqual program shows, however, that the stronger effect for combat veterans is only marginal and with a sample this size not statistically different from the other groups at the .05 level. Additional research should be conducted to determine whether the marginal effect for combat veterans seen in this data set holds true in other samples of Vietnam veterans.

The Kendall's tau association between drug use and demoralization tends to be somewhat stronger among both veteran groups (.21, $p < .0001$ among combat veterans; .20, $p < .001$ among all other veterans) than among the nonveterans (.11, $p < .0001$).[11] But, as tested by log linear analysis, these subsample differences in the strength of the association between drug use and demoralization are not statistically significant.

---

[8]While 50% claim to have used at least one illicit drug during the past two years, only 12% say they have used a hard drug such as amphetamines, barbiturates, or heroin. Over one third report they seldom drink at all.

[9]Kendall's tau is a nonparametric measure of association based on the amount of agreement between two sets of ordinal rankings. It is equivalent to Phi and to Pearson r in four-fold tables.

[10]In these analyses the drinking typology was collapsed to measure heavy drinking versus "other" and the demoralization scale was trichotomized.

[11]In these analyses the 7-category drug use typology was used and the demoralization scale was trichotomized.

Testing the Hypotheses That Heavy Drinking and/or Drug Use Is a Functional Alternative to Posttraumatic Stress Disorder

Table 6.4 displays data that can be used to test the hypotheses that heavy drinking, drug use in general, and hard drug use in particular act as functional alternatives to posttraumatic stress disorder (PTSD) among combat veterans. Only Vietnam veterans from the second wave of data collection, as described in Appendix A to this volume, are included in these analyses. In Table 6.4A, for example, noncombat Vietnam veterans and combat veterans are classified according to whether or not they currently are heavy drinkers and whether or not they currently exhibit PTSD according to the PTSD scale developed in Chapter 3. Thus, there are four possible patterns: the Vietnam veteran both drinks heavily and exhibits stress disorder (YY); he drinks heavily but does not exhibit stress disorder (YN); he does not drink heavily but exhibits stress disorder (NY); and he neither drinks heavily nor exhibits stress disorder (NN).

In testing the functional alternative hypothesis, the key cell to examine is the YN cell—heavy drinking but no stress disorder. Boulanger (1981a, 1981b) has reported that stress reaction among Vietnam veterans increases with exposure to combat. If, in fact, heavy drinking is a functional alternative to stress disorder among combat veterans (that is, the Vietnam veteran reacts to the stressor of combat either through PTSD or heavy drinking), the percentage of combat veterans in the YN cell would tend to be larger than the percentage of noncombat veterans in that same YN category. In other words, the percentage of veterans who are heavy drinkers but do not exhibit stress syndrome should increase as a function of exposure to combat in Vietnam.

Table 6.4A shows, however, that the percentage of combat veterans who are heavy drinkers without exhibiting stress disorder (18.8%) is not larger than but is essentially the same as that of noncombat Vietnam veterans (19.5%) in that same category. Based on these data, the hypothesis that heavy drinking is a functional alternative to PTSD for the combat veteran can be rejected.

Likewise, the data in Tables 6.4B and 6.4C show that drug use in general and the use of hard drugs specifically (i.e., amphetamines, barbiturates, heroin) do not act as functional alternatives to PTSD among combat veterans. In neither table is the percentage of combat Vietnam veterans in that category larger than the percentage of noncombat veterans.

DISCUSSION

The purpose of this study was to test the accuracy of several existing stereotypes concerning the postwar drinking and drug use behavior of Vietnam Era

TABLE 6.4
Tests of Functional Alternative Hypothesis (a)

A.		Exposure to Combat	
Heavy Drinking and Stress Disorder		*No*	*Yes*
YY (Heavy drinking; Stress disorder)		5.2	13.2
YN (Heavy drinking; No stress disorder)		19.5	18.8
NY (No heavy drinking; Stress disorder)		6.5	15.7
NN (No heavy drinking; No stress disorder)		68.9	52.3
	Total (b)	100.1% (74)	100.0% (193)

B.		Exposure to Combat	
Drug Use and Stress Disorder		*No*	*Yes*
YY (Drug use; Stress disorder)		5.2	16.3
YN (Drug use; No stress disorder)		33.8	25.0
NY (No drug use; Stress disorder)		6.5	11.7
NN (No drug use; No stress disorder)		54.6	46.9
	Total (b)	100.1% (74)	99.9% (194)

| C. *Hard Drug Use (amphetamines,* | | Exposure to Combat | |
barbiturates, or heroin) and Stress Disorder		*No*	*Yes*
YY (Hard drug use; Stress disorder)		2.6	8.2
YN (Hard drug use; No stress disorder)		16.9	13.8
NY (No hard drug use; Stress disorder)		9.1	19.9
NN (No hard drug use; No stress disorder)		71.5	58.2
	Total (b)	100.1% (74)	100.1% (194)

(a) Only Wave 2 respondents are included in these analyses. Stress disorder includes possible PTSD.

(b) Percentage does not total 100 because of rounding error.

veterans 10 to 15 years after their discharge. The Vietnam War had the unforeseen consequence of exposing a large number of men to a situation where illicit drugs were inexpensive and readily available and where norms against use were lax. As reports of widespread illicit drug use among U.S. soldiers in Vietnam and in other foreign military posts pervaded the media, the American public became increasingly concerned that Vietnam returnees would trigger a drug epidemic stateside. Despite little methodologically sound research to support these fears, the image of the Vietnam veteran addict or alcoholic has persisted in the minds of many Americans.

The research findings described in this chapter attest to the invalidity of several existing stereotypes concerning the drinking and drug use behavior of Vietnam Era veterans. Contrary to popular belief, the data suggest that in most respects the current drinking and drug use behavior of Vietnam Era veterans does not differ considerably from that of their nonveteran peers. While the results of a regression analysis suggest that Vietnam service may have affected the current drinking rates of veterans, Vietnam veterans are only somewhat more likely than others to drink heavily. Other regression analyses show that 10 to 15 years later neither military service nor exposure to the drug scene in Vietnam has had any lasting effect on the current drug use patterns of veterans. Nor has exposure to combat had any discernible effect on either the current drug use or drinking rates of Vietnam veterans.

As might be expected, however, heavier substance use among the entire generation of Vietnam Era men sampled is associated to some extent with other symptoms indicative of general psychological malaise or demoralization. Preliminary analyses suggest the possibility that the combat veteran may be more likely than his peers to turn to heavy drinking as a means of coping with anxiety and depression. Further research is needed before any conclusions can be reached. Finally, the data clearly do not support the theory that drinking, drug use in general, or hard drug use in particular is a functional alternative to posttraumatic stress disorder for the combat veteran. It appears that the major psychological response to the traumas of combat still exhibited by the veteran 10 to 15 years after the war is PTSD and not substance abuse.

APPENDIX 6.A
THE SOCIAL DESIRABILITY SCALE

The following items comprise the social desirability scale (Crowne & Marlowe, 1964). Response categories for each item are "yes, no, don't know". Social desirability scores are simply the total number of answers in the scaled direction. The standardized version of the scale is used in the analyses reported in this paper. Social desirability scale items:

1. You never hesitate to go out of your way to help someone in trouble.
2. You are sometimes irritated by people who ask favors of you.
3. You have never intensely disliked anyone.
4. You sometimes try to get even rather than forgive and forget.
5. There have been times when you were quite jealous of the good fortune of others.
6. You are always willing to admit it when you make a mistake.
7. You always try to practice what you preach.
8. There have been occasions when you took advantage of someone.
9. You would never think of letting someone else be punished for your wrongdoing.
10. You never resent being asked to return a favor.
11. You sometimes think that when people have a misfortune they only get what they deserve.
12. You like to gossip at times.
13. You have never been irked when people expressed ideas very different from your own.
14. You have never deliberately said something that hurt someone's feelings.
15. You sometimes feel resentful when you don't get your way.

7 Violence and Vietnam Veterans

Ghislaine Boulanger

One of the qualities most frequently associated with Vietnam veterans is their alleged proneness to violence. The media has repeatedly capitalized on this stereotype, emphasizing a criminal's service record in Vietnam. In the last few years, defense attorneys have pleaded that their clients are not guilty of particular crimes because they are suffering from stress reactions incurred as a result of their service in Vietnam. Apart from the anecdotal evidence supplied by the newspapers and the testimony of mental health professionals that is occasionally upheld in court, information about the incidence of postcombat violence and its relationship to posttraumatic stress disorder (PTSD) has been based mainly upon clinical impressions, with very little research to lend credence to such impressions.

PREVIOUS FINDINGS

Veterans and Violence

Many clinicians have speculated about the relationship between having been in combat and later being unable to restrain violent impulses. Basing their comments on clinical evidence, Horowitz and Solomon (1978) made the following observations about Vietnam veterans: "Problems of control over violent impulses are complicated whenever real violence has occurred, whenever human beings are dehumanized or devalued and whenever reality and fantasy images are confused" (p. 278). In a similar vein, Shatan (1978), who has worked extensively with Vietnam veterans in crisis, describes the "restructuring of the personality that permits violence to occur" (p. 45). Alternatively, Gault (1971) and Panzarella, Mantell and Bridenbaugh (1978) have argued that it is possible for some soldiers to experience and perpetuate violence in combat without manifesting any consequent perception or evidence of psychiatric disturbance.

Research into postcombat violence has focused more frequently on the veterans' attitudes to violence or their self images as violent men than on manifest violent behavior. For example, Brady and Rappoport (1973) compared the attitudes toward violence of middle aged males and females, college males and females, and enlisted Vietnam veterans and field grade officers. Age proved a significant variable: the older males and females and officers had higher violence scores than college students and veterans. Education was also important: those among the middle aged sample who had more than a high school education had significantly lower violence scores. However, it was also found that exposure to combat resulted in a more positive general and specific orientation to violence than any other interpretation. In another attitude study, Pollock, White, and Gold (1975) also found that exposure to combat was significant in determining attitudes toward violence. Combat veterans attending college differed significantly from their noncombat cohorts in their opinion that violence is necessary for certain groups to get their way.

Two studies that inquired into the veteran's perceived capacity for violence, but not into his violent behavior per se, established an association between the veteran's image of himself as violent and his exposure to combat. Strayer and Ellenhorn (1975) found that "self perceived hostility was significantly associated with severity of adjustment problems and the intensity of combat experience" (p. 89). Buchbinder and Shrauger (1979) found that hospitalized Vietnam veterans differed from combat veterans from other wars and noncombat veterans from earlier wars only in their perceived capacity for violence, with younger veterans scoring higher.

Parenthetically, it should be noted that immediately after World War II, Grinker and Spiegel (1963) observed a similar pattern of aggression and hostility in the verbalizations and behavior of recently returned combat veterans. Whether time away from combat is a factor in reducing the aggression associated with combat or whether the Vietnam veteran is generally more violent (as Buchbinder and Shrauger found) is considered in the course of this chapter.

Among the studies of manifest violence, Strange and Brown (1970) interviewed psychiatric inpatients. The sample was divided into those who served in Vietnam and those who did not, but no further controls for combat in Vietnam were introduced. The authors found that the behavioral expression of aggression was not increased among Vietnam veterans, although threats and preoccupation with such conflicts seemed more likely to occur. These data emphasized Vietnam veterans' preoccupation with violence, but by neglecting to control for combat the authors failed to establish whether such thoughts are acted upon more frequently by combat veterans.

In his study of Post Combat Violent Behavior (PCVB), Yager (1976) did control for combat. He contrasted PCVB combat veterans with non-PCVB combat veterans on a number of precombat variables. Getting into fights in childhood and volunteering for Vietnam differentiated statistically between the two groups. Yager also found that the occurrence of PCVB seemed to be a function of time. Most of the violent incidents occurred during the first 3 to 6 months immediately following combat and less frequently thereafter. Thus, Yager explained PCVB as a function of predisposition to violence, rather than as a function of deconditioned controls against violence resulting from the combat experience.

Explaining the psychological and behavioral sequelae of combat as a function of predisposition rather than as a direct effect of the combat experience itself has been a frequent goal of researchers, as was discussed in Chapter 4.

PTSD and Violence

The diagnosis of PTSD was recently introduced into the psychiatric nosology with the publication of the DSM III (APA, 1980). Of this diagnosis, which is discussed in more detail in Chapters 3 and 4 in this volume, the editors of DSM III note: "Increased irritability may be associated with sporadic and unpredictable explosions of aggressive behavior, even upon minimal or no provocation. This latter symptom has been reported to be particularly characteristic of war veterans with this disorder" (p. 237). Indeed, in what amounted to the first comprehensive description of this disorder, Kardiner (1969) specifically mentioned a "proclivity to explosive and aggressive reaction patterns" (p. 249). Haley (1978) speculates that "veterans' delayed stress response symptoms represent a breakdown of defenses, but are also defenses against repetition to completion of their violent impulses and ward off and numb intolerable ideas and emotions" (p. 263).

Just as there have been few studies about actual violence among Vietnam veterans, so Williams (1983), has commented on the paucity of investigations into the relationship between PTSD symptoms and violent behavior. However, Yager (1976), noted that many of the instances of PCVB he recorded occurred as a result of startle reactions and in situations that evoked unwanted combat memories. Thus, an alternative explanation to Yager's finding that PCVB is related to a violent predisposition may be that men with PTSD are more prone to PCVB. On the other hand, Roberts et al., (1982), found no significant differences in MMPI Manifest Hostility Scale scores between combat veterans with PTSD and those without. However, the authors note that their sample consisted of substance abusers whose psychopathology may have masked PTSD in some cases. In a recent report, Kadushin, Boulanger, & Martin (1981) found that at least one quarter of combat veterans from Vietnam continue to suffer from a disproportionate number of the symptoms of chronic PTSD. This chapter concludes with an analysis of the specific relationship between PTSD and violence among Vietnam veterans.

CURRENT RESEARCH OBJECTIVES

In the following analysis, a number of variables that account for differences between combat veterans with psychological or social problems and combat veterans without such problems are examined. However, before attempting to understand the context in which violent behavior occurs among men of the Vietnam generation, it is important to establish the incidence of such behavior among Vietnam veterans, particularly combat veterans, as compared with their nonveteran peers. Having determined whether or not differences exist between these populations, the present study will attempt an explanation of the conditions under which men are more likely to become violent. To take these conditions in roughly chronological order, it will be determined if the following factors contribute significantly to current violent behavior: a history of premilitary antisocial behavior, of having enlisted in the Armed Forces, of having had disciplinary problems while in the military, of having fought in combat, the passage of time since the combat experience; and finally having a disproportionate number of symptoms of PTSD.

Are Vietnam Veterans More Violent Than Nonveterans?

Respondents were asked a number of questions about violent behavior in which they might have engaged recently. Had they been involved in any fights in the last 5 years? The intensity and frequency of these fights was measured by the use of weapons and whether the opponent was forced to seek medical help, were assessed. Arrests for violent crimes after the respondents left the military, or, in the case of nonveterans, since they turned 21, were recorded, as were instances of wife abuse. Table 7.1 shows that Vietnam veterans generally do not differ significantly from era veterans or nonveterans on any of these dimensions except in the two questions that measure the intensity of the fights. However, when the control for combat is introduced, a different picture emerges. As can be seen from Table 7.2, significantly more combat veterans have been in fights in the last 5 years, have used weapons, have hurt someone so badly that a doctor had to be seen. Although the number of respondents who answered the questions about arrest is not sufficient for meaningful conclusions to be drawn, there appears to be a tendency for combat veterans to be arrested more frequently for crimes of violence than

TABLE 7.1
The Incidence of PCVB Among Vietnam Veterans and Controls

Type of Behavior	Percentage Saying Yes			χ^2 Significance
	Vietnam Vet	Era Vet	Nonvet	
Have you had a physical fight in last 5 yrs?	23.9 (276)	20.1 (273)	18.4 (452)	NS
Of those saying yes: Two or more fights in last 5 yrs?	42.0 (64)	52.0 (48)	50.0 (76)	NS
Have you used a weapon?	15.9 (276)	10.6 (273)	9.3 (452)	0.2
Did you hurt someone badly?	22.8 (276)	19.8 (273)	17.0 (452)	NS
Of those saying yes: Was he hurt so badly he had to see a doctor?	75.3 (73)	60.6 (66)	58.3 (108)	0.5
Have you been arrested for a violent crime since leaving military or since age 21?	8.5 (82)	5.1 (101)	5.6 (197)	*
Of those married: Have you ever hit your wife?	14.3 (230)	9.6 (208)	13.6 (346)	NS

*Insufficient data for significance test.

noncombat veterans and nonveterans. Eisenhart (1975) has commented on the dehumanizing process of basic training. It was suggested that this alone is sufficient to release a man from society's prohibitions against violence, but statistical tests not shown here reveal that today there is no difference in violence between the noncombat veterans, who have all been through basic training, and nonveterans, who, of course, have not. If men did become more violent as a result of basic training, their behavior has now returned to baseline. Combat veterans, on the other hand, continue to be more violent than their peers, even 10 to 16 years after returning from combat.

If the seven questions in Tables 7.1 and 7.2 are taken in the aggregate, an index of manifest violence can be constructed. The mean for this index is 1.02, the standard deviation 1.51. As this analysis continues with an examination of the conditions under which men are more likely to become violent, the index is dichotomized. Respondents with a score of zero through two are considered nonviolent; those with a score of three or more (more than one standard deviation above the mean) are termed violent.

Predisposition to Violence

To test the hypothesis that predisposition to violence accounts for the differences between combat veterans and others in the sample, it is first neces-

TABLE 7.2
Incidence of Violent Behavior According to Combat Status

| Type of Behavior | Percentage Saying Yes | | | χ^2 Significance |
	Combat Vets	Noncombat Vets	Nonvets	
Have you had a physical fight in last 5 years?	26.8 (198)	19.5 (348)	18.5 (452)	.04
Of those saying yes: Two or more fights in last 5 years?	46.2 (52)	56.7 (60)	50.0 (76)	NS
Have you used a weapon?	17.7 (198)	10.9 (348)	9.3 (452)	007
Did you hurt someone badly?	27.3 (198)	18.1 (348)	16.9 (452)	.02
Of those saying yes: Was he hurt so badly he had to see a doctor?	79.7 (59)	60.0 (80)	58.3 (108)	.001
Have you been arrested for a violent crime since leaving military or since age 21?	11.5 (61)	4.9 (122)	5.6 (197)	*
Of those married: Have you ever hit your wife?	13.6	10.9	13.6	NS

*Insufficient data for significance test.

sary to identify behaviors in childhood and adolescence that are associated with violent behavior in later life. Responses were sought to a number of questions about premilitary antisocial behavior. Three behaviors were significantly associated with the index of manifest violence. At least one quarter of those respondents who knew children who had been in trouble with the law while in school are violent today, whereas only 8% of those who did not know such children are violent today (Asymmetric Somers' D is .156, Significance < .0001). Of those respondents who got into trouble with the law themselves, a third are violent today, compared with only 11% of the respondents who did not get into trouble and are violent today (Somers' D .21, Significance < .0001). Of those who played hooky frequently, one third are violent today, while 14% of those who did not play hooky fall into this category (Somers' D .19, Significance < .0001). There was no significant difference between those who failed to graduate from high school and those who did not graduate in terms of later violence (Somers' D − .003).

Military Disciplinary Problems as Predictors of PCVB

Worthington (1978) found that antisocial behavior in the military accounted for postmilitary maladjustment, both he and Yager (1976) found that enlistees were more likely to be socially maladjusted on their return from combat. Therefore, the relationship between enlisting or having had disciplinary problems and a score of three or more on the index of manifest violence was investigated. Military respondents were asked whether they had enlisted, whether they had received Articles 15 or courts martial, and whether they had received dishonorable discharges. When each of these variables was cross-tabulated with the dichotomized violent behavior index, it was found that enlisting (Asymmetric Somers' D − .05 NS) and receiving a dishonorable discharge (Asymmetric Somers' D .11) are apparently not associated with postmilitary violent behavior (there were only seven such men in the entire sample and therefore significance levels cannot be given). But men who were court martialled (Asymmetric Somers' D .09, Significance < .05) or who received Articles 15 (Asymmetric Somers' D .14, Significance < .0001) are more likely to be violent today.

Distribution of Premilitary and Military Antisocial Behavior Across Sample Categories

Having established which premilitary and military variables predict violence, we now ascertain whether more of the respondents who engaged in antisocial behavior as children or had disciplinary problems while on active duty found their way into combat, as some have contended. Comparing the three significant preservice predictor variables across Vietnam Era experience, there is no significant difference in the number of respondents who had friends who got into trouble (chi square .35, 2 df), got in trouble themselves (chi square .19, 2 df), or played hooky frequently (chi square 1.12, 2 df) and subsequently became combat veterans, noncombat veterans, or nonveterans. It is concluded that predisposition to violence does not appear to have influenced a man's entry into combat. Nor are combat veterans any more likely to have enlisted (chi square .09, 1 df, NS), to have received Articles 15 (chi square .00002, 1 df, NS), or to have received dishonorable discharges (chi square .00008, 1 df, NS) than noncombat veterans. However, there is a slight tendency for combat veterans to have been court martialed more often than noncombat veterans (chi square 4.3, 1 df, Significance < .03).

The Interaction Between Combat and Predisposition To Violence

To review the findings so far: combat veterans have been found to be significantly more violent than noncombat veterans and nonveterans. Although a number of premilitary and military variables that predict violent behavior have been identified, the distribution of these predictor variables does not differ significantly between combat veterans and the rest of the sample; thus PCVB cannot be attributed to a predisposition to violence. However, it is possible that an interaction exists between the predictor variables and exposure to combat which would explain the above findings. If combat does intensify the predisposition to violence, significantly more combat veterans who had positive scores on the predictor variables would be violent than would noncombat veterans and nonveterans who had similarly high scores.

Table 7.3 shows that there is no significant difference between the current violence scores of nonveterans, combat veterans and noncombat veterans among those who got into trouble as adolescents or knew other adolescents who got into trouble; and in the case of playing hooky, significantly more of

TABLE 7.3
Percent of Currently Violent Respondents with Discipline Problems Before or During War According to Combat

		Status		
		Combat Vets	Noncombat Vets	Nonvets
Did you know kids who got in trouble when you were a kid?	Yes	25.8 (89)	23.8 (160)*	23.8 (214)*
	No	16.5 (109)	5.9 (188)	6.7 (238)
Did you get in trouble yourself?	Yes	35.7 (42)*	33.3 (78) *	31.1 (103)*
	No	16.7 (109)	8.5 (270)	10.0 (349)
Did you play hooky often?	Yes	13.6 (22)	34.5 (29)*	42.9 (42)*
	No	21.6 (176)	12.3 (318)	12.0 (409)
Did you enlist?	Yes	20.0 (20)	22.6 (31)	
	No	20.8 (178)	13.2 (317)	
Were you ever court martialled?	Yes	30.4 (23)	19.0 (21)	
	No	19.2 (172)	13.9 (21)*	
Did you receive any Articles 15?	Yes	26.1 (46)	27.9 (86)	
	Np	19.5 (128)	9.8 (245)	

*Significant difference at .05 level or above.

the noncombat respondents prove to be violent. However, there is a different interaction from the one anticipated. Among men not predisposed to violence, combat veterans are significantly more violent. To put this another way, those men who fought in combat are more likely to be violent independent of predisposition.

The relationship between enlistees and those with disciplinary problems and combat (below the dotted line) shows a slightly different pattern. There is an interaction between receiving a court martial and being in combat: more of the combat veterans who received courts martial are violent than the noncombat veterans. Combat veteran enlistees and those who received Articles 15 are no more violent than similar noncombat veterans. Here, as in the figures above the dotted line, combat veterans are more likely to be violent independent of disciplinary actions in the military. Among combat veterans, then, combat, not predisposition, appears to be the decisive factor in determining whether or not a man will become violent after the war.

The Relationship Between PTSD and PCVB

The Violence Index and the PTSD scale described in Chapter 3 have no common items, but they are significantly related to one another. In general 25.4% of the men in this sample who currently have a disproportionate number of stress symptoms are violent, as opposed to 18.2% who are possibly stressed and violent, and 9.1 percent who are not stressed and are violent (Asymetric Somers' D $-.106$, Significance $< .0001$). In other words, respondents with stress reactions are almost three times as likely to be violent as those who do not have stress symptoms.

When combat is introduced into the equation, Table 7.4 shows that the basic significant relationship between PTSD and violence remains the same, although it is somewhat stronger for combat veterans than it is for the controls. It is important to note however that among those men who do not have PTSD, irrespective of combat status, there is no significant difference in violent behavior.

A Causal Analysis of PCVB

To provide a fuller understanding of the conditions under which a man, particularly a veteran, is likely to become violent, each of the variables discussed earlier is now regressed onto the index of manifest violence. Thus, the relative contribution that each of the predisposing variables makes to current violent behavior can be assessed. Before we look at the findings, however, the treatment of the variables in the regression equation should be considered. The three prewar predisposing factors and the four variables indicative of disciplinary problems in the military are added together and used as two

TABLE 7.4
Percentage of Violent Veterans According to Combat and PTSD Status

	Percentage Violent		
$n =$	Combat Vets 198	Noncombat Vets 348	Nonveterans 452
Stress Reactions:			
YES:	31.6	26.7	19.4
POSSIBLY:	20.7	15.3	18.8
NO:	8.5*	9.4**	9.0***

*Asymmetric Somers' D .14, Significance .008.
**Asymmetric Somers' D .10, Significance .004.
***Asymmetric Somers' D .08, Significance .01.

continuous variables, called "prewar problems" and "military problems" respectively. Since the concern in this study is in part with those who have PTSD and not with those who may have a few unrelated anxiety or depressive symptoms, the PTSD Scale is treated as two dummy variables rather than as a continuous variable. Thus men who are stressed and those who are possibly stressed are contrasted with those who are not stressed. Then again, the violence index is skewed strongly in the direction of nonviolence. Only about 15% of the respondents score three or above. Fewer than 2% have a score of six or more (of a possible eight). Yet these extreme cases, persons who might be habitual offenders, weigh heavily in a regression analysis, as would persons with no violent behavior, who represent the other extreme. The skewness of the index is 1.66. When the natural logarithm of the measure is taken, the skewness is reduced to .811, giving a more reasonable measure and a bet-

TABLE 7.5
Variables with Significant Direct Effect on the
PCVB of Vietnam Veterans

	B	Beta	F	Sig.
Prewar problems	.119	.197	21.15	.001
Military problems	.116	.141	10.57	.001
Combat	.100	.090	4.32	.03
Age	−.102	−.094	4.99	.02
Stressed	.221	.174	13.07	.001
Possibly stressed	.136	.123	6.82	.009

Multiple R	.37885
R Square	.14353
F	13.40
Significance	.0001

ter chance that the predictor variables are not merely accounting for extremes. Finally, since a number of the researchers quoted earlier discovered a relationship between the veteran's age and violence, the respondent's age is introduced as a possible explanatory variable.

The results of the regression as presented in Table 7.5 confirm and summarize what has already been learned about the relationship of violence, prewar problems, military discipline problems, combat, and PTSD. Each of the variables has a significant direct effect on current violent behavior, and younger men who returned home from the war more recently are more likely to be violent today than are older men. However, comparing the size of the Betas, we conclude further that having PTSD is a greater determinant of current violent behavior than is age or having been in combat.

SUMMARY AND CONCLUSIONS

Despite considerable speculation about the relationship between combat and violent behavior, there is little empirical evidence to confirm these speculations; and no studies have contrasted the incidence of violence among combat veterans with noncombat veteran controls. Nor have observations about the relationship between PTSD and violence been tested empirically. The present study has investigated and substantiated the relationship between combat and violence and violence and PTSD and has established the incidence of violence among combat veterans with and without PTSD. It has been found that the incidence of violence can be increased by having been in combat but not by basic training alone. Today, 10 to 16 years after their military service ended, combat veterans are significantly more violent than controls. Consistent with earlier findings (Williams, 1983; Worthington, 1978), a number of predisposing premilitary and military factors indicative of a violent disposition were identified. However, when controls for combat were introduced, it was found that combat veterans are more likely to be violent independent of these predisposing factors.

This study does not claim that Vietnam veterans are any more violent than combat veterans from earlier wars. Studies undertaken at the time indicated that World War II veterans were preoccupied with violence just as Vietnam veterans claim to be (Gault, 1971). One possible explanation for an earlier finding (Brady & Rappoport, 1973) that Vietnam veterans are more preoccupied with violence than are combat veterans from earlier wars is that PCVB declines with the passage of time. While this hypothesis is apparently supported in the present study by the finding that younger veterans are more violent than those who returned home earlier, the hypothesis could be confirmed only by a longitudinal study. There are two possibly complementary explanations for the high incidence of violence among combat veterans; one is simply that "controls against violence can be deconditioned by warfare" (Haley, 1978, p. 278).

The second explanation is that violent acts are committed most frequently when the veteran is suffering from chronic symptoms of PTSD, which, in its turn, is caused by exposure to combat. Since it has already been established that significantly more combat veterans have symptoms of PTSD (Kadushin, Boulanger, & Martin, 1981), there is support for Haley's (1978) contention that "delayed stress symptoms represent a breakdown of defenses...against violence" (p. 264). In this study, a significant relationship between PTSD and violence has been demonstrated empirically. In general, respondents with PTSD are three times more likely to be violent than those with no stress symptoms.

In sum, the following profile of the violent veteran has been established. Younger men with a history of antisocial behavior before the war and a history of discipline problems during the war are, as has been argued previously, more likely to be violent today. But this study shows that independent of these obvious predicting factors, having been in combat and, most significant of all, having PTSD are sufficient in themselves to cause a veteran to become violent.

8 Is the Vietnam Generation Politically Alienated?

Helen Dermatis
Charles Kadushin

BACKGROUND TO POLITICAL ALIENATION AMONG VETERANS

The Unpopular War and the "Homecoming Syndrome"

 Much attention has been given to the image of Vietnam veterans as the losers of an unpopular war, unwelcomed and uncelebrated upon their solitary return home (e.g., Figley & Leventman, 1980; Marin, 1981; "Special report", 1981). This unfortunate situation is considered to be at least partly responsible for the current emotional plight of Vietnam veterans (Keane & Fairbank, 1983; Lipkin, Blank, Parsons, & Smith, 1982; Parsons, 1984).

It has also been proposed that men who underwent the searing experiences of the war in Vietnam may have acquired different political attitudes from those of men who did not serve in the military. Vietnam veterans may be more opposed to war and more politically alienated from the government that risked their lives than those who did not serve.

The following questions address issues central to the examination of the political impact of the Vietnam War on those who fought it: Do Vietnam veterans differ in their political attitudes from comparable nonveterans?; Do Vietnam veterans feel mistreated by the public (or does the public actually mistreat them)? If they are mistreated, does this give rise to negative psychological consequences for them?

Much rhetoric has been spent answering those questions. According to popular conception, the Vietnam War had a character unlike previous wars. It is alleged that in earlier wars in which the U.S. was involved, soldiers went into battle confident of their country's support. Vietnam veterans, however, did not receive much support for their military involvement. On the contrary, while Americans were engaged in active combat abroad, many of their peers at home took part in antiwar protests and demonstrations. The outcomes of previous wars were perceived as victories for the U.S. Our role in Vietnam and the outcome of that war were perceived as an American misfortune. On their return home following earlier wars, groups of soldiers received an enthusiastic welcome and were honored in parades and civic ceremonies. Vietnam veterans returning home, usually individually, received little recognition for having risked their lives for their country. Thus, in addition to the injuries of war, Vietnam veterans, much like rape and other crime victims, may suffer from the "second wound" (Symonds, 1980): societal reaction. In this case, the second wound or injury might be called the "Homecoming Syndrome."

The public perceived the unique circumstances surrounding the Vietnam War as having an adverse impact on those who fought it. Interviews with veterans revealed that they blamed themselves for having lost the war (Special report," 1981). Veterans who entered military training with a "gung ho" spirit soon lost their fervor, which gave way to cynicism and depression as well as to a disenchantment with the government ("Special report," 1981). Encountering a silent and indifferent reception upon their return home, (Clemons, 1970; Furlong, 1967; Marin, 1981; "Social issues," 1971), Vietnam veterans became even more embittered. One source of the Vietnam veterans' anguish was economic. Public reports indicated that Vietnam veterans received relatively fewer benefits following the completion of their tour of duty than had veterans of World War II and the Korean War ("Role of VA," 1977). Welfare recipients and prisoners were said to be treated more favorably than Vietnam veterans (Christian, 1981).

Many social scientists have expended considerable effort in speculating about the plight of Vietnam veterans without addressing a growing body of empirical data. For example, Polner (1971) proposed that American society, by its lack of responsiveness to the needs of returning Vietnam veterans, was guilty of a violation of a basic trust existing between a government and citizens who put themselves at risk for the nation's welfare. American society attempted to conceal its own embarrassment and dishonor for the outcome of the war by shifting the blame for the war from the governing system onto the veterans themselves (Figley & Leventman, 1980). Veterans were stigmatized as the losers of a war and consequently became targets of discrimination (Camacho, 1980). Vietnam veterans experienced bitterness and rage over their nation's having ordered them into battle and then scapegoating them when they returned home (Lifton, 1973). Veterans' readjustment to the civilian world was characterized by periods of disorientation, violent acting out, and apathy (Levy, 1973; Lifton, 1973; Pilisuk, 1975). Others have contended that the war not only gave rise to emotional disorders in veterans, but resulted in their losing trust in, and feeling alienated from, their government and their fellow citizens for not having supported them during the war and upon their return home. These views by social scientists corresponded to and largely reiterated the popular view of the Vietnam veteran as a politically and socially alienated individual.

Prior Research on the Effects of War on the Political Attitudes of Former Soldiers

To put all this speculation into perspective, we should note that it has been traditional for American social scientists to consider the political effects of war on the men who fought in it for at least 40 years. However, these studies have been based on empirical data, not on impressions. The first systematic series of studies (Stouffer, Lumsdaine et al., 1949; Stouffer, Suchman, et al., 1949) reported that soldiers who had been discharged had essentially the same attitudes toward most foreign policy issues as did soldiers who had not completed their overseas tour of duty. In addition, soldiers who had completed their overseas tour of duty and soldiers who were still fighting did not differ in the amount of cynicism expressed for U.S. involvement in the war. Most soldiers during and following World War II believed that the U.S. had entered the war either to stem the tide of Nazism and Fascism or to act in its own self-defense. Only a minority of soldiers at some point during their overseas military experience or following its completion regarded economic imperialism to be the primary underlying factor for the U.S. entry into World War II. Stouffer, Lumsdaine, et al. (1949) did report differences in opinion about postwar policy between soldiers who had already been sent back to the U.S. and those still overseas. Men who had already come home were less willing to support proposals for postwar American aid to Europe than were those soldiers who were still fighting in the war. In addition, Stouffer, Lumsdaine, et al. found that a majority of recently discharged World War II veterans reported more intense antimilitary feelings than did soldiers still engaged in combat. Furthermore, soldiers who had completed their tour of overseas duty expressed more doubt and skepticism about the value of fighting the war than did soldiers who were still engaged in combat.

The big political issues during the Korean war were anti-Communism and the degree of support in America for the Cold War. Perhaps because of McCarthyism, or because attention after the Korean war was directed to the "brainwashing" of captives, there seem to be no studies that specifically investigated the political impact of having served in that war. Indeed, from an official point of view it was not even a war but, rather, a "conflict." It remained for the war in Vietnam to revive studies of war and politics.

Strayer and Ellenhorn (1975) investigated antiwar sentiments among Vietnam veterans. Veterans were interviewed following their completion of service regarding the nature of their preinduction and postdischarge attitudes towards U.S. involvement in the Vietnam War. Strayer and Ellenhorn reported a major reversal in veterans' attitudes: prior to military induction, a sizable majority (67%) had been in favor of U.S. involvement in Vietnam; following completion of their tour of duty in Vietnam, an overwhelming majority (75%) were opposed to U.S. involvement in Vietnam.

The cited studies are based on the responses of World War II and Vietnam veterans obtained shortly after their discharge from military duty. To the extent that public opinion surveys ask and code veteran status, it is possible to search existing studies for differences between veterans of whatever war and nonveterans of comparable age. For example, Segal and Segal (1976) found no difference between veterans and nonveterans on a total of 21 out of 23 items covering trust in government and isolationism–interventionism. The items that indicated differences between veterans and nonveterans concerned stationing military troops and planes in Europe and replacing the draft with an all-volunteer army. Nonveterans were more likely than veterans to agree that stationing American troops and planes in Europe was of no help to the U.S. Nonveterans were also more likely than veterans to approve of replacing the draft with an all-volunteer army. In addition, Senter (1983), using samples of veterans from World War I, World War II, Korea, and Vietnam, reported that veterans were more likely than nonveterans to believe that the government was making sufficient effort to avoid war. Senter also found that veterans were more likely than nonveterans to oppose granting aid to North Vietnam.

Whereas those studies were based on samples of World War I, World War II, Korean War, and Vietnam War veterans, other studies have compared only Vietnam veterans with nonveterans on a host of attitudes: orientation to violence, level of trust in government, political cynicism, cosmopolitanism, and civic intolerance. Veterans were found to have a more positive orientation toward violence than did college students, but were not found to differ from middle-aged women (Brady & Rappoport, 1973). Other researchers reported results based on data collected at the beginning and end of the Vietnam War. This methodological approach allows for the direct comparison of both pre- and post-Vietnam War attitudes held by veterans and nonveterans. Bachman and Jennings (1975) found a trend among both veterans and nonveterans toward a declining trust in government, a decline that was more pronounced in the case of nonveterans.

Jennings and Markus (1977) investigated political cynicism among Vietnam veterans and nonveterans and reported that over the course of the Vietnam War, both groups exhibited a trend toward higher levels of political cynicism, with nonveterans exhibiting a steeper increase. Jennings and

Markus also found that the political outlook of both Vietnam veterans and nonveterans became more narrow (i.e., became less cosmopolitan), with nonveterans becoming even more "local" than veterans in their political frame of reference over the period spanning the Vietnam War. Vietnam veterans and nonveterans did not, however, differ in their of level of civic tolerance. Harris (1980) found that veterans differed significantly from nonveterans in their level of political alienation. Compared with nonveterans, Vietnam veterans claimed they had less control over the political process and were more cynical about the American political and social system. There is clearly little consensus in the conclusions drawn by these investigators. The different findings could be attributed to sampling differences, for some of the studies employed samples that were so small they were not representative of Vietnam veterans as a whole (Segal & Segal, 1976; Strayer & Ellenhorn, 1975); others sampled mainly enlisted men (Bachman & Jennings, 1975) or all-volunteer servicemen (Brady & Rappoport, 1973), thus limiting our ability to draw firm conclusions. In general, however, most of the research findings indicate few or no differences in political attitudes between veterans and nonveterans. Thus, there is little empirical support for asserting that the Vietnam War altered long-term political attitudes, but this conclusion awaits the corroboration of a nationally based sample.

Some research compares the public's and veterans' perceptions of the mistreatment of Vietnam veterans. Veterans and nonveterans felt that the welcome extended to Vietnam veterans on their return home was not as generous as that afforded servicemen returning home from earlier U.S. wars (Harris, 1980). Furthermore Harris (1980) found that the majority of Vietnam veterans believed that the benefits they were receiving were insufficient. In contrast, World War II veterans felt that the help provided them was adequate (Cantril & Strunk, 1951).

Even less empirical attention has been given to the ways in which veterans' political attitudes and perceptions of their homecoming influence their psychological state. In an echo of the German "stab in the back" legend (Dorpalen, 1964)—that the German civilian front lost World War II despite the bravery of the troops in the front lines—it has now become common in the United States to blame lack of support back home for the current emotional plight of Vietnam veterans (Keane & Fairbank, 1983; Lipkin, et al., 1982; Parsons, 1984). It is suggested that Vietnam veterans continue to suffer from stress reactions not only because of the rigors of combat and the nastiness of that particular war, but also as a result of the indifferent if not negative reception, or "dysreception," as Parsons (1984) refers to it, they received when they came home. Brass bands and ticker tape parades could have mitigated the horror of war.

In sum, the mythology of the Vietnam war suggests that the political situation surrounding the war should have had a major impact on Vietnam veteran readjustment. Yet to date there is only limited hard evidence to support such speculation. Further, whatever hard research does exist finds few and insubstantial associations between veteran status and political opinion.

The present study aims at filling this gap in our knowledge. We examine differences between Vietnam veterans and nonveterans in political attitudes, behaviors, perceptions of feeling unwelcome, and difficulty in readjusting to civilian life, but a new variable is added to this list: the level of psychological distress. If the widely held beliefs about Vietnam veterans are true, then veterans would be expected to differ from nonveterans in their political attitudes and behaviors. Further, political alienation, the veteran's perception that he had difficulty in readjusting, and his feeling unwelcome should result in an increased level of psychological distress.

CURRENT FINDINGS

Differences Between Vietnam Veterans and Nonveterans in their Political Attitudes

Unlike most of the previous research on Vietnam veterans, the present study obtained a multisite probability sample representing various military service categories (Vietnam versus service elsewhere versus nonveterans) and included veterans who were both enlistees and conscripts. A full description of the sample is found in the Appendix to this volume. Eighty-two questions on political attitudes and behaviors — including attitudes towards veterans and veteran readjustment, voting behavior, confidence in American institutions, attitudes toward particular expenditures in the Federal budget, and general political points of view on domestic and foreign issues — were administered to our sample of veterans and nonveterans. The Appendix 8.A at the conclusion of this chapter summarizes the particular questions. Thirty-two of these items were also administered, in equivalent years, by the National Opinion Research Center's Annual Social Survey (NORC). Before we report on differences between veterans and nonveterans, we can "calibrate" our data by reporting minor differences between our contextual sample and the NORC national samples.

Weighted to reflect the true distribution of the populations of the cities and regions sampled, our nonveteran sample is slightly more liberal than equivalent NORC national samples of men the same age. This is true despite controls for region and city size. The subject matter of our interview, the war in Vietnam, may have induced a slightly liberal slant to respondents' answers to questions on other issues. Though statistically significant, the differences are only a few percentage points. Further, the reported differences, or lack of them, between the veterans and nonveterans in our sample generally hold true for comparisons between men in the NORC sample of the same age groups whose social class, region, and city size have been adjusted to be the same as the Vietnam veterans and the Vietnam Era veterans in our sample.

Let us now look at the findings in detail. Vietnam veterans and Vietnam Era veterans differ from the nonveterans in our sample on 19 of the 82 political questions put to them, with the veterans generally more conservative than the nonveterans, as shown in Table 8.1, which summarizes the results of our analysis. (Since weighting mainly affects the comparison of our samples with national norms, and since we will now address only the present sample, all data here and in the rest of this paper are unweighted.) Since veterans as a group are lower in social class than nonveterans (as shown in Chapter 2, this volume), and since social class is related to most of the political issues we studied, the differences are those that remain after social class is controlled. There are few differences between Vietnam veterans and Era veterans except on issues directly related to Vietnam: Vietnam veterans, except those in the highest and lowest social class categories, are more opposed to amnesty for deserters than are either Era veterans or nonveterans; Vietnam veterans think their sons should serve in a new war, if necessary; and they are opposed to the U.S. establishing formal political ties with Vietnam. Veterans, regardless of place of service, want the government to spend more on veterans and to be more active in their behalf; they would also spend more money on defense and less on the environment than nonveterans, and, in an hypothetical case, would send troops to Yugoslavia if the Russians invaded it (but not, by the way, to Argentina — a question composed years before the recent crisis over the Falkland Islands). Veterans, however, are more cynical about the Armed Forces than nonveterans, disagreeing with statements that blacks are better treated in the military and that the Armed Forces provide better opportunities for job training than in civilian life. Finally, veterans are less active politically than nonveterans, except for those in the lowest social class, almost none of whom are politically active.

It should be remembered that the differences between veterans and nonveterans are not large; fewer than 25% of the responses show differences. It is important to note that if the veterans were extremely conservative before entering military service and now appear only generally conservative on issues relating to Vietnam, then the war indeed may have exerted a liberalizing effect. Since only postwar measures of political attitudes and behaviors were obtained in the present study, we cannot directly assess attitudinal or behavioral changes. At the very least, we can say that there is no evidence for the proposition that war experiences resulted in antiwar feelings, political liberalism, or greater political activity on the part of veterans. To be sure, the veterans may have been more conservative and more favorable to war and less active even before entering the military than men who did not serve and remain so even now. The present study, of course, has no evidence about prewar attitudes.

TABLE 8.1
Issues on Which Veterans Differ from Nonveterans at .01 Level or
More with Social Class* Controlled

General Political Views

Liberal, middle of road or conservative.

Nonveterans tend to be liberal; veterans, more middle of the road and conservative.

Presidential candidates are responsive to people's problems.

Nonveterans tend to disagree; veterans agree.

Government Effective in Helping Veterans with:

Educational costs; hospitalization and medical treatment; employment.

Nonveterans more strongly agree; veterans disagree.

Budget

Money being spent for natural environment.

Nonveterans think too little being spent; veterans think too much, with exception of lowest social class.

Money being spent for military.

Nonveterans believe too much being spent; veterans believe too little being spent.

Defense spending.

Nonveterans in favor of reducing defense spending; veterans strongly opposed.

Political Activity

Worked to help poor/disadvantaged.

Nonveterans tend to be more active than veterans, with exception of lowest social class.

Attended protest rally meetings; served as an officer of a social action organization; engaged in picketing or marching in behalf of a cause; supported cause by door to door canvassing, distributing leaflets and petitions.

Nonveterans tend to be more active than veterans with exception of lowest social class.

Vietnam War Issues

Resisters deserve amnesty.

Era veterans and nonveterans in favor of unconditional amnesty; veterans take position of no amnesty, with exceptions of highest and lowest social classes.

Son being called to serve in war.

Nonveterans believe son should not go war; veterans believe son should serve, with exception of lowest social class.

U.S. should establish relations with Vietnam.

Nonveterans and Era veterans believe U.S. should establish relations; Vietnam veterans believe U.S. should not.

TABLE 8.1 *(Continued)*

Military Issues

Blacks are treated better in the military.	Nonveterans disagree more than veterans, except at lowest social class.
Armed forces offer better opportunity to develop real job skills than does civilian life.	Nonveterans argue more than veterans, except at highest social class.
Should U.S. send troops to Yugoslavia if Russians invade?	Nonveterans are opposed to sending or have no opinion; veterans are more in favor, with exception of lowest social class.

*Social class defined as 4-valued index (education, income and occupation equally weighted).

Based on the degree to which answers to questions clustered together, we constructed five different indices, as shown in Appendix 8.B at the end of this chapter: lack of confidence in institutions, political alienation, difficulty in readjustment, feeling unwelcome, and belief that the government was not effective in helping veterans. Because indices are more reliable than answers to a single question, only indices will be used in the following analyses.

Let us discuss the more abstract constructs such as confidence and political alienation before turning to issues specifically related to veteran adjustment. The index on lack of confidence in institutions is simply a sum of all the questions about confidence. Though Bernard Barber (1983) has shown that confidence is multidimensional, and indeed questions on confidence both in our data and in the NORC studies are not highly clustered, they are nevertheless widely used in national surveys and often simply added up as we have done here. The national data show that "confidence," whatever it is, has been decreasing yearly. Its decline, however, cannot be laid to any differences in the Vietnam experience for men of that generation as seen in Table 8.2 since there is no difference in confidence between Vietnam veterans and all the other respondents in our sample.

The Alienation Index is composed of such items as: "The lot of the average man is getting worse"; "It is not what you know but who"; "Public officials don't much care"; "The government is run for a few big interests"; "Things are going pretty badly in this country"; and so on. The content of the items suggests that political and economic alienation are measured in about equal degrees. Table 8.2 shows that, taken together, these items do distinguish between veterans and nonveterans, with the former being somewhat more cynical than the latter.

Three indices cover veteran issues. The first is composed of three items about veteran readjustment: "People don't understand"; "Veterans feel left out"; and "Readjustment was more difficult than most people imagine." The

TABLE 8.2
Analysis of Variance Summary Table for Type of Veteran Status on Political Indices

	Means			
Political Index	Vietnam Veterans	Era Veterans	Non Veterans	F (2,1378)
Lack of Confidence in Institutions	3.46	3.33	3.39	.19
Alienation	4.83	4.92	4.53 (3)	5.27**
Difficulty in Readjustment	2.05	1.77	2.51	76.25 (1)***
Feeling Unwelcome	1.55	1.32 (2)	1.49	4.95**
Government not Effective in Helping Veterans	1.50	1.47	1.30 (3)	2.78

1) All significantly different from one another.
2) Significantly different from Vietnam veterans and nonveterans.
3) Nonveterans significantly different from Vietnam veterans and Era veterans.
*$p < .05$.   **$p < .01$.   ***$p < .001$.

full wording of the first two questions differs for veterans and nonveterans. Veterans were asked whether they felt they had trouble readjusting; nonveterans were asked for their perceptions of veteran readjustment. As shown in Table 8.2, nonveterans were more likely to agree that veterans were poorly adjusted — the widely held stereotype noted earlier. Compared with Vietnam veterans, Era veterans said they had less trouble readjusting.

A second index includes three items about feeling unwelcome. Again the nonveterans were asked for their perceptions; and veterans, for how they actually felt. Items (in brief) were: "Most people respect you for having served"; "The American people have made veterans feel at home"; and, "People made you feel proud." Table 8.2 shows that Vietnam veterans felt and nonveterans perceived just about the same degree of unwelcomeness. Era veterans felt better about things.

Finally, with respect to the government's not being effective in helping veterans with such matters as education costs, medical treatment, compensation for disabilities, loans, jobs, and drugs, veterans generally were more in agreement than nonveterans.

To what extent can the differences shown in Table 8.2 be explained by class, racial, or regional differences, or by population density factors, which tend to account for much of the variance in political attitudes in the United States? Table 8.3 explores these indices with these additional factors taken into account. To show the differences between veterans and nonveterans, we constructed "dummy" variables for combat veterans, noncombat veterans (who served in Vietnam), and Era veterans. The standardized coefficients shown in Table 8.3 for these categories are implicitly contrasted with the nonveteran category, which is not shown. Thus, on the third line, "Difficulty

TABLE 8.3
Political Attitude Indices Regressed on Class, Race, Region and Veteran Status

Political Attitude Indices	Predictor Variables[1]		Region				Veteran Status				
	Class	Race	West	South	Mid-West	City Size	Combat Vets	Noncombat Vets	Era Vets	R^2	F (9,137)
Lack of Confidence in Institutions	-.02	.01	-.07*	-.06*	-.08**	.05	.03	-.01	-.01	.01	1.44
Political Alienation	-.21***	.22***	.01	-.01	.04	-.07**	.07**	-.01	.06*	.13	23.95**
Difficulty in Readjustment	-.01	.08**	.01	-.03	.01	.01	-.15***	-.16***	-.32***	.11	19.89**
Feeling Unwelcome	.11***	.03	-.02	-.06*	-.02	.06*	.04[2]	.005	-.06*	.02	4.56**
Government not Effective in Helping Veterans	.09**	.04	-.11*	-.18***	-.16***	.01	.08**	.02	.07*	.04	7.35**

[1] Class defined as four valued index. Race defined as nonwhite vs. white. Region defined as West, South, Midwest vs. Northeast (New York Metropolitan Region). City size—metropolitan regions vs. all others. The values for predictor variables are standardized regression coefficients.

[2] Difference between combat veterans and era veterans sig at $p < .05$.

*$p < .05$.   **$p < .01$.   ***$p < .001$.

in Readjustment," combat veterans are 15 standardized units (standardization allows us to compare scales with different numbers of items and different distributions) lower on the "Difficulty in Readjustment" scale than nonveterans; noncombat Vietnam veterans are 16 units lower; and Era vets, 32 units lower. Even with class, race, region, and city size controlled, nonveterans were much more likely than veterans of all kinds to feel that veterans had trouble readjusting.

Only region makes a difference in lack of confidence in political institutions. (Every region is more confident than the New York Metropolitan region in our sample!) On the key index of alienation, low class and being black are the factors contributing to alienation — triple the effect of veteran status, with the latter remaining with small but statistically significant beta coefficients. Combat veterans and, curiously, Era veterans — even with class, race, region, and city size controlled — are slightly more alienated than other men.

Veteran status and race are the only factors that produce differing perceptions about readjustment difficulty; whereas social class, region, city size and being an Era veteran make something of a difference (not much) on the "Feeling Unwelcome" index. Men of higher social class were more likely to have felt unwelcome or to perceive that Vietnam veterans were unwelcome; southerners (as compared with others) were more welcoming, as were men in smaller cities. Finally, with all these factors controlled, Era veterans were less likely to feel unwelcome. With respect to the government's not being effective in helping veterans: the higher the class, the more men tended to agree. All the regions had a better opinion of the government than did New York, and combat veterans and era veterans had a poorer opinion of the government than nonveterans.

In sum, we have found veterans to be slightly more conservative than nonveterans, to be slightly more alienated, and to favor military spending and military intervention. They also would like more veteran benefits. None of these differences is large, however. The greatest difference is that although nonveterans endorse the stereotype of the veteran as a seriously troubled person, Vietnam veterans reject it.

The Effect of the Homecoming Syndrome on Current Adjustment of Vietnam Veterans

Let us now turn to the "Homecoming Syndrome" and its possible consequences for Vietnam veteran psychological adjustment. It has been alleged that on his return from Vietnam, the veteran felt unwelcome, lost confidence in American political institutions, became politically alienated, was not helped by the government, and, as a result of all this, had difficulty readjusting to civilian life. It is further alleged that these factors in the Homecoming Syndrome then contributed to and exacerbated any adverse psychological symptoms veterans may already have developed as a result of service in Vietnam. In this way, the Homecoming Syndrome may not be the original cause of PTSD, but it is certainly a major factor in its severity and persistence into the present. According to this view, the Homecoming Syndrome is in large measure responsible for the fact that Vietnam veterans have more psychological difficulties than American veterans of other wars. (See Boulanger, Chapter 4 this volume, for a discussion of this particular "fact".)

While we have already seen that, on the average, there are few major differences between Vietnam veterans and other men in their scores on the factors that make up the Homecoming Syndrome, it may well be that those individual Vietnam veterans who, more than others, did experience the Homecoming Syndrome were also those who suffered most from PTSD. Further, if the Homecoming Syndrome theory is correct, the effect of homecoming on PTSD should be greater among combat veterans than among others. Let us now turn to the data to test these hypotheses.

Table 8.4 indeed seems to support the hypothesis that the Homecoming Syndrome is related to PTSD during and right after the war, even more so to current levels of PTSD. Further, Table 8.4 shows that although exposure to combat does not intensify the relationship between PTSD and the Homecoming Syndrome in the short run, it does so in the long run. That is, when we look at current PTSD, the correlations between factors in the Homecoming Syndrome and PTSD are consistently higher for combat veterans than for others.

But what are the causal relationships? Perhaps a man's mental state leads to his political position, not the reverse. Perhaps a sense of alienation is part of the stress reaction syndrome rather than a cause of it. In short, we need to develop a model of how the various factors in the homecoming impinge on current levels of PTSD and test that model against our data. We have some-

TABLE 8.4
Correlations Between Political Scales and Stress

| | Stress During and Right after War | | Current Stress | |
| | Pearson R | | Pearson R | |
	No Combat	Combat	No Combat	Combat
Lack of Confidence in Institutions	.15	.22	.14	.29
Alienation	.23	.23	.24	.30
Difficulty in Readjustment	.35	.34	.25	.39
Feeling Unwelcome	.11	.15	.13	.24
Government not Effective in Helping Veterans	.18	.14	.13	.26

thing of a problem in doing so, since a sensible model would require firm data on the timing of effects and their consequences. That is, we would need to have data collected at the time of combat and at the time of reentry into civilian life, as well as at the present time. In fact, all we have is data collected at one point of time — the present. Some of the data (such as the combat scale) refer to past events, but these impressions of the past were gathered in the present. The questions about stress reaction were asked for the present time, for the period during combat, and for one year thereafter. A man's estimates of earlier symptoms — those experienced on the average 10 years prior to the survey — are probably less firm than his reports of current symptoms. Nonetheless, the material on participation in combat is quite vivid, refers to specific events and actions, and is probably reasonably valid. The elicitation of symptoms follows a discussion of the military experience and is probably colored by it — all to the good, considering our aim of establishing a reasonable time sequence for the effects of homecoming on current PTSD. Reactions to homecoming were elicited in the context of a general discussion of what men did and felt when they returned home. As we explained earlier, two scales were formed from the questions about homecoming issues: the degree to which veterans felt unwelcomed, and the degree to which they experienced problems in readjustment. Since the homecoming events took place after combat and after the experience of at least some of the PTSD symptoms elicited by the interview's referring to combat and one year thereafter, it seems reasonable to locate scales referring to homecoming in a time period somewhat after the veteran's first experience with PTSD symptoms. On the other hand, the alienation scale is clearly related to present feelings, and therefore should be located after homecoming. The only remaining issue is where to locate alienation in reference to current PTSD symptoms. To go along with the general argument that alienation leads to PTSD, let us assume that alienation is a result of all the experiences a man has had during his period of readjustment. Therefore, we locate the sense of alienation as having occurred before the current reports of PTSD symptoms. The time-line chart (Fig. 8.1) recapitulates this argument. The relative times are indicated by (t0) — the time period in Vietnam, (t1) — the homecoming, (t2) — the most recent past, and (t2+) as the present time. A full model requires that we take some causes of these symptoms and feelings into account. Clearly, the "cause" of being in combat is something beyond the range of our study (since we showed in Chapter 2, that such things as race and social class are not related to combat experience). But race, social class, and living in big cities are related to political attitudes, feelings of being unwelcome, and current levels of PTSD symptoms. Except for current social class, all these causal factors can be treated as "exogenous" variables; that is, they lie outside of the events within our model. Current social class, however, clearly can be affected both by earlier symptoms of PTSD and by problems in readjustment; the latter factors may affect the

```
Combat (t0)-> PTSD(t0,t1)->Readjustment (t1)->Alienation (t2)->PTSD (t2+)

                          Difficulties

                   ->Unwelcome (t1)
```

FIG. 8.1   PTSD Time-Line Chart

ability to obtain and keep a good job and the ability to obtain higher levels of education. Obviously, parental social class is also a cause of current social class levels. This completes the set of variables in our model. The model and the empirically derived relationships between variables in the model, given our hypothesized time sequence, are shown in Fig. 8.2. The arrows indicate a causal relationship and the numbers next to the arrows give the size of the relationship (path coefficient – beta weights in this case). If there is no arrow between variables, then the beta was not statistically significant at the .05 level.

Figure 8.2 shows first that PTSD symptoms at time t1 are the result of combat with nonwhite status also contributing to the presence of symptoms (see Chapter 2 for a discussion of the effect of being nonwhite on the Vietnam experience). Having PTSD symptoms at time t1, that is, during the war and for one year thereafter, is depicted as leading to a reduced social class level,

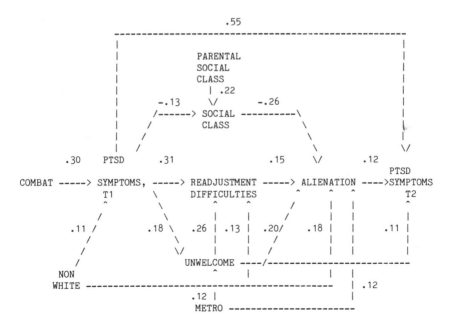

FIG. 8.2   Causal Model of Effects of Homecoming and Alienation on Post-traumatic Stress Disorder Symptoms

readjustment difficulties, and a sense of being unwelcomed. Men who returned to metropolitan areas were also more likely to feel unwelcomed than men who returned to smaller cities and rural areas. Readjustment difficulties are compounded by the sense of being unwelcomed and by being nonwhite. Current social class, in addition to being negatively affected by the presence of PTSD symptoms, is also positively affected by parental social class.

Alienation has the most complex set of causal factors with current social class, readjustment difficulties, being unwelcomed, being nonwhite, and living in metropolitan areas all contributing.

Finally, and most importantly for the purposes of this chapter, current levels of PTSD symptoms are explained primarily, (as one would expect) by past levels of PTSD symptoms; alienation and the sense of being unwelcome on one's return from military duty also contribute, however. While the best predictor of having current PTSD symptoms is having had PTSD symptoms on return to civilian life, and the best predictor of having had PTSD symptoms back then is having experienced combat, it is true that to some extent a sense of alienation and a sense of feeling unwelcome do contribute to a veteran's current PTSD symptoms. In turn, both the sense of alienation and feeling unwelcomed are to some extent caused by objective social circumstances as well as by a complex process related to a man's adjustment to PTSD symptoms.

CONCLUSION

The "stab in the back" theory (Dorpalen, 1964) has proved to be a vast oversimplification of the facts. The Homecoming Syndrome — alienation and feeling unwelcome — does have a modest effect on current levels of PTSD, once one considers initial levels of PTSD experienced during the war. There is no question, however, that the major origin of PTSD symptoms is the experience of combat. In turn, PTSD symptoms themselves may cause readjustment difficulties and lead to a sense of being unwelcome — hardly surprising when one thinks about the extreme difficulties some men with PTSD symptoms have in relating to other individuals, and to society more generally. So if combat veterans did develop PTSD symptoms and as a result had a hard time readjusting when they came back, then their further difficulties tend to lead to higher current levels of PTSD symptoms. Although this finding is not theoretically surprising, it is of considerable practical importance. To deal effectively with PTSD, we must find some way of breaking out of a vicious circle.

The "second wound" occurs partly as a result of the natural processes of coping with PTSD. This is not to say that we are further "blaming the victim," but that special efforts have to be made to overcome the veteran's sense of alienation and feeling unappreciated, and that these efforts must be separated from political factors. Of further practical political importance is that a sense of not being helped by the government — mainly, of course, not being helped by the VA — makes combat veterans worse off psychologically. The lack of long-term effects of the war on the political position and political attitudes of veterans is also noteworthy. Except for their desire for more government help to veterans, Vietnam veterans are no different in their politics from other men in their generation. The war certainly did not radicalize veterans. On the other hand, Vietnam veterans are not especially likely to be "Hawks" and are not a Pentagon constituency. There may be a message here, but it is not the one touted by either liberals, who expected the war to radicalize veterans, or by conservatives, who tend to blame liberals almost exclusively for the current plight of Vietnam veterans.

APPENDIX 8.A
LIST OF VARIABLES USED TO COMPARE VETERANS
WITH NONVETERANS

VETS DESERVE RESPECT
VETS SHOULD FEEL PROUD
PRES HELP IN VETS
AMER PEOPLE WELCOME
  VETS
PEOPLE AT HOME RESPECT
  FOR SVC
DID NOT WANT THANKS
PEOPLE AT HOME MADE YOU
  FEEL PROUD
PEOPLE AT HOME DID NOT
  UNDERSTAND
FELT OUT OF EVERYTHING AT
  HOME
READJUST IS HARDER THAN
  PEOPLE THINK
GOVT HAS RESPBLTY TO FIND
  VETS JOB
GOVT HELP VETS WITH ED
  COSTS
GOVT HELP VETS WITH MED
  AND HOSP
GOVT HELP DISABLD VETS
  WITH DISABTY

GOVT HELPS WITH LOANS FOR
  HOME
GOVT EFFECTIVE IN FIND
  VETS JOB
GOVT EFFECTIVE IN HELP
  VETS DRUG
REGISTERED TO VOTE 1976
  PRES
PRES CANDIDATES
  RESPONSIVE 1976
VOTE 1976*
WHO VOTE FOR 1976*
VOTE 1972*
WHO VOTE 1972*

VOTE 1968*
WHO VOTE 1968*
GENERAL POLITICAL
  OUTLOOK*
CONFIDENCE IN EXEC
  BRANCH*
CONFIDENCE IN ORG LABOR*
CONFIDENCE IN PRESS*

CONFIDENCE IN MILITARY*
CONFIDENCE IN CORPORATIONS*
CONFIDENCE IN ORG RELIGION*
CONFIDENCE IN EDUCATION*
CONFIDENCE IN MEDICINE*
CONFIDENCE IN TV*
CONFIDENCE IN SUPREME COURT*
CONFIDENCE IN SCIENCE*
CONFIDENCE IN CONGRESS*
CONFIDENCE IN FINANCE*
PUBLIC OFFICIALS DO NOT CARE*
THINGS ARE GOING IN US
TRUST GOVT
GOVT FOR ALL OR FEW
MONEY FOR UNEMPLOYMENT
MONEY FOR ENVIRONMENT*
MONEY FOR NATIONAL HEALTH*
MONEY FOR BIG CITIES*
MONEY FOR CRIME RATE*
MONEY FOR DRUG ADDICTION*
MONEY FOR BLACKS*
MONEY FOR MILITARY*
MONEY FOR WELFARE*
AVG MAN GETTING WORSE*
CORPORATIONS ARE COMPETITIVE
REDUCE DISTRIBUTION OF INCOME*
GOOD CHANCE TO GET AHEAD
EMPLOYERS HAVE LITTLE SYMPATHY
LEGALIZE MARIJUANA*
BLACKS TREATED BETTER IN MILITARY
REDUCE DEFENSE 25% WITHIN 5 YRS

MONEY REALLY IMPORTANT IN JOB
ARMED FORCES GOOD FOR TRAINING
FBI AND MIL INT ARE A THREAT
WHO YOU KNOW COUNTS IN JOB
MACHINES RUN OUR LIFE
WORKED ACTIVELY PETITIONS
ATTENDED PROTEST RALLY
PICKET OR MARCH FOR CAUSE
HELPED POOR OR DISADVANTAGED
CIVIL DISOBEDIENCE TO JAIL
OFFICER FOR SOCIAL ACTION ORG
WORKED FULL TIME FOR SOC CAUSE
LESS THAN HONORABLE DESERVE BENEFITS

RESISTERS DESERVE AMNESTY
DESERTERS DESERVE AMNESTY
LESS THAN HONORABLE DESERVE AMNESTY
SON WOULD NOT GO TO WAR
SON GO TO CANADA AS LAST RESORT
US SHOULD ESTABLISH REL WITH VIETNAM

EXPECT ANOTHER WAR NEXT 10 YEARS*
US TO YUGOSLAVIA IF RUSSIANS INVADE
US TO ARGENTINA IF ASKED

*NORC item

APPENDIX 8.B
LIST OF POLITICAL INDICES WITH INDIVIDUAL ITEMS

I. Lack of Confidence in Institutions

1. How much confidence do you have in the people running the Executive branch of the federal government?
2. How much confidence do you have in the people running organized labor?
3. How much confidence do you have in the people running the press?
4. How much confidence do you have in the people running the military?
5. How much confidence do you have in the people running the major companies?
6. How much confidence do you have in the people running organized religion?
7. How much confidence do you have in the people running education?
8. How much confidence do you have in the people running medicine?
9. How much confidence do you have in the people running TV?
10. How much confidence do you have in the people running the U.S. Supreme Court?
11. How much confidence do you have in the people running the scientific community?
12. How much confidence do you have in the people running Congress?
13. How much confidence do you have in the people running banks and financial institutions?

Response Categories

(1) A great deal of confidence
(2) Only some
(3) Hardly any confidence at all

The response (3) "Hardly any confidence at all," was scored as + 1. Scores range from 0-13.

II. Alienation

1. Most employers have little sympathy for the employees' point of view.
2. In spite of what some people say, the lot of the average man is getting worse, not better.

3. When it comes to jobs, it is not what you know but who you know that really counts.
4. These days, machines seem to run our lives.

Response Categories

(1) Agree strongly
(2) Agree mildly
(3) Neither
(4) Disagree mildly
(5) Disagree strongly

The responses (1)"Agree strongly" and (2)"Agree mildly," were scored as +1.

5. Would you agree or disagree that public officials don't care much about what people like you think?

Response Categories

(1) Agree
(2) Disagree

The response (1) agree was scored as +1.

6. Would you say that the government is pretty much run for a few big interests or would you say it is run for the benefit of all the people?

Response Categories

(1) Big interests
(2) All the people

The response (1) "Big interests," was scored as +1.

7. How do you think things are going in this country these days?

Response Categories

(1) Very well
(2) Fairly well
(3) Pretty badly
(4) Very badly

The responses (3) "Pretty badly" and (4) "Very badly," were scored as +1.

8. People like myself have a pretty good chance of getting ahead.

Response Categories

(1) Agree strongly
(2) Agree mildly
(3) Neither
(4) Disagree mildly
(5) Disagree strongly

The responses (4) "Disagree mildly" and (5) Disagree strongly," were scored as $+1$. Range of scores 0-8.

III. Difficulty in Readjustment

Veterans

1. People at home just didn't understand what you have been through in the armed forces.
2. Having been away for a while, you felt left out of everything that was going on at home.
3. Readjusting to civilian life was more difficult than most people imagine.

Nonveterans

1. People at home just didn't understand what veterans had been through in the armed forces.
2. Having been away for a while, veterans felt left out of everything that was going on at home.
3. Readjusting to civilian life was more difficult for veterans than most people imagine.

Response Categories

(1) Agree strongly
(2) Agree mildly
(3) Neither agree nor disagree
(4) Disagree mildly
(5) Disagree strongly

The responses (1) "Agree strongly" and (2) "Agree mildly," were scored as $+1$. Range of scores 0-3.

IV. Feeling Unwelcome

Veterans

1. Most people at home respect you for having served your country in the armed forces.
2. The American people have done everything they can to make veterans feel at home again.
3. People at home made you feel proud to have served your country in the armed forces.

Nonveterans

1. Most people at home respect veterans for having served their country in the armed forces.
2. The American people have done everything they can to make veterans feel at home again.
3. People at home made veterans feel proud to have served their country in the armed forces.

Response Categories

(1) Agree strongly
(2) Agree mildly
(3) Neither agree nor disagree
(4) Disagree mildly
(5) Disagree strongly

The responses (4) "Disagree mildly" and (5) "Disagree strongly" were scored as $+1$. Range of scores 0-3.

V. Government Not Effective In Helping Veterans

1. How do you rate the effectiveness, in general, of the government in covering educational costs for veterans?
2. How do you rate the effectiveness of the government, in general, in providing hospitalization and medical treatment to disabled veterans?
3. How do you rate the effectiveness of the government, in general, compensating veterans for wartime disabilities?
4. How do you rate the effectiveness of the government, in general, in providing loans for the purchase of homes and farms?

5. How do you rate the effectiveness of the government, in general, in helping veterans to find jobs?
6. How do you rate the effectiveness of the government, in general, in treating veterans for drug problems?

Response Categories:

(1) Agree strongly
(2) Agree mildly
(3) Neither
(4) Disagree mildly
(5) Disagree strongly

The responses (4) "Disagree mildly" and (5) "Disagree strongly,"were scored as + 1. Range of scores 0-6.

APPENDIX 8.C
DATA FOR PATH MODEL SHOWN IN FIG. 8.2

MEANS AND STANDARD DEVIATIONS

PTSD2	2.224	.770	PTSD SYMPTOMS, TIME 2
PTSD1	2.485	.696	PTSD SYMPTOMS, TIME 1
CLASSR	2.363	.972	RESPONDENT'S SOCIAL CLASS
METRO	.691	.463	METROPOLITAN AREA RESIDENCE
NOWHITE	.337	.473	BLACK AND HISPANIC
PCLASS	2.548	.874	PARENTAL SOCIAL CLASS
READJUST	1.913	1.096	READJUSTMENT DIFFICULTIES
ALIEN	4.428	1.950	ECONOMIC AND POLITICAL ALIENATION
UNWELCOM	1.407	1.087	FELT UNWELCOME UPON RETURN
COMBAT	.357	.480	COMBAT (HEAVY, MEDIUM, LIGHT/NONE)

CORRELATIONS

	PTSD2	PTSD1	CLASSR	METRO	NOWHITE	PCLASS
PTSD2	1.000	.589	− .169	.097	.182	− .101
PTSD1	.589	1.000	− .151	.034	.126	− .081
CLASSR	− .169	− .151	1.000	.139	− .174	.228
METRO	.097	.034	.139	1.000	.180	.044

NOWHITE	.182	.126	.174	−.180	1.000	−.309
PCLASS	−.101	−.081	.228	.044	−.309	1.000
READJUST	.289	.373	−.108	.060	.200	−.121
ALIEN	.252	.185	−.295	−.083	.250	−.104
UNWELCOM	.236	.181	.037	.122	.104	.018
COMBAT	.202	.304	−.036	.039	.049	−.052

	READJUST	ALIEN	UNWELCOM	ALLCOMBA
PTSD2	.289	.252	.236	.202
PTSD1	.373	.185	.181	.304
CLASSR	−.108	−.295	.037	−.036
METRO	.060	−.083	.122	.039
NOWHITE	.200	.250	.104	.049
PCLASS	−.121	−.104	.018	−.052
READJUST	1.000	.265	.326	.148
ALIEN	.265	1.000	.241	.031
UNWELCOM	.326	.241	1.000	.101
COMBAT	.148	.031	.101	1.000

11 SOCIAL SUPPORT

Charles Kadushin

Social support and social networks have become catch-words in both popular parlance and the behavioral science literature. Both support and networks are almost automatically regarded as an obvious "good." In fact, "networking" may well be regarded as the social intervention of choice in the eighties, since it is cheap, voluntary, and effective and appeals to both the radical right and the radical left. In the next three chapters, we challenge the notion that social support and networks are universally helpful. Focusing on the interactions between Vietnam veterans and their families and friends, we show that the impact of social networks depends not only on their structure and intensity, but on the context in which the networks that surround the veterans are situated. While we stress the importance of both social network analysis and social support mechanisms for understanding the situation of Vietnam veterans, the main thrust of our work is that the conditions of network formation and social support need to be carefully examined before the consequences of the networks and support systems surrounding veterans and their peers can be properly evaluated. Two sets of myths will be subjected to test. One set concerns social support in general; the second concerns the particular nature of the social support available to Vietnam veterans. We will proceed from the specific to the general and begin with a review of myths about the effects of support on Vietnam veterans.

The most pervasive myth, that the problems of Vietnam veterans differ from those of American veterans of previous wars because the American public did not support the war in Vietnam and did not properly welcome veterans when they came home, is so ubiquitous and so important that it deserves a chapter of its own — "Is the Vietnam Generation Politically Alienated?" Given this context, we deal with the specifics: the effects that particular partners, relatives, friends, and professionals had on Vietnam veterans.

There are four myths. The most fundamental is that given the unpopularity of the war and the possibility that Vietnam veterans committed atrocities, very few veterans had the opportunity to talk about the war, or at least to talk about it in any meaningful way. This lack of conversation is partially tied to the lack of a hero's welcome and the lack of ceremonies celebrating the reintegration of veterans into civilian life. If the war was dastardly and unpatriotic, then it is literally unspeakable. The classic "war stories," in which men celebrate their heroism and masculinity in battle, are absent.

Three corollary myths follow from this position. If men did discuss the war, then their friends, partners, and relatives did not understand them and were not able to offer effective social support. Further, professionals themselves, sharing the negative reaction to the war in general and to the horrors of guerrilla combat in particular, were unwilling to listen or at least were not helpful. Finally, given all this, only other Vietnam veterans could really help and really understand. Our analysis shows that although these myths are exaggerated and, in fact, depend somewhat on the context in which returning Vietnam veterans found themselves, there is some truth to these stereotypes. On the other hand, most men did have a chance to talk to at least someone about the war, and, in many instances, such discussion is associated with lower levels of current distress. Most important is the context in which the discussion took place and the type of person who was the partner — which brings us to the second set of myths those about the universal effectiveness of social support.

The study of social support has burgeoned in recent years. We have seen a number of major reviews, collections of articles, and critiques of the literature (eg., Cobb, 1976; Cohen & Syme, 1984; Gottlieb, 1981; Kaplan, Cassell, & Gore, 1977; Leavy, 1983; Sarason, 1985; Thoits, 1982; Wortman, 1984). The present study was designed in 1975, well before the current rush of literature. In characterizing social support, it relies heavily on network structure for understanding the impact of a veteran's friends on his adjustment but focuses more on quality for evaluating the effect of marital support. The sheer amount or extent of the support is also evaluated for the case of friends.

While structure, quality, and quantity of support are all important in principle and probably should all be measured in future studies, current literature suggests that the most disappointing aspect of social support has been its network, or structural, aspects. In the first blush of enthusiasm for social network analysis, researchers and practitioners alike thought that various structural aspects of social networks (aspects to be described later) would have a great impact on health and well being: in fact, many studies have come up empty handed. Our analysis suggests that the lack of results — positive or negative — is the result of inadequate understanding and conceptualization of the interpersonal environment of individuals. It is to this conceptualization that we now turn.

The "interpersonal environment" — that is, the set of all persons who interact with — have some direct relationship to a given focal person (Rossi, 1966), is critical to the analysis of support systems. Surprisingly, there are between 500 and 2,000 or more persons in a typical interpersonal environment (de S Pool & Kochen, 1978). The interpersonal environment includes all the people who comprise what network experts call the "first order zone," that is, the people directly connected with the focal individual (Barnes, 1969). The first task in studying social support systems is to determine which members of the interpersonal environment are relevant to the problem or situation at hand.

The interpersonal environment may be only a part of the set of social influences on the person. The concept of "networking" suggests that for many purposes individuals mobilize friends to contact other friends who are not known by or accessible to the original person. Utilizing these "friends of friends" to gain an advantage or a favor is said to be a characteristic mode of operation for Mediterranean societies (Boissevain, 1974). "Weak ties" — those persons connected to others whom we do not know very well — can also be very important to the conduct of social relations in our own society (Grannovetter, 1973). The second task in studying support systems and networking is, therefore, to determine in what way these "friends of friends" need to be taken into account in understanding individual behavior. Is the social system that surrounds individuals the kind in which "everyone knows everyone else," or is it more loosely structured, so that we can expect specialized chains and circles to form around different purposes? Social support in close-knit societies may work in a different way from social support in more loosely structured systems.

Not all members of the interpersonal environment occupy the same social status; some are kin or spouses, while others are friends, who may be male or female. There are professionals whose very business it is to be helpful. Some professionals are members of the interpersonal environment; others must be reached through a networking process. A third task in studying social support and networking systems is to differentiate between the various types of actual or potential helpers — for example, what are the situations in which a spouse is more effective than a friend, and vice versa? And when are professionals more useful than friends? Different types of persons in the interpersonal environment may perform different functions: spouses may encourage, friends may help to find resources, professionals may offer specialized therapy (Litwak & Szelenyi, 1969). The matter of sheer availability may also be critical. A casual friend who lives near by may be more helpful for some purposes than an intimate who lives across the country. The ability or willingness to stay with a problem over the long haul is also important. For example, Litwak (1979) suggests that kin may be more willing than intimate friends to help a person deal with a long term hospitalization. The substitutability of one type of supporter for another is of concern to us here: if wives are not supportive, can friends take up the slack? Finally, the consequences of support may not be additive. Support from one's wife combined with support from one's friends may not be twice as good—all one might need is support from one quarter or another, with any further support superfluous.

We need to determine the extent to which each of the identified supporters in the interpersonal environment is perceived to be supportive or helpful. In the end, the payoff is the extent to which supporters and others in the interpersonal environment make a difference: are men with social support of one kind or another who have interpersonal environments of one kind or another better off in various ways or worse off? In evaluating the impact of the interpersonal environment, it is extremely important to realize that interpersonal relationships always take place within a broader social context. Social relations in a large city may be different from those in a small town; this will affect the nature and consequences of the interpersonal environment.

Although most of the literature on social support assumes that it has positive benefits (for exceptions, see Kadushin, 1983b; Kobasa & Puccetti, 1983), this is not our assumption. One can obviously have too much of a good thing so that support becomes oppressive rather than helpful. Supporters may offer the wrong kind of help, making matters worse than they were before. It is also possible that persons will seek out others with similar problems. This can lead not only to mutual support, but to mutual exacerbation. Finally, it is obvious that if people with problems seek out the help of others, then acts of social support must be correlated with having a problem. This is been especially obvious in studies of help given to the aged. Older people with more problems are likely to have been offered more, and specific, help. Even if help is mainly efficacious, there will be a spurious positive correlation between having a problem and having received social support. If the sequence of events is not taken into account, social support will apparently lead to negative effects.

There is considerable attention in the social support literature on the so-called buffering effect, which is reviewed by Martin in his chapter. Briefly, the matter concerns whether social support is equally effective for those who have and who have not been exposed to a stressor, or whether social support is mainly effective among those who have been exposed to a stressor. More broadly, various aspects of social structure can affect individuals in the following three ways: (a) they can create situations that are more or less stressful. (b) they can mandate practices that immunize the individual against, or, conversely, sensitize him to stressors in the environment; (c) they can produce structures that alleviate or exacerbate existing disorders. In sum, the effort in our analysis of social support systems of veterans is to specify the conditions under which various kinds of support are effective or perhaps even harmful for various kinds of outcomes.

The following chapters on social support deal with a number of different aspects of this complex problem. Kadushin's chapter serves as an introduction, identifies general types of interpersonal environments, and assesses the degree to which they are helpful to veterans under various conditions. Martin's contribution focuses on a comparison of spouse and friend support and shows under what conditions and for which purposes each is helpful. Cantor's chapter centers on one particular type of friend — the women friends of the men in our sample. Throughout, we are concerned with specification: the conditions under which the particular social support structure is useful, when is it not, and the different outcomes it effects.

9 The Interpersonal Environment and Vietnam Veterans

Charles Kadushin

THE COMMUNITY CONTEXT

The major concern of this chapter is the effect of the larger social context of the interpersonal environment on the adaptations of Vietnam veterans. The interpersonal environment has been defined as the set of all persons who interact with or have some direct or indirect relationship with the focal individuals — in this case, our respondents. We have already seen that the political environment has some effects as it impacts on Vietnam veterans, especially on those who have returned home with problems. The concerns, as well as the assistance, of the larger community are passed on to veterans through their interpersonal environment.

There is probably no single concept in social science that has generated more stereotypes and more myths than the concept of "community" (Wellman, 1979). Consider two kinds of larger social environments within which a person's own interpersonal environment functions. One type is the mythical village, or folk society. In this community, everyone knows everyone else. The norms are clear, violations of standards are immediately observed and redressed, individuals know where they stand in the community, and help for problems is readily available (Wellman, 1979). In this traditional community, we expect that warriors will be surrounded by others who will ease their transition from the state of war to the state of peace. There will be readjustment rituals and help for those who have difficulty in readjustment (Smith, 1981).

At other extreme is the modern urban specialized community, epitomized by such metropolises as New York City. These "communities" emphasize

121

multiple, cross-cutting circles or regions of solidarity coexisting with loose, anonymous, and incompletely connected systems of relationships (Simmel, 1955; Kadushin, 1966). While on one hand the metropolis provides great personal flexibility — one can simultaneously be a member of a Wall Street brokerage firm and play the bass fiddle in a jazz club on weekends — social support comes from a more limited specialized group, and it may require considerable social skill or "networking" ability to make and retain contact with this group. Thus, a veteran may be supported by other veterans but not necessarily by other circles to which he may belong. In fact, many of the first veteran self-help or "rap" groups were formed in large cities such as New York (Egendorf, 1975).

These two polar types of community systems — the traditional village and the metropolis — may both be supportive, but in different ways and under different circumstances. In smaller communities, if everyone in the interpersonal environment indeed knows everyone else, then we may assume that something like traditional society is operating. On the other hand, even if everyone in the interpersonal environment of a veteran in a metropolis knows everyone else this may not guarantee that they all share the same norms and belong to the same moral "community." They may merely be a pocket of people linked only by virtue of knowing the focal individual. Specialized circles may take on different meanings depending on the larger context. In smaller cities, people might have to go out of their way to find others with similar interests and statuses. In the metropolis, such specialized circles are more easily found. We predict that a dense interpersonal environment in a smaller city will be associated with better postwar adjustment of Vietnam veterans and that, similarly, being surrounded by a circle of veterans will be helpful in metropolitan cities. In both cases, we are talking of ameliorating the consequences of battle stress which occurred some years before our interview. These predictions do not deal with the number of friends or the quality of the relationship between the respondent and his friends. Rather, we merely stipulate that the friends are there, that each has a certain status, and that they are related to one another in certain ways. Once the general effects of interpersonal environments are demonstrated, expand our concerns and investigate what happens when friends talk about Vietnam and how professional sources of help differ from informal ones.

THE DATA: INDICATORS OF TYPES OF INTERPERSONAL ENVIRONMENTS

In studying interpersonal environments, we necessarily concentrate on a small subset of relationships relevant to the particular problems or interactions with which we are concerned. In the present study, we asked respondents for the names of their "best friends" when they were 18 to 20 years old (when they registered for the draft). Up to three names were taken. Men were also asked for their closest friends or buddies while they were in the military or over the equivalent time period for those who were not in the service. We also ascertained whether respondents were still in touch with these past friends and whether they were currently considered friends. When the interview touched on the men's current situation, we asked who had found them their current job (if anyone); who their partner or spouse was; who their current best friends were (up to four); and if none of those was a Vietnam veteran, the names of some Vietnam veteran friends. For each person mentioned by the respondents we obtained the following additional information: sex; veteran status; whether or not the topic of Vietnam was discussed; occupation; how long the friend known our respondent; how they had met; how often they continued to be in contact; where the person lived; whether that friend was among the three persons to whom the respondent then felt closest; whether the friend was the one person to whom the respondent would turn if he had a serious personal problem; and whether the friend knew any of the other friends. In the present case, we focused on veteran status and whether any of the up to nine persons present in the interpersonal environment know one another.

All told, the average number of persons in the present interpersonal environment in this study was 5.3. A man was said to have a circle of Vietnam veteran friends if a greater proportion than the average (33%) of his spontaneously mentioned current friends were Vietnam veterans. In addition, we were interested in the density of the respondent's interpersonal environment. This was calculated as the number of connections (persons who knew one another) divided by the number of possible connections. The lower third of the distribution of densities is said to represent a low density. The top two thirds of the distribution is said to have a dense interpersonal environment; that is, the respondent is treated as if he lives in a world in which everyone knows everyone else.

Following the same logic, let us assume that if the men have a dense interpersonal environment and live in a medium- or smaller-sized city or rural area, their social environment is somewhat like traditional society; otherwise, it is not. Similarly, if the men have a circle of veteran friends in metropolitan centers, this circle may represent a naturally occurring support system; conversely, if they have a circle of Vietnam veteran friends in a smaller city, this circle may have resulted from their having purposely sought out other Vietnam veterans. Finally, we should note that the consequence of concern to us here is the current prevalence of Posttraumatic Stress Disorder (PTSD) (see Chapter 3, this volume).

RESULTS

We suggested that density would be effective only in settings reminiscent of traditional societies, such as smaller cities. Indeed, a national study of mental health in America concludes that "people who live in small cities – not in the most densely populated metropolitan regions nor in rural areas – have the most integrated context for social support" (Veroff, Douvan, & Kulka, 1981, p.515). A negative association between density of the interpersonal environment and mental disorder was found, as predicted, in data gathered by the Legacies project in 1977 in Brooklyn and Southern Westchester County, New York, and in Bridgeport, Connecticut (Kadushin, 1982). Although Brooklyn is part of New York City, in many respects it is a collection of smaller, working-class ethnic communities more typical of smaller towns and traditional communities.

In the present data set we regard Atlanta, Chicago, and Los Angeles as metropolitan communities; and we assume that Columbus, Georgia, rural Georgia, South Bend, Indiana, and rural Indiana are more typical of smaller communities and more likely to contain within them some pockets of traditional societies. Table 9.1 shows the the relation between low and high density and PTSD for men who have or have not experienced combat in Vietnam and for those who now live in smaller cities and rural areas. Because the multiplicity sampling used in gathering data on veterans distorts the proportion of men with large numbers of kin living in the area (especially parents), and these kin are related to social support systems, we present in the following analysis weighted data which correct for the overrepresentation of men with parents living in the area. We also have removed from the analysis the 46

TABLE 9.1

Effects of Low and High Density on Three Classes of PTSD Symptoms, for Veterans now Living in Nonmetropolitan Areas, Who were Exposed or Not Exposed to Combat in Vietnam

		PTSD Symptom Class							
		I		II		III			
				Possibly		Not			
		Stressed		Stressed		Stressed		Total	
Combat	Density	%	N	%	N	%	N	%	N
No	Low	9	(3)	31	(10)	59	(19)	99	(23)
	High	17	(8)	29	(14)	54	(26)	100	(48)
Yes	Low	30	(7)	52	(12)	17	(4)	99	(23)
	High	8	(2)	50	(12)	42	(10)	100	(24)

Mexican Americans in the sample, all of whom were in Los Angeles. All showed elevated levels of PTSD, and no effects of exposure to combat. We had great difficulty in obtaining an adequate sample of Hispanics in Los Angeles, and suspect this sample to be biased and unrepresentative.

It is evident that living in a world in which one's friends know one another is associated with fewer PTSD symptoms among those men who were exposed to combat. Note that the "buffering" effect is present in these data; the "small town," in which everyone knows everyone else, has no effect for those not exposed to combat. Their psychological symptoms are not associated with density. Further, combat has the expected effect of increasing the the proportion of men with PTSD symptoms when density is not taken into account. The same table, when displayed for men now living in metropolitan areas, shows no effects due to density. Table 9.1 also shows what has already been shown, namely, that men who have experienced combat have a higher proportion of PTSD symptoms.[1]

We can gain insight into what it means to be in a situation of high social density by looking at some class differences in the effects of density on current levels of PTSD among combat veterans. One might expect that working class men would be more attuned to traditional "communities." Indeed they are. Those working class men who live in an interpersonal environment in which everyone knows everyone else have fewer PTSD symptoms. The effects of density do not hold for men with professional occupations. For them, having a circle in which everyone knows everyone else does not indicate that these others are really a "community," but rather that they represent an intersection of circles uniquely put together by the respondent. Our findings also suggest that being black does not imply any greater sense of "community" than being white. Controls for race do not affect our findings.

We proposed that in metropolitan areas, a circle of Vietnam veteran friends might prove helpful to veterans who would otherwise have displayed high levels of PTSD as a result of combat. The positive effects of social support are well known and are explored further in the next chapter. With respect to Vietnam veterans, much has been made of the positive effects of "rap" groups (Egendorf, 1975; Lifton, 1973; Williams, 1980). That social support might also be associated with negative effects has been less discussed, but it takes little imagination to suggest that there might be conditions under which social support will be associated with high symptom levels rather than with lower ones. "Networking" might lead veterans with problems to seek out other such veterans. Thus we might observe a spurious association between

---

[1]An analysis of these data using MULTIQUAL (Bock, 1975; Bock & Yates, 1977), a loglinear related method, shows that a model that contrasts the effect on PTSD of low and high density for combat veterans in nonmetropolitan areas and for combat generally for all areas fits the data very well (for details, see Kadushin, 1983a).

PTSD and social support, spurious because if we could control for such networking activity, the association would disappear. Second, it is entirely possible that veterans who become involved with other veterans become "professional" Vietnam veterans, who develop secondary gains from this association
and who become reluctant to give up their symptoms.

Both possibilities, the positive and negative association between veteran
circles and PTSD, are demonstrated in Table 9.2. The positive association is
found among combat veterans in nonmetropolitan areas. Over 30% of combat veterans who "hang out" with Vietnam veterans, as compared with about
10% of those who do not, have high current levels of PTSD symptoms. The
negative association is found among combat veterans in metropolitan areas.
There we find that almost 40% of veterans who do not hang out with other
Vietnam veterans have high levels of PTSD symptoms, whereas fewer than
20% of combat veterans who do associate with other Vietnam veterans currently have a high level of PTSD symptoms.[2]

How do we account for these differences between metropolitan and
nonmetropolitan areas? The positive effects of merely having veteran friends
in metropolitan areas may well stem from the fact that these friends are more
"sophisticated" and represent a variety of potential resources rather than being a set of friends who merely share a common misfortune and who reinforce one another in their misery. To find support for this hypothesis, we separated the veteran friends of men in metropolitan areas into those whom the
respondent had first met either through relatives or through the
neighborhood—homebodies, we might call them-and compare them with
"sophisticates"—men whom the respondent got to know through other
sources such as work, school, and the like. Then the positive effects of having
a circle of veteran friends were limited to the sophisticates—the quintessen-
tial urban men. The negative effects in smaller cities and rural areas may be
caused by "misery loving company." To find veterans in these less populated
areas may take more effort. Veterans with problems may be more motivated
to take the extra effort to search for other veterans. It is not that knowing
other veterans necessarily makes men worse off, but that men with problems
are also those who search for other veterans.

Are there other factors we should have taken into account in explaining
our findings? The obvious ones are class, race, and geographic mobility.
Race and class have few effects. Men who moved away from home after age
18 (after their military experience) are no different from men who returned to
their home town. Finally, since combat and having veteran friends are
unrelated, there is no way that our findings can be interpreted as resulting
from "drift": that is, it is not true that combat leads to having fewer friends

---

[2]These differences are statistically significant.

TABLE 9.2

Effects of Membership in Veteran Circles on Three Classes of PTSD Symptoms, for Veterans now Living in Metropolitan and Nonmetropolitan Areas, Who Were Exposed or Not Exposed to Combat in Vietnam

		PTSD Symptom Class							
		I		*II*		*III*			
				Possibly		*Not*			
		Stressed		*Stressed*		*Stressed*		*Total*	
Combat	*Vet Circle*	*%*	*N*	*%*	*N*	*%*	*N*	*%*	*N*
		Nonmetropolitan							
No	No	9	(4)	30	(13)	60	(26)	99	(43)
	Yes	18	(7)	33	(13)	49	(19)	100	(39)
Yes	No	11	(3)	48	(15)	42	(13)	100	(31)
	Yes	32	(6)	47	(9)	21	(4)	100	(19)
		Metropolitan							
No	No	22	(20)	26	(24)	52	(47)	100	(91)
	Yes	12	(8)	30	(20)	58	(38)	100	(66)
Yes	No	37	(16)	44	(19)	19	(8)	100	(43)
	Yes	18	(6)	47	(16)	35	(12)	100	(34)

and also to higher levels of PTSD. The correlations between current patterns of friendship and PTSD do not appear to be spurious.

FRIENDS AND PROFESSIONALS: WHO IS MORE HELPFUL?

Thus far we have shown the effects of the social structure on the interpersonal environment and of the presence in the environment of certain types of people on the prevalence of PTSD symptoms. No one has actually done anything, however. Suppose these others in the interpersonal environment talk with our respondent about Vietnam, or at least listen to him? One of the more common myths is that having someone to talk with about Vietnam is very helpful to Vietnam veterans. Our data suggest that talking to just anyone is not especially useful and is not associated with lower probabilities of PTSD symptoms, a point elaborated in the next chapter. Talking with a Vietnam veteran, however, is quite a different matter. Just about all the veterans in our sample report talking with friends who are Vietnam veterans about Vietnam, as one might expect. We find that talking about Vietnam with a good friend who is a Vietnam veteran has an effect almost identical to those findings already reported, namely, that such talk is especially useful for veterans in big cities. Nonetheless, talking about Vietnam with nonveteran friends is not altogether without consequence. This brings us to some rather astounding findings.

We need now to consider the likelihood of consulting professional help for mental problems. In collecting the second set of data from the Midwest, the South, and the West, we asked an extensive series of questions about seeking professional help. An error in data collection caused us seriously to under-report visits to mental health professionals; we can report only on visits to professionals generally. With this caveat, let us briefly review some of the findings on veterans seeking professional help for mental problems.

None of the usual correlates of help-seeking for psychological problems (Veroff, Kulka, & Douvan, 1981) — occupation, education, income, region of the country, ethnicity, marital status, and so forth — are significant in this sample, and gender is of course irrelevant. Help seeking is strongly related, however, to PTSD symptoms. This is partially an artifact because unless a veteran reported some symptoms (not all of which were PTSD symptoms), he was not asked about help-seeking. On the other hand, studies of people who do seek help for psychological problems show that almost all who come for help prepare some "presenting problem" as their reason for seeing the mental health professional (Kadushin, 1969). Very few people just "drop in" on a psychiatrist or psychologist. In contrast, the interpersonal environment is always there. Not only are there no significant demographic correlates of talking to one's friends or having a circle of Vietnam veterans, but being stressed or possibly stressed upon coming home from Vietnam is not significantly related to these factors in the interpersonal environment. People can and do "drop in" on friends without having a "presenting problem."

Since only those with problems seek professional help, let us confine further analysis only to those who were stressed or possibly stressed when they returned home; and to make sure we are dealing mainly with PTSD reactions to combat, only combat veterans will be considered. Again, the larger social context is extremely important. We found that among combat veterans city size does make a difference: stressed combat veterans in metropolitan areas are much more likely to seek help, but stress is not a factor in seeking help in the smaller cities.

Aside from PTSD symptoms, the main correlate of seeking professional help is talking about Vietnam with friends who are not Vietnam veterans. Table 9.3 shows that over 60% of men in metropolitan areas who talked with their nonveteran friends sought professional help, compared with fewer than 30% of those who did not talk with their friends. In nonmetropolitan areas the figures are in the same direction, but the difference attributable to discussion is smaller, partly because fewer men seek help in the first place.

Talking with Vietnam veteran friends did not appear to encourage veterans to seek professional help. Indeed it may have had the opposite effect, as shown in Table 9.4. In metropolitan areas, men who did not talk with veteran friends were more likely to seek professional help. Perhaps Vietnam veteran friends, especially those in big cities, do not believe professionals can help. This is certainly one underlying assumption behind rap groups. On the other hand, if nonveterans hear a combat veteran talking about Vietnam, they may think the veteran is emotionally disturbed and should seek professional help.

To what extent is the Vietnam veteran's impression that professional help for PTSD is useless grounded in fact? Table 9.5 suggests that combat veterans who were stressed when they returned home, and who saw at least one professional in the meantime, are still stressed or possibly stressed today. About half of those who visited at least one professional for help with psychological problems are stressed or possibly stressed today, compared with only one quarter of those who did not seek professional help. Does seeing a

TABLE 9.3

Percent Vietnam Combat Vets at "Risk"* Who Sought Professional Help for Mental Problems, According to City Size and Whether They Talked With Nonveteran Friends About Vietnam

		City Size			
		Metropolitan		Nonmetropolitan	
		%	(n)	%	(n)
Talked to NON-VET Friends	No	28	(11)	12	(12)
	Yes	64	(41)	27	(18)
Somers' D		.36 sig @.05		.15 (NS)	

*Stressed or Possibly Stressed After the War.

TABLE 9.4

Percent Vietnam Combat Vets at "Risk"* Who Sought Professional Help for Mental Problems, According to City Size and Whether They Talked With Veteran Friends About Vietnam

		City Size			
		Metropolitan		Nonmetropolitan	
		%	(n)	%	(n)
Talked to VETERAN Friends	No	63	(42)	16	(21)
	Yes	30	(10)	33	(9)
Somers' D		− .36 sig @.05		.16 (NS)	

*Stressed or Possibly Stressed After the War.

TABLE 9.5
Percent Vietnam Combat Vets "At Risk"* Who Are
Currently Stressed, According to Whether They Have
Sought Professional Help

		%	(n)
Sought Professional Help	No	26	(47)
	Yes	49	(36)
Somers' D		−.23 Sig @ .05	

*Stressed or Possibly Stressed After the War.

professional make people worse? Unlikely, but the data do suggest that men who were once stressed and who continued to be stressed, and who therefore sought professional help, are still not better. It may be that people with more severe and more continuing problems are those who went for help, but that does not change the fact that they are still stressed. (For an alternative explanation of the professional's apparent failure to treat PTSD symptoms successfully, see Boulanger, 1985). Only by assigning stressed combat veterans at random to professional sources could we conclusively decide whether the professionals help, make no difference, or make matters worse. In any case, though their logic may be fallacious, it is easy to see why Vietnam veterans, as a result of evidence they can directly observe, think professionals do not help.

DISCUSSION

The key difference between professional help and the interpersonal environment is availability. When the right kind of interpersonal environment is readily available, it seems helpful. By "right kind" of environment, we mean Vietnam veterans who understand the experience of combat and who do not think a man is "crazy" because he wants to talk about his experiences in Vietnam, yet are not so crippled themselves by the experience that they have become "professional" Vietnam veterans. On the other hand, nonveterans may have a great deal of difficulty in listening to accounts of combat trauma; their reaction is to send combat veterans away to talk to professional listeners. Even mental health professionals tend to be repelled by the experiences of victims of war, the Holocaust, or rape. It may be that the professionals seen by the Vietnam veterans in our sample had similar difficulties and thus were unable to help.

Especially important in understanding how the interpersonal environment can help veterans is realizing that friends and relatives are helpful only under certain conditions. The entire community, if it is cohesive, may be helpful in smaller cities. In big cities there are not the same kind of integrated social relations, and merely because one's friends happen to know one another is no indication that the social system can act with any unity or purpose. In fact, we saw that well-meaning friends can be harmful. They can recommend professionals who apparently are not of much help; and, in certain contexts, they can constitute a community of "professional" Vietnam veterans who simply reinforce each other's misery. On the other hand, the right blend of Vietnam veterans can help one another. In short, forming effective support groups or taking advantage of the natural ones which may exist is far from a cut and dried procedure. The next chapter, on wives and friends, drives some of these points home, as we see that wives are not always helpful—and friends, if they are not available, are of little use.

10 Effects of Support on Demoralization and Problem Drinking

John L. Martin

INTRODUCTION

Interest in the role of the supportive social network in models of health and illness is reflected in a large and fast-growing body of literature on social support. The focus of this literature is broad and includes studies of the influence of supports on a variety of health outcomes, including mental health (Brown & Harris, 1978; Gore, 1978; Henderson, Byrne, & Duncan-Jones, 1981); physical health and medical complications (Gore, 1978; LaRocco, House, & French, 1980); psychiatric status (Henderson, 1980); pregnancy complications (Nuckolls, Cassel, & Kaplan, 1972; Sosa, Kennel, Klaus, Robertson, & Arretia, 1980), and mortality risk rates due to a variety of causes (Berkman & Syme, 1979). These studies of social support have been based not only on general populations (Henderson, Byrne, & Duncan-Jones, 1981), but on more homogeneous groups as well, including working-class women (Brown & Harris, 1978); recent mothers (Turner & Noh, 1983); unemployed men (Gore, 1978); the elderly (Lowenthal & Haven, 1968); and adolescents (Kaplan, Robbins, & Martin, 1983).

Methodological and conceptual problems make it difficult to draw definitive conclusions regarding the etiologic role of supports in the process leading to illness (see Thoits, 1982, and Gore, 1981, for reviews of these problems). However, the evidence tends to converge on the idea that social supports are positively related to health, and this relationship may be especially strong for individuals made vulnerable to illness as a result of acute stressful life events, long term difficulties, or other predisposing factors (Brown, Bhrolchain, &

Harris, 1975; Eaton, 1978; Gore, 1978, 1981; Turner & Noh, 1983). A theory of this "stress-buffering" role of social supports (Cassel, 1974; Cobb, 1976; Gore, 1981) has been fairly well developed around this evidence of the increased importance of social support for highly stressed individuals, and this theory forms the basis of the study reported in this chapter.

Although much has recently been written documenting the disproportionately high rate of psychological problems found among Vietnam veterans in general and high combat veterans in particular, systematic research aimed at specifying social factors that might effectively reduce or ameliorate these problems is relatively sparse. It is suprising that more work focused specifically on the veteran's social context has not been done since the members of the interpersonal environment form the essential network within which readjustment and reintegration must take place. Furthermore, given the potentially negative effects of war combat on mental health, the role of social supports as a buffer is not only an important practical problem, but an important theoretical problem.

Evidence from World War II indicates that combat exposure is an extremely stressful event, capable of producing acute psychotic symptoms in previously sound individuals (Grinker & Spiegel, 1963; Swank, 1949). Evidence from the Vietnam war indicates that combat can also cause insidious psychiatric dysfunction reflecting posttraumatic stress disorder (see Boulanger in this volume as well as Figley, 1978; Frye & Stockton, 1982). Although a significant minority of Vietnam veterans who saw combat were, and continue to be, "psychiatric casualties," a majority of these men are healthy and well functioning. They not only coped successfully with the stressor of war but have overcome the stigma associated with participating in that war. The question here is: To what extent do socioenvironmental factors account for this difference in current adjustment levels?

Based on evidence just outlined, the guiding hypothesis of this analysis is that support characteristics of the interpersonal environment play a major role in determining current levels of mental health among Vietnam veterans exposed to combat in the war. In the exploration of this hypothesis, the analytic approach corresponds to the approach taken by researchers examining the stress-buffering effects of supports. That is, the relationship between social supports and indicators of mental health will be examined, focusing on the degree to which combat exposure influences this relationship. To the extent that distress associated with combat exposure is reduced or eliminated by social supports, the stress-buffering hypothesis will be confirmed, indicating that supports play a central role in determining current levels of mental health. On the other hand, to the extent that distress is not reduced or eliminated, the role of supports in determining current levels of psychological functioning will be called into question.

THE STRUCTURE OF THE SAMPLE

Sampling procedures and the characteristics of the sample are described in detail in Appendix A to this volume. Our main concern here is to describe the demographic and social status characteristics of the sample as they apply to the present analysis.

Marital Status

Table 10.1 shows the breakdown of the entire sample of 1,381 respondents by marital status. Two major subsamples were derived from this distribution. The first, hereafter called partnered respondents, is composed of married men and men who are not married but living with a partner, ($n = 979$, 71%). The second group, hereafter called unpartnered respondents, is composed of divorced, separated, and never-married men ($n = 399$, 29%). The three widowed men were excluded from the analysis altogether since they had extremely elevated scores on all indicators of mental health, they were all nonveterans, and they clearly represent a distinct group, given widowhood at the age of 35 or younger.

The analysis is structured around partnered and unpartnered status for two reasons. First, marital status is consistently related to a variety of health outcomes. Being married is associated with better mental health (Gove, 1972), better psychological well being (Gurin, Veroff, & Feld, 1960), and lower mortality risk rates (Berkman & Syme, 1979; Gove, 1973). These studies show that the benefits of being married are especially strong for males, and therefore marital status is a critical variable to consider. Because men who were not married but living with a partner did not differ from their married peers on either the dependent or independent variables, the two groups were combined.

The second reason for organizing the analysis around partner status is that applicable indicators of social support differ, with the presence or absence of

TABLE 10.1
Breakdown of Total Sample by Marital Status

Marital Status	N	Percent
Married	919	66.5
Living with a partner	60	4.3
Divorced	108	7.8
Separated	42	3.1
Widowed	3	0.3
Never married	249	18.0
Total	1381	100.0

a partner (as detailed later in the description of support measures). Partner support, obviously applicable only to those having a partner, has been shown to be a key resource in coping with various stresses and strains (Kessler & Essex, 1982). In fact, in an earlier analysis of these data (Martin, 1981, Kadushin et al., 1981), it was shown that partner support was entirely responsible for the observed significant marital status difference in mental health in this sample. Respondents with a low level of partner support were actually more symptomatic than were unmarried respondents, whereas those with relatively high levels of partner support were significantly less symptomatic, as expected. These considerations led to dichotomizing the sample into two partner statuses and constructing measures of support applicable to each.

Combat Exposure

The second major variable around which the analysis is structured is combat exposure. For the purposes of this study, the finer distinctions between heavy and light combat made by the continuous combat scale (see Appendix B to this volume) were not of interest. Instead, it was desirable to specify a single group of respondents who had clearly experienced the stressors of combat in Vietnam. It was not possible simply to utilize the entire group of Vietnam veterans for this purpose because a number of Vietnam veterans never saw combat, or saw it so infrequently that they could not legitimately be considered exposed to the stresses of combat. Thus, Vietnam veterans who scored less than three on the combat scale were not considered to have been exposed to the stressor of war. This small group was combined with veterans who had served elsewhere and with nonveterans to form the group designated as "not exposed" to combat stress. Vietnam veterans scoring three or higher on the Combat scale were considered exposed to the stressor of war and form the contrasting group of "exposed" respondents. Among partnered respondents, 195 (20%) are in the exposed group, and 784 (80%) are in the not exposed group. Among unpartnered respondents, 63 (16%) are in the exposed group and 336 (84%) are in the not exposed group.

Social Status Control Variables

Three social status indicators are included in all analyses as control variables. Age is a dichotomous variable in which zero (0) represents respondents between the ages of 24 and 30 ($n = 580$, 42%) and one (1) represents respondents between the ages of 31 and 35 ($n = 798$, 58%). Respondent race is also a dichotomous variable in which zero (0) represents those who identified themselves as non-white ($n = 494$, 36%) and one (1) represents those who identified themselves as white ($n = 884$, 64%).

The third variable, socioeconomic status (SES) is a composite indicator based on three variables: income level, occupational prestige, and education. Each variable was scored from one to five in the direction of higher SES. These three variables were summed, resulting in a continuous distribution ranging from three to 15 ($M = 9.20$, $SD = 2.80$.)

INDICATORS OF SOCIAL SUPPORT

Issues surrounding the measurement of social support are many and varied. Although recent efforts, which are both psychometrically sophisticated and based on prespecified measurement models. (e.g. Henderson et al., 1981; McFarlane, Neale, Norman, Roy & Streiner, 1982; Phillips & Fischer, 1981), will undoubtedly go a long way toward resolving some of these issues, there is no current consensus on how best to tap the support construct.

One main dimension along which prior measures of support have been operationalized involves intimacy. At one extreme are measures based on the emotionally supportive quality of a single confidant (e.g. Brown, Bhroluchain, & Harris, 1975; Lowenthal & Haven, 1968). At the other extreme are measures based on additive indices tapping mainly the quantity of a variety of relationships both close and distant (e.g. Lin, Simeone, Ensel, & Kuo, 1979; Phillips & Fischer, 1981). The latter type of index is associated more with integration into, and involvement with, a social network through which support during times of stress is assumed to be provided.

For the purposes of this analysis, support was measured in both ways. The first, and primary, type of support involves a close confidant. The second type of support involves contact with close personal friends. The specific measures as they apply to partnered and unpartnered subgroups of this sample are described below.

Intimate Support

The partner support scale was designed to measure the supportiveness of the partner relationship for the respondent and was based on items judged to be face valid indicators of the presence or absence of a supportive partner (see Kessler & Essex, 1982, for an example of a similar measure.) Items tap feelings of affection for, and comfort with, one's partner; agreement in decision making; satisfaction with the relationship; and the use of the partner as a confidant for help with personal problems. The six items of the scale are provided in Appendix 10A. Responses to each item were scored from one to five in the direction of high support. Items were summed, resulting in a continuous distribution ranging from nine to 30 ($M = 23.29$, SD

$= 3.91, n = 979$). The alpha coefficient for the six items is .60, indicating an acceptable level of internal consistency reliability for the partner support scale.

Network Confidant Support

As a parallel measure to the partner support scale representing intimate support, a simpler indicator of intimate support for unpartnered respondents was used. This indicator is based on responses to the interview question, "Who would you turn to for help with a serious personal problem?" Respondents who named a person whom they previously had nameded as part of their social network of friends received a score of one (1) on this network confidant variable. Respondents who either named no one or named someone outside their network of friends received a score of zero (0) on this variable.

Scored in this way, the network confidant variable taps the presence or absence of a confidant in the social network of close friends. Although many of those receiving a zero on this indicator named someone such as a therapist, priest, or parent as the person to whom they turned for help, they are distinct from those assigned a one on the variable because their main confidant was not part of their immediate circle of spontaneously named close friends. A confidant residing outside the circle of friends may be less accessible for help with serious day-to-day problems, compared with a confidant who is integrated within the immediate social network. Of the 399 unpartnered respondents to whom this measure applies, 184 (46%) received a score of one (1) on the network confidant measure, and 215 (54%) received a score of zero (0) on this measure.

Friend Support

The measure of friend support, which is applicable to both partnered and unpartnered subgroups, is based on the amount of contact respondents had had with close friends over the previous year (cf. Berkman & Syme, 1979). Information about each friend was elicited according to the method developed by Schulman (1972) and more fully elaborated by Fischer and his colleagues (Fischer et al., 1977; McCallister & Fischer, 1978; Phillips & Fischer, 1981). The one piece of information used in this friend support scale was the frequency of contact respondents reported having with each friend. Each friend named received one of the following weights: 2.5 if seen once a week or more; 1 if seen once every 2 to 3 weeks; 0.5 if seen once a month; and 0 if seen less than once per month. These weights were summed across the total set of friends (which ranged from 0 to 11), resulting in a continuous distribution of friend support scores ranging from 0 to 19. The mean of this friend support measure is 6.26, $(SD = 3.60, n = 977)$ for partnered respondents, and 6.60, $(SD = 3.44, n = 395)$ for the unpartnered.

MENTAL HEALTH INDICATORS

Two indicators of mental health that focus on psychological distress are used here. One involves demoralization symptomatology; the other, perceived problems with drinking. Indicators tapping these two domains were chosen because psychiatric epidemiological evidence suggests that when studying males it is important to consider disorders more typically expressed by men (Dohrenwend & Dohrenwend, 1976; Mechanic, 1978). Studies indicate that as a group males typically express distress through of higher levels of "acting-out" disorders, such as alcohol and drug abuse and antisocial personality problems. In contrast, females tend to express distress in terms of depressive symptomatology and demoralized mood. This sex difference although consistent, does not mean that men don't become depressed or that women don't experience problems with alcohol and drugs. It does mean, however, is that we should not focus exclusively on one commonly measured type of disorder, such as depression or demoralization, when studying a sample of males, because we may fail to detect psychological distress expressed through acting-out problems. Examining two distinct mental health indicators is also useful for determining the generalizability of our findings regarding social supports, across different outcomes.

Demoralization

Twenty-three items taken from the Psychiatric Epidemiology Research Instrument (PERI) make up the demoralization scale used here, and correspond closely to the way in which Dohrenwend and his colleagues (Dohrenwend, Oskenberg, Shrout, Dohrenwend, & Cook, 1981) have operationalized this construct (Frank, 1973). These items tap the following symptom areas: poor self-esteem, helplessness/hopelessness, suicidal ideation, sadness, anxiety, confused thinking, and psychophysiological problems. For each item, respondents were asked whether in the previous 12 months the symptom had occurred very often, fairly often, sometimes, almost never, or never. Items were keyed in the direction of high demoralization and summed. Scores range from 0 to 92, with a mean of 18.75 $(SD = 11.72)$ among partnered respondents and 22.04 $(SD = 12.06)$ among the unpartnered. The internal consistency reliability of this scale is high; alpha = .91.

Perceived Problem Drinking

The problem drinking scale used here is designed to measure the extent to which drinking is a problem for respondents. The five items that make up this scale (listed in Appendix 10.B) tap the regularity of drinking, intensive periods of drinking, and feelings of dependency on alcohol. Items were scored zero (0) or one (1) in the direction of problem drinking, and summed. The continuous distribution of scores ranges from zero to five. The internal consistency reliability of this scale is high, given its brevity, (alpha = .73). The mean level of problem drinking for partnered respondents is 1.58 (SD = 1.49, n = 950). For unpartnered respondents, the mean level of problem drinking is 2.11, (SD = 1.65, n = 392).

SUMMARY OF THE SAMPLE AND MEASURES

A summary of the measures as they apply to partnered and unpartnered respondents is shown in Table 10.2.

It can be seen from the table that significant differences between partnered and unpartnered respondents exist only for the two mental health indicators,

TABLE 10.2
Comparison of Dependent and Independent Variables Across
Partner Status (a)

| | Partnered Status | |
Variable	Partnered	Unpartnered
Combat Exposure (b)	20%	16%
	(195/979)	(63/399)
Demoralization (c)	18.75	22.04
	(975)	(398)
Problem drinking (d)	1.58	2.11
	(950)	(392)
Friend support (e)	6.26	6.60
	(977)	(395)
Partner support	23.29	—
	(979)	
Network confidant	—	46%
		(184/399)

    (a) Valid Ns for each variable are shown in parentheses.
    (b) Percent exposed to combat. Chi square = 3.176, df = 1, p = N.S.
    (c) t = 4.68, df = 1371, $p < .0001$.
    (d) t = 5.74, df = 1340, $p < .001$.
    (e) t = 1.62, df = 1370, p = N.S.

demoralization and problem drinking. These differences are in the expected direction, with partnered respondents having a lower mean level of both types of problems compared with unpartnered respondents. No significant differences between the two groups exist for either the proportion exposed to combat or mean friend support.

RESULTS

Relationships Among Predictor Variables

Prior to conducting the main analyses we examined the interrelationships among the main predictor variables within each partner status in order to establish their degree of overlap. For partnered respondents the correlation between partner support and friend support is small and nonsignificant ($r = .07$), indicating that the two support measures are independent. For unpartnered respondents the correlation between network confidant and friend support is also small and nonsignificant ($r = .064$), indicating that these two support measures are also independent.

Turning to the influence of prior combat exposure on current levels of support, we tested for mean differences between exposed and nonexposed respondents within each partner status. These results are summarized in Table 10.3. It is clear that combat exposure has no significant influence on levels of supports for either partnered or unpartnered respondents.

It thus cannot be claimed that the stressor, which occurred (on average) 6 years prior to the interview, exercises a causal influence on these types of social supports. In addition, the number of years elapsed between leaving Vietnam and being interviewed, which ranged from 3 to 13, had no influence on support levels or on outcomes, as indicated by within group analyses conducted on combat exposed respondents.

Combat Exposure, Supports, and Mental Health

Partnered Respondents

Having established that the main predictor variables are independent of one another, the effects of these three variables on demoralization and problem drinking were tested using the general linear regression model shown in the following equation:

$$\begin{aligned}
D = a &+ b_1(C_1) + b_2(C_2) + b_3(C_3) \\
&+ b_4(X_1) + b_5(X_2) + b_6(X_3) \\
&+ b_7(X_1 \times X_2) + b_8(X_1 \times X_3) + b_9(X_2 \times X_3) \\
&+ b_{10}(X_1 \times X_2 \times X_3)
\end{aligned}$$

TABLE 10.3
Differences Due to Combat on Measures of Support, for Partnered
and Unpartnered Groups (a)

	Exposure Status			
Partner Status	Not Exposed		Exposed	
Partnered	M	SD	M	SD
Partner support (b)	23.35	3.79	23.06	4.36
	(784)		(195)	
Friend support (c)	6.24	3.64	6.33	4.30
	(782)		(195)	
Unpartnered	M	SD	M	SD
Network confidant (d)	48%	–	38%	–
	(160/336)		(24/63)	
Friend support (e)	6.57	3.55	6.80	2.84
	(332)		(63)	

(a) Valid Ns are shown in parentheses.
(b) $t = -0.92$, $df = 977$, p = N.S.
(c) $t = 0.30$, $df = 975$, p = N.S.
d) Percent with a network confidant. Chi square = 1.94, $df = 1$, p = N.S.
e) $t = 0.50$, $df = 393$, p = N.S.

This equation indicates that distress (D), (demoralization and drinking), are a function of: C_1, respondents' age; C_2, respondents' ethnicity; C_3, respondents' SES; X_1, combat exposure; X_2, partner support; and X_3, friend support. In addition, outcomes are also a function of the multiplicative interaction terms among the three main predictors, X_1, X_2, and X_3. The coefficients b_1 through b_{10} are regression weights associated with each predictor term and "a" is a constant representing the value of the distress measure when C_1 through C_3, and X_1 through X_3 are all equal to zero.

The relationship between the interaction terms in the model and the hypotheses of interest are as follows: The two-way interaction terms, exposure × partner support and exposure × friend support, represent tests for the homogeneity of slopes between the measures of support and health outcomes, for exposed and nonexposed groups. These interactions correspond to tests of the stress buffering hypothesis. A significant F-test associated with either of these terms indicates that the support–distress relationship is significantly different for these two groups. The two-way interaction, partner support × friend support, represents a test of whether the relationship between distress and each support indicator is contingent on the level of the other support indicator. The three-way interaction, exposure × partner support × friend support, represents a test for the presence of an interaction between any two variables as a function of the third variable. A significant F-test associated with this term indicates the most complex situation, where the influence of any one variable is dependent on the level of the other two.

Demoralization.   Table 10.4a shows the results of testing the model on demoralization scores for partnered respondents. Both combat exposure and partner support are significantly related to demoralization in the expected direction. The nonstandardized regression coefficients (*b*) indicate that combat exposed respondents have significantly elevated levels of demoralization and that partner support is inversely related to demoralization. In addition, the significant two-way interactions between each support measure and combat indicate significant differences in slopes between partner support and demoralization, and friend support and demoralization, as a function of combat. These effects are in the predicted direction, such that a unit increase in each type of support reduces demoralization levels significantly more for exposed, than nonexposed respondents.

The situation is somewhat more complicated, however, for the significant three-way interaction term. In order to interpret the meaning of this interaction, each support measure was dichotomized at its median, and covariance adjusted demoralization means for high and low levels of each type of support were computed (controlling for status variables). These means, shown Table 10.4b, indicate that it is the relatively specialized function of friend support that accounts for this complex effect. That is, variation in friend support is significantly associated with demoralization only for respondents exposed to combat who also have relatively low levels of partner support. Under no other combinations of combat and partner support does friend support exercise an effect.

Problem Drinking.   Equation 1 was again used to test the predictive power of supports and combat in relation to problem drinking. The results of testing the full model provided no support for the hypothesized slope differences due to combat between either type of support and problem drinking; Neither the exposure × partner support interaction, ($F = 2.84, p < .10$), nor the exposure × friend support interaction ($F = 0.84$), were significant. Nor was the three-way interaction significant ($F = 0.96$). However, a significant partner support × friend support interaction was present. Thus, the three nonsignificant interaction terms were deleted from the model and the reduced equation tested. These results are shown in Table 10.5a. The significant main effects shown here indicate that combat exposed respondents have significantly higher scores on problem drinking compared to nonexposed respondents. Friend support is also associated with problem drinking, but this relationship is in the opposite direction of what we expected: Increasing levels of friend support are associated with increases in problem drinking.

TABLE 10.4a

Regression of Demoralization on Combat, Partner and Friend
Support with Age, Race and SES Controlled
(Partnered Respondents)

Main Effects	F (a)	b
Combat exposure	10.84**	31.16
Partner support	10.33**	−0.65
Friend support	1.04	0.70
Interactions		
Combat × Partner support	10.23**	−1.32
Combat × Friend support	6.03*	−3.35
Partner × Friend support	1.65	−0.37
Combat × Partner × Friend	6.43*	0.15

TABLE 10.4b

Covariance Adjusted Demoralization Means Using Combat
Exposure, Partner Support, and Friend Support as Predictors,
After Controlling for Age, Race and SES
(Partnered Respondents)

Classification	Adjusted Demoralization Mean	n
Combat exposed respondents	20.21	194
High partner support	16.61	100
High friend support	16.34	56
Low friend support	16.88	44
Low partner support	23.82	94
High friend support	20.68	44
Low friend support	27.01	50
Nonexposed respondents	18.63	779
High partner support	15.76	415
High friend support	14.96	217
Low friend support	16.56	198
Low partner support	21.52	364
High friend support	21.62	164
Low friend support	21.41	200

(a) $df = 1,962$, for each effect.

** $p < .002$.

* $p < .02$.

TABLE 10.5a
Regression of Problem Drinking on Combat, Partner and Friend
Support with Age, Race and SES Controlled
(Partnered Respondents)

Main Effects	F (a)	b
Combat exposure	4.01*	0.24
Partner support	1.45	−0.03
Friend support	6.40**	0.20
Interaction		
Friend × Partner support	4.35*	−0.01

TABLE 10.5b
Covariance Adjusted Problem Drinking Mean using Combat,
Partner Support and Friend Support as Predictors, After
Controlling for Age, Race and SES (Partnered Respondents)

Classification	Adjusted Problem Drinking Mean	n
Exposed respondents	1.79	191
Nonexposed respondents	1.55	757
High friend support	1.84	463
Low friend support	1.50	485
High partner support	1.41	494
High friend support	1.49	258
Low friend support	1.33	236
Low partner support	1.92	454
High friend support	2.19	205
Low friend support	1.66	249

(a) $df = 1,940$, for each effect.
* $p < .05$.
** $p < .02$.

In addition to these main effects, the significant partner support × friend support interaction indicates that the effects of friend support are dependent on the level of partner support. In order to clarify this interaction, we again dichotomized the sample on each support measure and computed covariance adjusted means for each group. These means are shown in Table 10.5b. It can be seen that only under the condition of low partner support is friend support directly associated with problem drinking. In contrast, under the condition of high partner support, friend support has no significant effect.

Unpartnered Respondents

The same model applied to partnered respondents was applied to unpartnered respondents. For this group, however, partner support was replaced with network confidant support. In addition, we dichotomized the friend support distribution for this group, and used this dichotomized version of the variable in the actual tests. Thus, for unpartnered respondents, the three main predictors — combat, network confidant support, and friend support — are all dichotomized variables.

Demoralization. Testing the full model on demoralization for unpartnered respondents, we found no significant effects due to the exposure × friend support interaction ($F = 0.10$), friend support × confidant interaction ($F = 2.13$, $p < .15$), or the three-way interaction ($F = 1.63$, $p < .20$). However, a significant exposure × confidant interaction emerged. Thus, the three nonsignificant interactions were deleted from the equation, and the reduced model tested. These results are shown in Table 10.6a.

From the tests of main effects it can be seen that, unlike for partnered respondents, combat has no influence on demoralization for unpartnered re-

TABLE 10.6a
Regression of Demoralization on Combat, Partner and Friend
Support with Age, Race and SES Controlled
(Unpartnered Respondents)

Main Effects	F (a)	b
Combat exposure	0.17	−3.62
Network confidant	0.02	0.28
Friend support	0.02	−0.15
Interaction		
Combat × Network confidant	6.57*	8.62

TABLE 10.6b
Covariance Adjusted Demoralization Means using
Combat, Network Confidant, and Friend Support as
Predictors, After Controlling for Age, Race and SES
(Unpartnered Respondents)

Classification	Adjusted Demoralization Mean	n
Exposed respondents	22.74	63
Confidant present	27.19	24
Confidant absent	18.29	39
Nonexposed respondents	22.05	331
Confidant present	22.19	159
Confidant absent	21.91	172

(a) $df = 1,386$, for each effect.
* $p < .01$.

spondents. Nor does either support indicator influence demoralization in a direct manner. Although the significant exposure × confidant support interaction indicates the presence of a slope difference due to combat, the direction of the confidant support effect on demoralization is the opposite of what we expect. The covariance adjusted demoralization means shown in Table 10.6b reveal the source of this paradoxical support effect. For the combat exposed group, the presence of a network confidant is significantly associated with increased demoralization. Demoralization is not influenced at all by the presence of a network confidant among nonexposed respondents.

Problem Drinking.   With regard to problem drinking, the full model was tested on unpartnered respondents, and these results are shown in Table 10.7a. Although combat has a significant main effect on problem drinking for this group, the results are complex, as indicated by the significant three-way interaction. Covariance adjusted means, presented in Table 10.7b, indicate the source of this interaction. Among combat exposed respondents who have a high level of friend support, we find that the absence of a network confidant is associated with significantly higher levels of problem drinking, relative to when such a confidant is present. For no other combination of exposure status and friend support is there an association between confidant support and problem drinking for unpartnered respondents.

CONCLUSION

Although these findings are complex, it is reasonable to conclude that combat veterans tend to be more reactive to the support characteristics of their interpersonal environment, than either noncombatant veterans or non-veterans. Evidence from three out of four models tested converge on this conclusion. However, the nature of this reactivity varies, depending on whether we take demoralization or problem drinking as the outcome measure of distress. Although these two measures are significantly correlated in this sample ($r = .25$), each tends to respond differently to variations in intimate and network supports.

With respect to demoralization among partnered respondents, combat veterans as a group are more demoralized, but the presence of a supportive spouse or partner is a powerful resource capable of reducing this type of distress. Furthermore, when an adequate level of partner support is lacking, support through contact with friends "fills in" and eliminates demoralization associated with combat. These results do not mean that support from friends and from spouses is an interchangeable social resource; the presence of an unsupportive spouse or partner is, itself demoralizing, and friend support does not alleviate this distress. On the other hand, demoralization associated

TABLE 10.7a
Regression of Problem Drinking on Combat, Partner and Friend
Support with Age, Race and SES Controlled
(Unpartnered Respondents)

Main Effects	F (a)	b
Combat exposure	5.93*	0.39
Network confidant	0.31	− 0.19
Friend support	0.10	− 0.20
Interactions		
Combat × Network confidant	0.53	0.66
Combat × Friend support	0.25	0.76
Confidant × Friend support	1.23	0.47
Combat × Confidant × Friend	4.33*	− 2.01

TABLE 10.7b
Covariance Adjusted Problem Drinking Means Using Combat,
Network Confidant, Support as Predictors, After Controlling for Age,
Race and SES (Unpartnered Respondents)

Classification	Adjusted Problem Drinking Mean	n
Combat exposed respondents	2.61	62
High friend support	2.51	36
Confidant present	1.96	17
Confidant absent	3.05	19
Low friend support	2.71	26
Confidant present	2.93	7
Confidant absent	2.47	19
Nonexposed respondents	2.01	327
High friend support	2.03	173
Confidant present	2.07	88
Confidant absent	1.90	85
Low friend support	1.99	154
Confidant present	1.89	70
Confidant absent	2.09	84

(a) $df = 1,380$, for each effect.
* $p < .05$.

with combat exposure can be reduced by the presence of either type of support. Partnered respondents exposed to combat are consistently more sensitive to both types of support as compared with nonexposed peers, insofar as demoralization is concerned. Problem drinking, on the other hand, responds differently to social supports for this group. Combat exposure has no influence on the relationship between either spouse support or friend support and problem drinking. Whereas combat veterans as a group score higher on this outcome, they do not differ from their nonexposed peers in terms of the conditions under which friend support influences problem drinking. For all partnered respondents, a combination of low partner support and increases in friend contact is strongly associated with increased problem drinking. However, when partner support is high, friend support is not associated with problem drinking either directly or inversely.

With unpartnered respondents, complex results were found for both demoralization and problem drinking. Prior combat exposure has no direct impact on demoralization for this group. Combat does, however, have an influence on the association between the presence of a network confidant and demoralization. But this effect is the opposite of what we expected; the presence of a confidant is associated with increased demoralization for combat veterans.

It is notable that this finding parallels one reported by Carveth and Gottlieb (1979), who found a direct relationship between their measure of supportive friend contact and demoralization-like distress. In an attempt to interpret this direct relationship, both Carveth and Gottlieb (1979) and Gore (1981) propose that distress precedes and determines help-seeking, hence at some time in the coping process there will be a direct causal relationship between distress and support. Applying this reasoning to the present finding, it may be that unpartnered respondents who turned to someone in their network for help with personal problems were experiencing difficulties with which they were coping at the time of the interview. In contrast, those who named either no one, or someone such as a therapist, parent, or more distant friend may not have been experiencing personal problems and thus responded to the question in a more detached or "theoretical" way rather than in an immediate and practical way.

Whatever reason underlies this paradoxical effect, the evidence indicates that those who named a network confidant are demoralized, compared with those who did not. Given the available data, we cannot determine whether these network confidants are effective sources of social support. The fact that this direct relationship between naming a network confidant and demoralization was found only among combat exposed respondents suggests that the distress experienced by these men may have arisen from the combat experience. We may indeed be tapping the coping process described by Gore (1981) and Carveth and Gottlieb (1979), rather than a negative or deleterious social support effect.

How, then, should we interpret the inverse relationship found between the presence of a network confidant and problem drinking for combat exposed respondents with a high level of friend contact? The answer may lie in the fact that our network confidant indicator is actually detecting a form of coping with demoralization or other related problems for combat veterans. This idea is supported by the paradoxical results presented in Table 10.6, as well as by the fact that the zero-order correlation between this indicator and demoralization is .33 ($p<$ .007, n = 63) for combat veterans, but is small and nonsignificant for nonexposed respondents (r = .004, n = 315). Thus, the results presented in Table 10.7 may indicate that coping attempts made in the context of a network in which one's confidant resides, and with whom one is in frequent contact, helps guard against problem drinking. In contrast, coping attempts made in the context of a network in which one's confidant resides, but with whom one has little contact, may promote problem drinking.

Overall, the results presented in Table 10.7 indicate that for combat veterans frequent contact with a set of friends including a confidant represents a positive social structure that works against problem drinking. In contrast, frequent contact with a set of friends that does not include a confidant (either because one doesn't have one or one doesn't need one) represents a social structure that promotes problem drinking.

Taken together, these findings suggest that future research in the area of social supports should pay close attention to the way in which supports are measured and the outcomes to which they are applied. Persons made vulnerable to illness outcomes by severe stressors such as combat exposure are likely to be more sensitive to variations in their social environment and may respond to questions regarding help seeking quite differently from less vulnerable individuals. In addition, the modifying influence of particular social structural characteristics on the support–distress relationship needs to be more carefully examined. Very few studies to date have taken account of the interactive effect of multiple support indicators. The relatively frequent occurrence of these interactions in this study indicates that the effects of social support may be conditional not only on prior exposure to life stressors, but also on the availability of other types of social resources.

APPENDIX 10.A

The partner support scale consists of six items. All items were scored one through five in the direction of high support. For items 2 and 5, numeric responses were assigned values from one through five, based on the best resulting alpha coefficient.

1. When it comes to making important decisions, do you and your spouse/partner almost always agree (5); occasionally disagree (4), frequently disagree (2); almost always disagree (1); or does one of you make the important decisions without discussing them with the other (3)?

2. About how many disagreements did you and your spouse/partner have during the past week, even minor ones?

3. How often do you feel uncomfortable with you wife/partner would you say very often (1); fairly often (2); sometimes (3); almost never (4); or never (5)?

4. Do you feel affectionate towards you wife/partner would you say very often (5); fairly often (4); sometimes (3); almost never (2); or never (1)?

5. Using the numerical scale on this card (1-7), all things considered, how satisfied are you with your marriage/relationship?

6. If you need help with a personal problem, who would you turn to? Spouse/partner named (5); person other than spouse/partner named (1).

APPENDIX 10.B

The problem with drinking scale consists of the following five items.

1. In the past two years, have there been periods of time when you drank regularly? That is, at least one evening per week you would drink at least a six pack of beer, a bottle of wine, or several drinks of liquor? No (0), Yes (1).

2. Has there been a period in the past two years when you drank at least a six pack of beer, a bottle of wine, or several drinks of liquor almost every day? No (0), Yes (1).

3. In the past two years, how often have you drunk to the point where you felt high or "tight?" Never, once or twice, three or four times (0), five times or more (1).

4. Have you ever felt that you might become dependent on alcohol? No (0), Yes (1).

5. Have you ever thought you were drinking too much and ought to cut down or quit? No (0) Yes (1).

11 Women Friends of Men

Sheryl Canter

The presence or absence of women friends is an important part of the study of support networks. Friendships with women are generally considered to be more intimate than those with men. What little research there is in this area supports the notion that men are more willing to confide in women than in men. Komarovsky (1974) reports that for a sample of male undergraduates, female friends are the preferred confidantes when compared to parents, siblings, and male friends. A similar finding was reported by Olstad (1975). In a study of friendship among middle-aged and elderly adults, Booth and Hess (1974) found that many more men than women report cross-gender friendships. Although patterns of self-disclosure were not considered in this study, it is possible that the special role of women as confidantes accounts for the asymmetry. Belle (1982) gives evidence that women, both at home and at work, are the primary providers of social support — often to the detriment of their own health and well being.

However, friendship with women, as distinguished from a primarily sexual relationship, is not accepted in all spheres. Some men are more likely than other men to have women friends. Also, as this study shows, the quality of a man's relationship with his wife can vary widely, depending on personal attitudes, structural features of his social environment, or the experience of combat. In considering the possibility that female friendship may affect the occurrence of posttraumatic stress disorder (PTSD) in Vietnam veterans, we must be aware that many combat veterans say that they cannot talk about Vietnam to women (Williams, 1980). Thus, for the special stressor we are considering, women may not be of help. In this chapter, we examine the features of the person and the environment that tends to encourage or discourage friendship with women among men of the Vietnam generation. We discuss in what ways friendships with women differ from friendships with men, and what consequences these differences may have for the quality of life.

SUBJECTS

Married men and single men are considered separately, since the presence of a spouse fundamentally alters the way in which a man relates to women. Men who are separated, divorced, widowed, or cohabiting with women are excluded from the analysis, because these situations have ambiguous consequences for friendship with women. In all, 914 married men and 247 single men are considered.

DEPENDENT VARIABLES

Three dependent variables are considered: the number of current friends who are women; the number of "best friends" who are women; and whether or not the person named as a confidante is a woman.

Current Friends

In the course of the interview, respondents were asked about many different people in their lives. These included friends at age 18, friends at the time of the Vietnam war, current friends, confidantes, and "best friends." All friends with whom the respondent was still in contact formed the friendship pool. Unless otherwise stated, the respondent's wife and anyone else living with him are excluded. On average, respondents named five friends. There was no difference between married and single men in the total number of friends named. However, 15% of the friends of single men are women, versus 7% for married men, ($t = 5.67$ - separate variance estimate, $p < .001$). The cultural norm of fidelity and the suspicion with which women friends of married men are viewed may account for this difference. Another possibility is that girlfriends of single men, who could not be identified in this data set, elevate the proportion for single men, thus making the result artifactual.

However, there is evidence that married and single men differ in the manner in which they meet their women friends. To analyze the source of friendship, men who met the majority of their women friends through other friends and relatives (via introduction) were distinguished from men who met the majority of their women friends through work, school, hobbies, or other organized activities (goal-oriented settings). Among single men, 70% ($n = 76$) are most likely to meet women at work or school whereas only 57% ($n = 129$)

of married men are most likely to meet women in this way, (adjusted chi square = 5.29, $p < .03$). This perhaps indicates that married men are more likely to befriend a woman whom their wife knows and approves. A constraint of this sort would place married men at a disadvantage for acquiring women friends.

Only 9% of married men and 22% of single men report more than one woman friend. Seventy-six percent of married men and 57% of single men report no women friends at all.

Confidantes

Respondents were asked whom they would turn to for help with a serious personal problem. They could name a friend, a relative, a professional (such as a therapist or clergyman), or no one at all. Approximately 40% of respondents did not name a friend as helper. For those respondents who did, the proportion of helpers who are women is 66% ($n = 393$) for married men and 27% ($n = 31$) for single men, (adjusted chi square = 57.77, $p < .0001$). If the helper of a married man is a woman, there is a 96% chance that she is his wife.

Because the helper may be the respondent's wife or roommate, the proportion of all friends who are women, including wives and roommates, must be used for comparison. Considering only those men who named a friend as helper, the proportion of friends who are women is 24% for married men and 16% for single men. Thus women are overrepresented among helpers for both married and single men. A female friend is more likely to be a confidante than a male friend, whether the man is married or single. This confirms the notion that women are frequently the providers of social support. However, it does not tell us why this is so. It may simply be due to social convention, or it may imply that women are more skilled than men at providing support, perhaps because they have more practice (see Belle, 1982).

Best Friends

Respondents were asked to name the three people of all those named during the interview to whom they were closest. Three-quarters (76%) of the married men named their wives among their three closest friends. In addition, approximately 15% of married respondents named women other than their wives as closest friends. Since this percentage remains constant regardless of whether the wife is named, men who do not name their wives tend to name men instead.

For married men, 30% of best friends are women, which is high compared with the 22% of all friends, including wives and roommates, who are women. The tendency to name one's wife is responsible for this effect. When men who name their wives are excluded, only 6% of the best friends of married men are women. For single men, 17% of best friends and 16% of all friends, including cohabitants, are women. Thus, the women friends of single men are more likely to be confidantes but are not more likely to be named as best friends. Perhaps cultural norms prevent them from being named disproportionately. Alternatively, it may be that other characteristics of friendship, such as companionship or shared interests, are more important to single men than is the opportunity to confide personal problems. The tendency for married men to name their wives may be an acknowledgment of the special emotional support provided — or more cynically, it may simply reflect a cultural norm for doing so.

ANALYSIS

The analysis is divided into two parts: variables predictive of friendship with women and the consequences of friendship with women.

Who Has Women Friends?

Nonveterans have significantly more women friends than do Vietnam veterans or Vietnam Era veterans (adjusted chi square = 10.28, $p < .006$). Further analysis shows this difference is not due to differences in social class between the two groups. However, when men 24–30 years old are compared with men 31–35 years old, we find that the effect is significant only for younger men. Because the period when younger men were in the service is an important time for making friends, being away for 2 years in a largely male environment probably accounts for the difference. Had the younger veterans been at school or working at home, the difference would probably not exist. There are no differences between those veterans who went to Vietnam and those who did not, nor does exposure to combat affect the number of women friends. Therefore, for most analyses, veterans and nonveterans were pooled in order to add power to the analysis.

By far the most important factor in predicting who has women friends is the respondent's attitude towards women. Five attitudinal questions were included in the interview. The respondent was asked to indicate agreement or disagreement on a 4-point scale (higher numbers indicating disagreement) with the following statements:

1. A husband has no obligation to tell his wife of financial plans.
2. The initiative for dating should come from the man.
3. Women should assume their rightful place in business and the professions with men.
4. Women need and want protection.
5. Men should be given job preference.

Disagreement with all items but No.3 was taken to indicate a more liberal attitude. An index was formed by adding the responses to the five questions (No. 3 coded in reverse). Only respondents answering all five questions were included. Since the mean score is 13.498, scores of 5-13 are considered "traditional," while scores of 14-20 are considered "liberal."

The more liberal his attitude toward women, the more likely a man is to have women friends. Twenty-three percent ($n = 153$) of men with traditional attitudes have one or more women friends whereas 34% ($n = 223$) of men with liberal attitudes have one or more women friends (adjusted chi square = 16.29, $p < .0002$). This is true for both married and single men, regardless of veteran status.

In addition, attitude toward women has a subtle relationship to marital satisfaction. Respondents were asked to rate their marital satisfaction on a 7-point scale where (1) means completely satisfied and (7) means completely dissatisfied. Scores of (1) or (2) are taken to indicate marital satisfaction. For both traditional and liberal men, naming one's wife as a closest friend or helper is associated with marital satisfaction. Of men who name their wife as closest friend, 78% ($n = 492$) rate themselves as satisfied with their marriage, whereas only 68% ($n = 136$) of men who do not name their wife rate themselves as satisfied, (adjusted chi square = 7.99, $p < .005$). Of men who name their wives as helper, 82% ($n = 307$) rate themselves as satisfied compared to only 70% ($n = 369$) of men who do not name their wives, (adjusted chi square = 17.75, $p < .0001$). However, these effects are particularly marked among men with traditional attitudes towards women, as seen in Table 11.1. Apparently, more traditional men expect their wives to play the role of helpmate. If they are not able to turn to their spouses for support, they are more dissatisfied than liberal men, since their role expectations, as well as their emotional needs, are unmet.

Although liberal men are more likely to name their wives as closest friends or helpers, they are not more likely to be satisfied with their marriages. The lack of difference in marital satisfaction between traditional and liberal men, despite the difference in their tendency to name their wives, is due to the interaction noted above.

TABLE 11.1
Percentage Satisfied with Their Marriages

| | Attitude Toward Women | | | |
| | Traditional | | Liberal | |
	%	n	%	n
Wife Closest Friend	79	(244)	77	(239)
Wife not Closest Friend	66	(76)	70	(55)
Wife the Helper	86	(148)	79	(152)
Wife not the Helper	67	(187)	73	(171)

One might suppose that age would be a factor in whether men hold traditional or liberal attitudes toward women. To test this hypothesis, age was split into two groups: 24–30 and 31–35. Table 11.2 shows that when married respondents in each age group are compared, older men are found to be slightly less liberal than younger men. But when single men are compared, we find that older men tend to be more liberal than younger men. In fact, older single men tend to be more liberal in their attitude toward women than younger men, married or single. Apparently, for men in the older age group, not being married implies a certain rebelliousness or tendency to deviate from convention and tradition. Older single men also tend to have proportionately more women friends than younger single men (though fewer friends in total), as shown in Table 11.3. Whereas younger men seem to value companionship more highly, older men may be attracted to the potential for emotional intimacy offered by friendship with women.

Social class, measured as a linear combination of income, educational level, and occupational prestige, is related to the number of women friends in two ways, as shown in Table 11.4. First, 39% ($n = 213$) of lower class men hold liberal attitudes as opposed to 58% ($n = 461$) of higher class men, (adjusted chi square $= 46.14$, $p < .0001$). Second, there is evidence that the social environment can limit opportunities for friendship with women. After controlling for attitude towards women, 5% fewer lower class men have one

TABLE 11.2
Percentage with Liberal Attitudes

	Age Group				Row Total
	24–30		31–35		
	%	n	%	n	n
Marital Status					
Married	51	(158)	48	(272)	430
Single	49	(79)	64	(50)	129
Column Total		237		322	559

TABLE 11.3
Percentage with One or More Women Friends

	Age Group				Row Total
	24–30		31–35		
	%	n	%	n	n
Marital Status					
Married	24	(75)	24	(142)	217
Single	37	(61)	53	(42)	103
Column Total		136		184	320

or more women friends. This difference is not statistically significant, probably because of the small sample size.

Since men most often meet their women friends at work or at school, lower class men may have fewer women friends because they often work at male-dominated blue collar jobs and tend to have limited educations. This hypothesis is supported by the data. Among higher classes, 66% ($n = 173$) meet women most often at work or school, whereas only 52% ($n = 80$) of lower class men meet most of their women friends in this way, (adjusted chi square $= 6.83$, $p < .009$). Black and Hispanic respondents appear initially to have fewer women friends, but when race is controlled for class this difference disappears.

Table 11.5 shows that the size of the city in which the respondent lives is related to the number of women friends in a manner similar to class. Metropolitan residence engenders a more liberal attitude toward women, and may also provide structural incentives for friendship with women. After controlling for attitude toward women, we found that an additional 5% of men living in metropolitan areas have one or more women friends. (Again, the difference is not statistically significant, most likely because of the small sample size.)

The data in Table 11.5 suggest a manner in which city living might promote friendship with women. Fifty-four percent ($n = 505$) of respondents living in metropolitan areas are liberal in their attitude towards women, whereas only

TABLE 11.4
Percentage with One or More Women Friends

	Class				Row Total
	Lower		Higher		
	%	n	%	n	n
Attitudes					
Traditional	21	(69)	26	(84)	153
Liberal	30	(61)	35	(162)	223
Column Total		130		246	376

TABLE 11.5
Percentage with One or More Women Friends

	City Size				Row Total
	Metro		Non-Metro		
	%	n	%	n	n
Attitudes					
Traditional	25	(104)	21	(49)	153
Liberal	35	(175)	29	(48)	223
Column Total		279		97	376

42% ($n = 169$) of nonmetropolitan residents are liberal (adjusted chi square = 15.49, $p < .0002$). The tendency for metropolitan residents to hold more liberal attitudes is found in both lower and higher classes. However, residence in a metropolitan area increases the probability of one or more women friends for higher classes only.

One explanation for this is the class phenomenon noted earlier. However, it is only among higher class *married* men that metropolitan living increases the number of women friends, as suggested by Table 11.6. It may be that for married men the anonymity of city life facilitates friendship with women. The effect would not be found among lower class men since they generally reside in more closely knit neighborhoods, where the structural anonymity associated with city life does not exist.

The Effects of Friendship With Women

Two scales measuring the respondents' emotional well being are used to assess the effects of friendship with women. The first is a categorical measure Two scales measuring the respondents' emotional well being are used to assess the effects of friendship with women. The first is a categorical measure of chronic PTSD. The second is a demoralization scale, measured continuously, which is sensitive to chronic depression and other problems of day-to-day life. Descriptions of the stress scale and the demoralization scale may be found in Chapters 3 and 10 respectively.

The Effects of Stress on Friendships With Women

There is a nonsignificant tendency for stressed respondents to have more women friends. However, stressed men are significantly more likely to turn to men for help than are nonstressed respondents (chi square = 7.73, $p < .03$; see Table 11.7). These tendencies seem to hold for both married and single

TABLE 11.6
Percentage with One or More Women Friends

| | Class | | | | Row Total |
| | Lower | | Upper | | |
	%	n	%	n	n
Married					
Metro	18	(32)	30	(127)	159
Nonmetro	19	(25)	20	(33)	58
Single					
Metro	38	(34)	46	(44)	78
Nonmetro	38	(13)	50	(12)	25
Column Total		104		216	320

For upper class married men, adjusted chi square = 5.70, $p < .02$. All other comparisons between metropolitan and nonmetropolitan residents are nonsignificant.

TABLE 11.7
Posttraumatic Stress and Women Friends

	Percentage with One or More Women Friends*		Percentage of Helpers Who Are Women**	
	%	n	%	n
Stressed	32	(58)	49	(57)
Possibly Stressed	26	(94)	58	(137)
Not Stressed	25	(112)	64	(198)

*chi square = 3.17, p = ns.
**chi square = 7.73, p = .0210.

men, although the sample size is too small to permit proper analysis. This finding is consistent with that discussed earlier that combat veterans are not able or prefer not to discuss Vietnam with women. Kadushin (Chapter 9) reports that combat veterans suffering posttraumatic stress often turn to other combat veterans (who are male) for help. The sample is too small, however, to analyze separately the effect on stress reaction of those combat veterans who do turn to women for help.

We might then consider only those veterans who were not suffering acute posttraumatic stress when they returned from Vietnam. Perhaps having women friends would prevent these men from developing a delayed stress reaction. When men who reported an absence of stress during the period of their involvement with the military are considered separately, it at first appears that turning to women does help prevent a delayed stress reaction. However, it is only among married men, whose female helpers are generally their wives, that turning to women helps (see Chapter 10 of this volume for a discussion of the effects of spouse support on mental health). For single men who did not experience acute PTSD, 66% (n = 25) of those with a male helper remained unstressed whereas only 58% (n = 7) of those with a female helper remained unstressed (p = ns). Again, the sample size is very small, but the data do not support the notion that having women friends helps avoid delayed stress reactions in single men.

The Effects of Demoralization on Friendships With Women

A regression of demoralization on the proportion of friends who are women reveals a positive relationship (F = 5.13, $p < .03$). For both married and single men, demoralization is associated with more women friends. Since people with everyday emotional problems (as opposed to PTSD) may tend to discuss themselves and their lives more than people without such problems, demoralized men may attract those willing to listen and sympathize. That is, they attract women.

It at first appears that for married men naming a woman as helper is associated with less demoralization. However, we must recall that most married men turn to their wives for help, and naming someone other than one's wife can indicate a lack of marital satisfaction. Men who do not rate themselves as satisfied with their marriage tend to be more demoralized than those who do ($t = 7.33$ - separate variance estimate, $p < .001$). When only men who are satisfied with their marriage are considered, there is no difference in demoralization between those who name women and those who name men. It may be that marital satisfaction has such a powerful effect on demoralization that all other influences are superfluous. Or perhaps the same characteristics in a woman that contribute to marital satisfaction also prevent demoralization, thus making it impossible to examine the two separately.

For single men, naming a male helper is not symptomatic of a major life problem; thus the efficacy of male and female helpers can be compared. The evidence is that single men with female helpers are just as likely to be demoralized as those with male helpers — no more, no less. This is a curious nonresult, since a woman is more likely than a man to act as a confidante. If women are not superior helpers, why do men turn disproportionately to them for social support? It may be that male helpers are just as effective as female helpers and the disproportionate tendency to turn to women is due to a social norm for doing so.

Another possibility is that men are more receptive to help when it is offered by their wives. Married men are less likely to be demoralized than single men, ($t = 4.28$ - pooled variance estimate, $p < .001$). They are also, as previously noted, far more likely to turn to women for help. It is to be expected that the relationship between married men and their female helpers (their wives) is more intimate than that between single men and their female helpers. Since previous research has shown that women actually experience more physical and emotional problems when married (see Belle, 1982), we may assume that it is intimacy with women and not marriage itself that accounts for the difference. Assuming that single men do not simply like women less, it may be that men allow themselves to be vulnerable (and thus to be helped) only when the women friends are their wives. The potential for women friends to be of help is not utilized by single men.

SUMMARY

Among men of the Vietnam generation, several features of the person and the environment affect the number of women friends. Younger veterans have fewer women friends than nonveterans, but whether or not a veteran saw combat does not influence the number of women friends he has today. Men with liberal attitudes are more likely to have women friends. There is no difference in this regard among combat veterans, veterans who did not see combat, and nonveterans. Liberal attitudes are associated with metropolitan residence and higher social class, but both of these seem to be associated with having more women friends, even when attitude toward women is controlled for. Race does not affect the number of women friends a respondent has when class is controlled.

Married men have proportionately fewer female friends than single men. The women friends of married men are more likely to be met through relatives and friends than those of single men. Higher class married men living in metropolitan areas have more women friends than those in nonmetropolitan areas, and more than lower class men in either metropolitan or nonmetropolitan areas. Possibly this is due to the anonymity of city life for men in higher classes.

Friendship with women is qualitatively different from friendship with men. Women friends are more likely to serve as confidantes for both married and single men. A married man who names a woman as the person he turns to for help is almost always referring to his wife. Similarly, since the wife is often named as a best friend, women are overrepresented as best friends among married men. For single men, women are not overrepresented as best friends, even though they are disproportionately named as helpers. Possibly single men consider characteristics of friendship other than emotional intimacy (such as comfortable companionship) when they name their three closest friends.

There is no evidence that friendship with women is especially helpful in coping with demoralization or in preventing the incidence of chronic PTSD, except within the framework of a supportive marriage. Since previous research has shown that marriage is a cause rather than an alleviator of stress for women, the emotional benefits of marriage for men are probably due to intimacy with women rather than marriage per se.

Men who were exposed to combat in Vietnam, particularly those suffering from PTSD, are more likely to confide in other men rather than women. This finding is consistent with previous research. Since combat is an experience that almost no American woman has had, veterans may find more comfort and understanding in discussions with other men. One might hypothesize that if the men were suffering PTSD for reasons other than combat (e.g. assault or natural disaster), this pattern would not be found.

Very little research has been done on patterns of cross-gender friendship. This study, which views the topic from only the male perspective, leaves many questions unanswered. For example, we do not know whether women are as likely as men to turn to their spouse for help. It may be that women also prefer to turn to women. Nor do we know whether a woman would be as likely as a man to name her spouse as one of her three closest friends. If she did not name her husband, would she also tend to be less satisfied with her marriage? It is possible that women expect to give more emotional support than they receive and thus would not be less satisfied.

This study provides further evidence that women are more likely than men to be the providers of social support. It does not, however, tell us why this is so. It is possible that confiding in women is merely a social convention. But since conventions arise for a reason, it may also be that women are more emotionally supportive than men. If this is so, we must then explain why only married men seem to benefit from female supportiveness, and then only when it is provided by their wives. It is possible that men are unwilling to take the emotional risks necessary in order to be helped outside the safety of marriage. Future research might examine the conditions, presumably existing within marriage, under which a supportive friend is allowed to be of help. Such research into the dynamics of truly "helpful" relationships could have implications for the helping professions as well as for would-be friends. The self-help groups formed by Vietnam combat veterans are effective because they take advantage of the natural rapport among veterans.

Appendix A

THE COMMON DATA BASE

The data on which all the findings in this book are based were collected in the following way.

From December 1976 through June 1977, 380 cases were drawn from Brooklyn, Southern Westchester County, and the Bridgeport, Connecticut, metropolitan area. Men eligible to be drafted for the war in Vietnam were the target group, which meant, effectively, that men born in the years 1940–1953 were to be selected for the sample. Equal numbers of men 28 years and younger, and 29 and older were targeted, and the sample was split between veterans and nonveterans, half the latter having served in Southeast Asia. An almost equal number of blacks were also targeted. The sample was located through the use of "reverse" telephone directories. Census tracts in which there was a high proportion of blacks were selected for the black subsample. In Westchester County and Bridgeport, a sufficient number of eligible blacks could not be located in this way and an informal multiplicity sampling was invoked to find additional black respondents. After telephone screening, appointments were arranged with respondents for a personal interview, which lasted up to six hours. The telephone screening interviews also provided us with the normative distribution of the types of persons selected for the sample. In this way, we could introduce appropriate weights when the analysis called for them.

An additional 1,001 persons were sampled between December 1978 and October 1979. This second wave of data collection took place in seven sites across the United States. In the South: Atlanta, urban Columbus (Georgia) and a rural area surrounding Columbus were sampled. In the Midwest; Chicago, South Bend, Indiana, and the rural area surrounding South Bend were sampled. Los Angeles County was selected as representative of the West Coast, containing both metropolitan and suburban areas and a mixture of white and blue collar respondents. In this second wave of data collection, 55% of the sample were to be veterans, half of whom were to be Vietnam theater veterans; there were to be 25% blacks within each site (except in South Bend, where there simply were not enough blacks); and 25% Mexican American in Los Angeles County. The age distribution was split so as to match the first sample.

The strategy was to develop a sample in which the readjustment problems of veterans could be examined not only on a national level but also contextually. For example, this strategy offered an opportunity to consider whether veterans in large urban settings might experience different adjustment problems from those of veterans in smaller metropolitan or rural areas. This strategy proved extremely important in the analysis since the effects of social support systems, and to some extent medical help, were dependent on local context. As it turned out, weighting used to produce population estimates for each location sampled also yielded overall estimates of veteran and nonveteran characteristics that were very close to those provided by national probability samples (Boulanger, 1981a, 1981b), thus supporting the mix of the different types of contexts in the original design.

The entire design depended on developing an effective screening method to locate the types of persons described in the sample. The screening also had to yield weights for each of the strata so that population estimates could be achieved. Whereas the first wave data collection procedures in 1976–1977 in the Northeast had used reverse telephone directories and geographic strata derived from these directories to increase the efficiency of locating minority respondents, the second wave of sampling, in 1978–1979, used random digit dialing, with augmentation of residential and minority strings. In addition, the informal multiplicity sampling used in the first wave for some cells was formalized and developed to obtain unbiased population estimates (for details see Rothbart, Fine, & Sudman, 1979). This method was used for about 50% of the Vietnam veterans in the second series of data collection and provided considerable savings in costs; it also allowed us to locate veterans who had no permanent residence.

It is important to stress that all interviews in both sets of data collection were face-to-face, in-person interviews with respondents obtained through telephone screening. In some cases, interviews were arranged in the research project's local offices; in other cases, interviews were in the respondents' homes. The second data collection interviews were slightly shorter than the first; generally between 2 and 4 hours. Portions of the interview dealing with the answers to open-ended questions were taped and transcribed.

The quality of a survey is primarily dependent on low refusal rates. In order to obtain their cooperation with such a long interview, respondents were paid $25. In the first survey, the refusal rate, weighted to reflect the true proportion of the various strata in the population, was 25%. This included refusals of close to 50% in some minority district strata but much lower rates in other strata.

The second wave of data collection considerably improved upon the first. Refusals in telephone screening can occur anywhere in the chain that locates the eventual respondent. A member of the household called can refuse the call, the selected respondent can refuse to be interviewed, or the called number may never be answered. In some cases, the number can be validated by the telephone company as not assigned or nonworking, but in other cases the number must be listed as a nonresponse. Our estimate of the number of telephones that were never answered is about 10%. On answered calls refusal rates averaged 7.8%, varying somewhat by interviewing site. Once a respondent was located, the refusal rate averaged 15%. None of these figures includes the Mexican American population, because special efforts had to be made to secure them. Consequently, we cannot with confidence generalize to the Mexican American population of Los Angeles. On the whole, we are satisfied that within the context of the long interview and the difficult screening, the sampling was about as good as could be managed, with the exception, as noted, of the Mexican American sample in Los Angeles. For some purposes, the Mexican American sample is omitted from the analyses.

All the analyses in the book that utilize the concept the Posttraumatic Stress Disorder (PTSD) are confined to data collected in the second wave of data collection.

Appendix B

THE COMBAT INDEX

The Combat Index used in this analysis is based on a series of questions about individual acts that the respondent might have engaged in or been engaged in by the enemy. Specifically, each Vietnam veteran respondent was asked whether he:

> was part of a land or naval artillery unit that fired on the enemy.
> flew in aircraft over South or North Vietnam.
> was stationed at a forward observation post.
> received incoming fire from enemy artillery, rockets, or mortars.
> was on unit patrols that encountered mines and booby traps.
> was on a unit that received sniper or sapper fire.
> was on unit patrol that was ambushed.
> was in a unit patrol that engaged the Vietcong (or guerilla troops) in a firefight.
> was in a unit patrol that engaged the NVA (organized military forces) in a firefight.
> saw Americans killed or injured.
> saw Vietnamese killed or injured.
> killed anyone or thought he killed someone.

Respondents who had taken part in any of these activities were asked whether they had these experiences rarely, sometimes, often or very often. These four "frequency counts" were given values from one (rarely) to four (very often), and each of the original responses was multiplied by the frequency. There are two exceptions to this, artillery and forward observation, which were both halved in value.* The alpha reliability of the Combat Index was .95.

For most analytic purposes the scale is divided into the following three unequal parts:

0–2.99	No Combat	19% of respondents
3–16.99	Low Combat	40% of respondents
17.00 and above	Heavy Combat	40% of respondents

To qualify for a score of 17, the threshold for heavy combat, at the very least the combatants must have engaged in each of the activities sometimes, five of them often, or four of them very often.

---

*These two items were downvalued because in the factor analysis of the combat items, all other items loaded at .55 or above on a single factor. These two items had low factor loadings of .16 and .19.

Afterword —
Who Can Take Away the Grief
Of A Wound?

Chaim Shatan

In Henry IV Part I, during the battle of Shrewsbury, Shakespeare's Falstaff—in his renowned speech on honor—asks whether honor can "take away the grief of a wound?" For many Vietnam veterans, the grief of their wounds and the wounds of their grief appear to be continuing sources of stress. In the same way, the veterans themselves have been a cause of ongoing concern, embarrassment, neglect, and distrust to all sectors of the United States. This ambivalent attitude has generated many myths — fictions — and has stimulated much serious research and produced important data — facts. The authors' confrontation of these myths and realities is timely in view of not only the existing problems of Vietnam veterans, but also current diagnostic research and treatment developments. Their closely reasoned and well-documented study is far more than a critical or in-depth review. Clinicians and researchers will be happy to have their earlier leaps of intuition confirmed by such careful investigation and analysis. In the future, it will be harder to explain away earlier claims about the deleterious effects of war on behavior as mere hunches that are difficult to establish.

The long-term effects of war, especially the Vietnam war, on participants are critically important to document. Since it would be easy to polemicize these questions, the authors' data-intensive treatment is a landmark. It will be much less easy for such crucial ideas about men at war, and the psychological aftereffects of combat, to disappear once again from the body of knowledge. Fortunately, the authors go into detail about their sample, how it was selected, how data was gathered, and how morbidity was assessed.

This book suggests a number of reasons for the existing and continuing concern about Vietnam veterans. In addition, these veterans have finally come out of the woodwork in the wake of the antiwar movement of the 60s. This has led significant numbers of the population finally to grasp the fact that war in general, the military in general, and guerrilla warfare in particular are "bad for your health."

Certain aspects of the Vietnam combat experience have a fundamental bearing on the authors' findings. During the late 60s and early 70s, the particular nature of Vietnam jungle warfare was brought home to the American public nightly on television along with their supper. There are aspects of combat that nearly always evoke psychological reactions among the survivors. (I refer to guerrilla war veterans as combat survivors rather than veterans, since they survived in relatively small enclaves surrounded by a hostile sea of the general population.) Many combat survivors have made the sensory experience of combat palpable to me. They have told me what it is like to live in the split time zone of an ambush that lasts only 15 seconds. Darkness, silence, isolation are instantly annihilated in the spasms of fear and foreboding. Flashes of light and explosions accompany floods of light and startling sensations. You are sweating while shivering and cold to the bone. Heavy, pulsating strokes are banging out a deafening rhythm. It is the beating of our own heart against your chest. Time is compacted and will not move on. There is no past and no future. Each second is a separate parcel of time. At that moment the whole world feels as though it "slides through a membrane." Reality is torn asunder leaving no boundaries and no guideposts. Death comes from everywhere and nowhere. Death is the reality now. You yourself feel unreal. To feel real again, you must embrace the ever-presentness of death by wrapping it in yourself and poisoning your sense of self with a reservoir of evil and destructiveness. Only that way can inner and outer reality feel at one again. Otherwise, your perception is maladapted to reality. Reality becomes a vast web of suffering in which you are enmeshed. . . . This total experience of a catastrophic, manmade environment is the reality of the combat "stress."

Specific features of guerrilla warfare nearly always evoke reactions among the combat survivors. The loss of one's entire symbiotic unit — a loss that may occur more than once — is a devastating stress. Audie Murphy, the most decorated American hero of World War II, and his cook were the sole survivors of his unit in Southern France. The rest were casualties, killed, wounded, or captured. Murphy had severe posttraumatic stress disorder, a fact never publicized. It was known from his nightmares, from the fact that he always slept with a German Mauser under his pillow, and from the risky undertaking that eventually led to his death in his early 40s. Similarly, I knew a Korean war veteran who was the sole survivor of the destruction of his unit three times over in the retreat from the Korean DMZ to Pusan. Twenty-two years after the Korean war, this man said, "You never get over your experiences. You just learn to live with them." Is it more than coincidental that his occupation as a civilian was that of an exterminator? No, it is not coincidental if we recall that by 1970 40% of all deaths among World War II veterans were violent and over 50% of the deaths of the younger Korean war group were violent — from suicide, homicide, or one-car automobile accidents.

The long-term effect of the loss of one's unit was already noted in World War II. Another devastating aspect of combat, recognized in World War II and reiterated in Vietnam, was the impact of the loss of the unit leader — especially the loss of a respected leader, a worshipped leader. Most traumatic was the repeated loss of unit leaders.

Certain combat assignments are well known threats and hazards to the psychological well-being of the warrior. These include the assignment of "medic" or corpsman. Among medics, the "first casualty" was anticipated with extreme anxiety. It was common practice in Vietnam to end the medic's tour of duty after less than the customary 12-month rotation. The intense stress of dealing with casualties wore down the ability to be a medic after as few as 7 months. Long-term phobic reactions to blood, food, medications, and bandages are not uncommon. I have interviewed people with such reactions. Another particularly stressful assignment was burial detail and graves registration, a euphemism for identifying bodies or parts of bodies and making arrangements to "ship" them to the next of kin.

Besides the military occupational status or assignment, the degree and nature of combat were also crucial. In riverine warfare along the streams, brooks, and rivers of Vietnam, small groups of men on tiny gunboats penetrated deeply into territory where there was no support. The likelihood of being ambushed was greater than in most other combat. The dangers and responsibilities of "walking point" for a platoon or a squad weigh heavily on many men to this day, especially if a "wrong" decision on their part resulted in deaths and injuries. Similarly, the job of assigning privates to dangerous roles continues to burden many sergeants and other noncoms who made such decisions.

Controversy has surrounded the issue of predisposition and combat stress. Disagreement stems from the failure to recognize that overwhelming traumatic stress creates its own predisposition — that gross stress reactions are fertile ground for future emotional disturbances which have a discrete clinical picture and typical course. This book goes a long way to settling the controversy by demonstrating that combat is the crucial variable creating predisposition to stress disorders. The authors provide a quantitative analysis of the frequency and nature of these postcombat symptoms and syndromes. Their work supports the pioneering observations of Archibald et al. (1965) with World War II veterans and Niederland (1972) with concentration camp survivors. Years ago, these writers suggested that a preexisting disorder was largely irrelevant in postcombat stress disorder. Not the warmth of the reception the men received on their return home, but the amount and type of combat to which they were exposed; not the stability of their family background, but the intensity of the combat appears again and again to be the most fundamental issue in assessing predisposition.

During the Second World War, Grinker and Spiegel came to the McGill University Medical School to lecture about their pivotal book *Men Under Stress* (1945). I was a medical student there at that time and was impressed by their repeated emphasis that "every man is a law unto himself. Every man has his own breaking point." While noting that every stressed person manifests a different degree of disorder, a different "incubation period" or time of onset, a different duration of distress, or for that matter of any apparent disorder at all, they underscored the fact that symptoms following supreme stress appear in persons with varying predispositions. In other words, the specific stress of privation is the crucial variable predisposing to and predictive of morbidity. The syndromes are essentially independent of a person's prior psychiatric history. When the stressor is strong enough, one is at risk no matter how stable a family one has come from. The authors make this point tellingly.

Compared with other conflicts, the war in Vietnam did have some aspects that were unique. First was the role of military psychiatrists, a group of professionals who came to be held in very low esteem by the "grunts." After all, their function was to help maintain the fighting strength of the military forces rather than to treat individual men in distress. Accordingly, during the Vietnam war their role was that of psychiatric military officer rather than mental health professional. They reported consistently lower rates of psychiatric symptoms than has since proven to be the case. Vincent Wallen, an air force psychologist in Tokyo during the Vietnam war, described this "lulled combat psychiatry" in *Psychiatric News* (official organ of the American Psychiatric Association). He found that many warriors invalided from Vietnam to Japan with diagnoses of suspected ulcers, arthritis, and the like were actually suffering from gross stress reactions. The erroneous reports generated by the medical corps created false impressions, which in turn affected the attitudes of the mental health professions in the United States. This biased some of the earlier research into postwar adjustment.

Another factor specific to Vietnam is the possible collapse of the United States Armed Forces in the field. The absence of group cohesion and the short rotations were not the only elements involved in this collapse. Fraggings were surely an important measure of collapse, as mentioned by the authors. There is also a question that is difficult to investigate concerning the existence of private armies in Vietnam along the lines of the army depicted in the film *Apocalypse Now* and led by Kurtz. Recently, a V.A. psychologist called to tell me a leader of one such private army had been admitted to his hospital and had provided extensive evidence for the existence of these groups. Calling them "armies" may be an exaggeration—the largest group was said to number 100 to 200 and the other three about 50 each. Purportedly, they consisted of Americans, South Vietnamese, Montagnards, and

Vietnamese civilians who took to the highlands in an attempt to protect themselves against all comers. Of course, this may be a myth — but one that, like the other myths and fictions explored in this volume, merits investigation.

Last, but not least, there is considerable journalistic documentation about the opposition of enlisted men to their leaders in Vietnam. What was it about the situation in Vietnam that engendered this insubordination? Many enlisted men discovered as soon as they arrived in Vietnam that the myth and the reality of the American mission in that country were far apart. As one man said, "When I saw all the kids missing arms and legs in Saigon, I knew I shouldn't be there." Men were quick to recognize that in this most industrialized of all modern wars, the level of violence was completely out of proportion to the stated objectives. Peace symbols worn by troops in the field reflected the existence of the largest antiwar movement known among American troops in any American war. The Vietnam Veterans Against the War, a movement formed at that time, was highly effective and of lasting significance. A similar protest had occurred during a similar jungle war, the Filipino war. In 1899, the Minnesota Volunteers were horrified at the mass destruction and massacre that were part of army policy in putting down the Filipino "insurrection." By applying pressure through their congressmen, senators, and newspapers, they were able to mandate the official return of 2,000 of these volunteers to their home state.

One more myth, of primary group cohesion, is dealt a blow by the research in this volume. The blow is long overdue. The "symbiotic combat unit" of World War II and the buddy system of Korea (especially fostered by the Marine Corps) were significantly weakened in Vietnam. One element that contributed to the weakening of ties between troops in Vietnam was the 12-month rotation and DEROS (Date of Estimated Return From Overseas). This led to the practice of sending out and bringing back troops one at a time rather than in units. An example of the weakened ties within groups and between individuals was the "FNG" syndrome: individual men newly arrived in units were made to feel unwelcome.

Although many men developed strong ties in Vietnam, they were also aware that the closer they might become, the more likely they would be to experience severe emotional disturbances after combat, especially heavy combat. This is the syndrome we refer to today as PTSD. I have written and spoken about the fact that we are more affected by the loss of someone to whom we are closely attached. In Vietnam, the military tried to train troops to deny both grief and intimacy in the hope that denial of death would increase combat effectiveness and survival. In fact, the trainers succeeded to a limited extent in training troops in "anti-grief" (E. James Lieberman). Both anti-grief and anti-intimacy were expressed by calling men who cried, or showed other signs of mourning, "girls," "women," "ladies," or "hogs." Men who showed intimacy to each other were often called "fags," a term also applied to Vietnamese men by Americans. Americans were warding off their perception of the ease with which physical intimacy was expressed by Vietnamese men to each other. Anti-grief and anti-intimacy were also fostered in the midst of combat during services conducted for beloved comrades or sergeants. In order to stifle the grief and mourning, officers transformed memorials into calls for rituals of vengeance, calls to convert the impacted grief into ceremonial revenge. I have referred to this as "militarized mourning." The My Lai massacre was preceded by such a memorial vengeance call on the part of Lt. Calley's commanding officer, Capt. Medina.

The editors' introduction discusses the fiscal and political implications of recognizing that war is "bad for you." I am still struck by a mystery: the period from 1968 to 1980, which included the height of the Vietnam war, was the time when psychiatric diagnosis and treatment in the United States were governed by DSM II. DSM II had nothing to say about Traumatic Stress Disorders. DSM I (1950 to 1968) stood in sharp contrast. Much influenced by psychiatrists who had served during and after the Second World War, it emphasized the role of Gross Stress Disorders in the aftermath of combat. It has been suggested that the belated recognition of PTSD saved the government hundreds of millions of dollars. To this day, I have not yet found anyone to take responsibility for the disappearance of stress disorders from DSM II. The Vietnam Veterans Working Group, which I co-founded in 1975, collaborated extensively with the DSM III task force. However, we had nothing to do with the invention of the term "Posttraumatic Stress Disorder," a term I find unfortunate. I would have preferred Postcombat Stress Disorder or, if we include survivors of other disasters, Postcatastrophic Stress Disorders. The words trauma, stress, and stressors are bloodless compared with disaster and catastrophe. While they satisfy nosologists, they also create confusion. The term "psychic trauma" was originally devised by Freud and his followers to describe "ordinary" psychic wounds, such as the loss of a parent or a sibling, abandonment, the failure of a relationship, or the loss of one's station in life, not massive communal disaster.

In Chapters 3 and 4, the authors find that a significant number of men who did not serve in Vietnam also suffer from posttraumatic stress disorder. They report that basic training did not seem to result in long-term stress reactions. However, both anecdotally and clinically, it has been my impression that the degree and intensity of basic training can be a significant stress for some men. When we presented our basic PTSD formulation to the American Psychiatric Association annual meeting in Toronto in 1977, this was brought to our attention repeatedly. As far as nonveterans and nonsurvivors with PTSD are concerned, we must look for both direct and indirect victims of manmade disaster. I emphasize manmade disaster because there is evidence from such natural disasters as the 1975 Darwin (Australia) tidal wave to show that recovery essentially occurs within a year. By contrast, we know that that there was an important manmade component in the Buffalo Creek flood, just as there was in the Three Mile Island disaster. There was advance warning that the Buffalo Creek dams would collapse, but the coal mine companies did little or nothing. This failure, known to the victims, was an important element in the manmade underpinning of the delayed and chronic postcatastrophic disorder.

I have seen a significant number of adults who, as very young children, were victims of extraordinarily severe child abuse. I have also seen others who, in childhood, suffered from multiple traumatic events in the immediate family: several deaths, operations, and accidents occurring close together in time. They did not come for treatment when they were children, although some of them were symptomatic. However, their symptoms did not fall in the adult PTSD category. As usual, in the evaluation of childhood disorders, we need to be aware of the differences between child and adult symptomatology. A hyperalert adult nonveteran patient with PTSD had a significant learning disability and attention deficit as well as school refusal after his massive preschool traumata. His incipient PTSD went unrecognized.

This volume helps to slay the myth that massive psychic trauma does not have enduring psychological consequences. It is my conviction that in manmade catastrophe in particular, the stressor or stressors themselves create the predisposition for later disordered stress responses. The person burdened with this particular psychic wound is in a constant state of subclinical hyperarousal. Traumatic triggering factors tend to arouse this latent hyperalertness. Such factors act as autonomous fragments that carry the total emotional charge, or "cathexis," of the original stressful situation. Postcombat stressors are residues symbolizing or representing socially sanctioned collective human destructiveness, whether overt or covert. Vulnerability to such stress is heightened by the regression that accompanies combat training, combat itself, and incarceration, a regression that may continue long after the stressful event.

The authors' breakdown of PTSD signs and symptoms into seven categories is clearly useful for research. It should prove helpful for clinicians confronted by a welter of symptomatology that is not always best conceptualized by the current DSM III. I am impressed by the authors' differentiation between acute and chronic symptomatology, although DSM IIIR plans to eliminate this distinction. As for latency or delay, it is more appropriate to regard this issue as one of subclinical symptomatology. Frequently, patients do not report moderate symptoms, or those whom they consult are not aware of the relationship of symptoms to etiology. In my writing, I describe the restructuring of the personality into a "combat personality," which remains prone to violence given the right conditions. I also discuss the dissonance between the perceptual worlds of precombat, combat, and postcombat reality.

This book demonstrates clearly that combat, particularly in the presence of PTSD, is the single most important factor predisposing veterans to violence even 16 years after combat. This makes them more likely to be arrested — something that was demonstrated in the late 70s by the Massachusetts State Commissioner of Corrections. He found a significantly higher percentage of Vietnam veterans than all other veterans in the total Massachusetts prison population. However, I am not sure that postcombat violent behavior (PCVB) is a result of startle reactions or situations that evoke unwanted combat memories. The authors have shown that PTSD and PCVB are associated. The questions remains, What is the nature of that association? For example, is counterguerrilla warfare more predisposing to PTSD and therefore to PCVB? What of the combat veteran's inability to consummate grief for those close comrades whom he lost in warfare? What of the possibility that startle reactions may trigger vengeance and that combat memories may impel one to seek combat? This last point raises the issue of addiction to combat, which is beyond the scope of this book. Important new research by Van Der Kolk seems to confirm my impression that, as one Vietnam veteran said, "When some veterans are wounded they retreat, others cut themselves, and still other veterans cut other people."

Not many years ago, the assertion that combat was grossly stressing, and could lead to dynamic signs, symptoms, and syndromes years after the event, was hotly denied — probably for reasons of policy. The quantitative descriptions in this volume not only reinforce the recognition of what was once denied but also lead to new theoretical insights and clarifications. As veterans and survivors age and their endurance and adaptability wane, such clinical data and statistics may accumulate again — unless their current problems receive the attention they warrant.

For those who would pursue the path opened by Boulanger and Kadushin, the next assignment has at least two parts. One is to investigate whether survivors of combat and other manmade catastrophes experience more adverse psychological reactions that do survivors of natural disasters. Stress disorders in the wake of manmade disaster appear to follow a different clinical course from those that follow natural disasters of "acts of god." Once clinical patterns form, they are remarkably persistent long after the immediately precipitating events have ended. Many are disturbed by the idea that manmade disaster, which ruptures the fabric of human trust, has an impact more severe and more enduring than random natural disaster or "acts of god." With the methods employed by Boulanger, Kadushin, and the other contributors to this volume, we can gather data that allow us to apply not only our knowledge but our compassion to this issue.

The second part of the assignment is the study of the core aspect of what I call the "basic wound" of catastrophic stress. I believe that this basic wound is the new, permanent adaptive lifestyle that grows out of catastrophe. These are syndromes of disordered adaptability. The total climate of a death camp, the total impact of combat, predisposes to fundamental changes in styles of thinking, feeling, and action. The survivors of socially sanctioned collective human destructiveness develop new, inflexible styles of reacting. When they reintegrate, it is often at a regressed—hence more vulnerable—level of adaptation. This new adaptive lifestyle affects many members of entire social groups. It makes symptoms and syndromes possible. It is the background for frightening incursions of the past into the present, whether in the form of fears, anxieties, numbing and denial, startle reactions, or flashbacks. In a nutshell, the manmade disaster that is combat and the new adaptive lifestyle that follows combat create the substrate upon which are displayed the personality changes that we call symptoms and signs of posttraumatic stress disorder—symptoms, syndromes, and vulnerabilities superbly documented by the authors of this volume.

SELECTED PUBLICATIONS
OF CHAIM SHATAN

The grief of soldiers: Vietnam combat veterans' self-help movement. Special Report. *American Journal of Orthopsychiatry, 43*.

Through the membrane of reality: Impacted grief and perceptual dissonance in Vietnam combat veterans. (1974). *Psychiatric Opinion, 4*.

Entrails of power: Bogus manhood and the language of grief. (1977). In Hiller & Sheets (Eds.), *Women and Men: The Consequences of Power*. Cincinnati, OH: University of Cincinnati Press.

Bogus manhood, bogus honor: Surrender and transfiguration in the U.S. Marine Corps. (1977). *Psychoanalytic Review, 4*. Also in Goldman and Milman (Eds.) *Psychoanalytic Perspectives on Aggression*. Dubuque, IA: Hall, 1978. Also in *Sociological Abstracts*, (1981).

The emotional context of combat continues. (1978). In C. R. Figley (Eds.), *Stress Disorders Among Vietnam Veterans*. New York: Brunner/Mazel.

Militarized mourning and ceremonial vengeance. (1982). (German translation published as "Militarisierte Trauer und Rachezermoniell." In Passet & Modena (Eds.), *Krieg und Frieden aus psychoanalytischer Sicht (War and Peace from a Psychoanalytic Viewpoint*. Basel: Stromfeld. (Presented at International Psychoanalytic Conference on War and Peace, Zurich, 1983.

Have you hugged a Vietnam Veteran today? The basic wound of catastrophic stress. (1985). In W. E. Kelly, (Ed.), *Posttraumatic Stress Disorder and the War Veteran Patient*. New York: Brunner/Mazel.

References

Allerton, W. S. (1969). Army psychiatry in Vietnam. In P. G. Bourne (Ed.), *The psychology and physiology of stress*. New York: Academic Press.

American Psychiatric Association (1954). *Diagnostic and statistical manual of mental disorders (1st Edition)*. Washington, DC.

American Psychiatric Association (1968). *Diagnostic and statistical manual of mental disorders (2nd Edition)*. Washington, DC.

American Psychiatric Association (1980). *Diagnostic and statistical manual of mental disorders (3rd Edition)*. Washington, DC.

Archibald, H. C., Long, D. M., Miller, C., & Tuddenham, R. D. (1962). Gross stress reaction in combat—a 15 year follow-up. *American Journal of Psychiatry, 119,* 317-322.

Archibald, H. C., & Tuddenham, R. D. (1965). Persistent stress reaction after combat: A twenty year follow-up. *Archives of General Psychiatry, 12,* 475-481.

Atkinson, R. M., Sparr, L. F., Sheff, A. G., White, R., & Fitzsimmons, J. T. (1984). Diagnosis of posttraumatic stress disorder in Vietnam veterans. *American Journal of Psychiatry, 141*(5) 694-696.

Bachman, J. G., & Jennings, M. K. (1975). The impact of Vietnam on trust in government. *Journal of Social Issues, 31,* 141-155.

Badillo, G., & Currey, D. G. (1976). The social incidence of Vietnam casualties: Social class or race?. *Armed Forces and Society, 2,* 397-406.

Baraga, E., Van Kampen, M., & Watson, G. (1983). *Defining PTSD. Are the DSMIII criteria necessary and sufficient?* Unpublished manuscript.

Barber, B. (1983). The meaning of trust. In B. Barber (Ed.), *The logic and limits of trust*. New Brunswick, NJ: Rutgers University Press.

Barnes, J. A. (1969). Networks and political process. In J. C. Mitchell (Ed.), *Social networks in urban situations* (pp. 51-76). Manchester, England: University of Manchester Press.

Baskir, L. M., & Strauss, W. A. (1977). *Reconciliation after Vietnam. A program of relief for Vietnam era draft and military offenders*. Notre Dame, IN: University of Notre Dame Press.

Baskir, L. M., & Strauss, W. A. (1978). *Change and circumstance the draft, the war and the Vietnam generation*. New York: Random House.

Belle, D. (1982). The stress of caring: Women as providers of social support. In L. Goldberger & S. Breznitz (Eds.), *Handbook of stress* (pp. 496-505). New York: Free Press.

Bentel, D. J., & Smith, E. F. (1971). Drug abuse in combat: The crisis of drugs and addiction among American troops in Vietnam. *Journal of Psychedelic Drugs, 4,* 22–30.

Berkman, L. F., & Syme, L. S. (1979). Social network, host resistance, and mortality: A nine-year follow-up study of Alameda County residents. *American Journal of Epidemiology, 109,* 186–204.

Blank, A. S. (1982). Apocalypse terminable and interminable - operation outreach for Vietnam vets. *Hospital Community, 33,* 913–918

Blake, J. A. (1978). Death by hand grenade: Altruistic suicide. *Suicide and Life Threatening Behavior, 8,* 40–59.

Bock, R. D. (1975). *Multivariate statistical methods in behavioral research.* New York: McGraw-Hill.

Bock, R. D., & Yates, G. (1977). *Multiqual: Log-linear analysis of nominal or ordinal qualitative data by the method of maximum likelihood.* Chicago: International Education Service.

Boissevain, J. (1974). *Friends of friends: Networks, manipulators and coalitions.* New York: St. Martin's Press.

Booth, A., & Hess, E. (1974). Cross-sex friendship. *Journal of Marriage and the Family, 36,* (1), 38–47.

Borus, J. R. (1973). Adjustment issues facing the Vietnam returnee. *Archives of General Psychiatry, 28,* 501–506.

Borus, J. R. (1974). Incidence of maladjustment in Vietnam returnees. *Archives of General Psychiatry, 30,* 554–557.

Boulanger, G. (1981). *Conditions affecting the appearance and maintenance of traumatic stress reactions among Vietnam veterans.* Unpublished doctoral dissertation, Columbia University.

Boulanger, G. (1985). Post-traumatic stress disorder: An old problem with a new name. In S. M. Sonnenberg, A. S. Blank Jr. & J. Talbot (Eds.), *The trauma of war: Stress and recovery in Vietnam veterans problems of Vietnam veterans.* Washington, DC: American Psychiatric Press.

Boulanger, G. (in preparation). *PTSD: Recent research into the psychological aftermath of wars and other disasters.*

Brady, D., & Rappoport, L. (1973). Violence and Vietnam: A comparison between attitudes of civilians and veterans. *Human Relations, 26,* 735–752.

Brille, N. Q., & Beebe, G. W. (1955). *A follow-up study of war neuroses (Veterans Administration Medical Monograph).* Washington DC: US Government Printing Office.

Brown, C. W., & Moskos, C. C. (1976). The American volunteer soldier: Will he fight? *Military Review, 56,* 8–17.

Brown, G. W., Bhrolochain, M. N., & Harris, T. (1975). Social class and psychiatric disturbance among women in an urban population. *Sociology, 9,* 225–251.

Brown, G. W., & Harris, T. (1978). *Social origins of depression.* New York: Free Press.

Buchbinder, J., & Shrauger, J. (1979). *An empirical investigation of the hypothesized post Vietnam syndrome.* Paper presented at Annual meeting of the American Psychological Association, New York.

Buck, P. (1985). Adjusting to military life: The social sciences go to war. In Merritt Rose Smith (Ed), *Military enterprise and technological change: Perspectives on the American experience.* Cambridge, MA: MIT Press.

Burgess, A., & Holmstrom, L. L. (1974). Rape trauma syndrome. *American Journal of Psychiatry, 131* (9), 981–985.

Camacho, P. (1980). From war hero to criminal: The negative privilege of the Vietnam veterans. In C. R. Figley & S. Leventman (Eds.), *Strangers at home: Vietnam veterans since the war* (pp. 267–275). New York: Praeger.

Cantril, H., & Strunk, M. (1951). *Public opinion 1935–1946.* New Jersey: Princeton University Press.

Card, J. (1983). *Lives after Vietnam.* Lexington, MA D.C. Heath.

Carveth, W. B., & Gottlieb, B. H. (1979). The measurement of social support and its relation to stress. *Canadian Journal of Behavioral Science, 11,* 179-186.

Cassel, J. (1974). Psychosocial processes and stress: Theoretical formulation. *International Journal of Health Services, 4,* 471-482.

Christian, D. (1981, September). A Vietnam hero finds the real war is on the home front. *People* pp. 49-50.

Clemons, N. L. (1970, February 25). Johnny marches home 1970 style. *Wall Street Journal,* p. 22.

Cobb, S. (1976). Social support as a moderator of life stress. *Psychosomatic Medicine, 38,* 300-314.

Cohen, S., & Syme, L. (1984). *Social support and health.* New York: Academic Press.

Crowne, D., & Marlowe, D. (1964). *The approval motive.* New York: Wiley.

Dasberg, H. (1982). Belonging and loneliness in relation to mental breakdown in battle. In C. D. Spielberger, I. G. Sarason & N. A. Milgram (Eds.), *Stress and anxiety* (pp. 142-150). New York: Hemisphere Press.

DeFazio, V. J., Rustin, S., & Diamond, A. (1975). Symptom development in Vietnam era veterans. *American Journal of Orthopsychiatry, 45,* 158-163.

de S Poole, I., & Kochen, M. (1978). Contacts and Influence. *Social Networks, 1,* 5-52.

Dohrenwend, B. P. (1977) Social Psychiatry Research Unit. *Appendix I to the measurement of psychopathology: The Psychiatry Epidemiology Research Interview. A report on twenty-two scales.* Unpublished memorandum.

Dohrenwend, B. P. (1979). Stressful life events ad psychopathology: Some issues of theory and method. In J. E. Barrett (Ed.), *Stress and Mental Disorder.* New York: Raven Press.

Dohrenwend, B. P., & Dohrenwend, B. S. (1965). The problem of validity in field studies of psychiatric disorder. *Journal of Abnormal Psychology, 70* (1), 52-89.

Dohrenwend, B. P., & Dohrenwend, B. S. (1976). Sex differences and psychiatric disorders. *American Journal of Sociology, 81,* 1447-1454.

Dohrenwend, B. P., Oksenberg, L., Shrout, P. E., Dohrenwend, B. S., & Cook, D. (1981). What brief psychiatric screening scales measure. In S. Sudman (Ed.), *Proceedings of the Third Biennial Conference on Health Survey Research methods* (pp. 188-198). Washington, DC: NCHS.

Dohrenwend, B. P., Shrout, P. E., Egri, G., & Mendelsohn, F. (1980). Measures of nonspecific psychological distress and other dimensions of psychopathology in the general population. *Archives of General Psychiatry, 37,* 1229-1236.

Dorpalen, A. (1964). *Hindenburg and the Weimar Republic.* Princeton, NJ: Princeton University Press.

Eaton, W. W. (1978). Life events, social supports and psychiatric symptoms: A re-analysis of the New Haven data. *Journal of Health and Social Behavior, 19,* 230-234.

Egendorf, A. (1975). Vietnam veterans, rap groups and themes of postwar life. *Journal of Social Issues, 31,* 111-124.

Egendorf, A. *Legacies in Vietnam* (1981). Vol. IV Dealing with the war: A view based on the individual lives of Vietnam veterans. Washington, DC: US Government Printing Office.

Egendorf, A., Kadushin, C., Laufer, R. S., Rothbart, G., & Sloan, L. (1981). *Legacies of Vietnam* Vol. I Summary of findings. Washington, DC: US Government Printing Office.

Eisenhart, R. (1975). You can't hack it little girl: A discussion of the covert psychological agenda of modern combat training. *Journal of Social Issues, 31,* 13-23.

Eitinger, L. (1980). The concentration camp syndrome and its later sequelae. In J. Dimsdale (Ed.), *Survivors, victims and perpetrators* New York: Hemispheric Publishing.

Erikson, K. (1976). *Everything in its path: Destruction of community in the Buffalo Creek flood.* New York: Simon & Schuster.

Fairbairn, W. R. D. (1952). *Psychoanalytic studies of the personality.* London: Routledge, Keegan Paul.

Faris, J. (1977). An alternative perspective to Savage and Gabriel. *Armed Forces and Society, 3,* 457–462.

Figley, C. R. (1978). *Stress disorders among Vietnam veterans: Theory, research and treatment.* New York: Brunner/Mazel.

Figley, C. R., & Eisenhart, W. (1975, August). *Contrasts between combat and non-combat: Vietnam veterans regarding selected indices of interpersonal adjustment.* Paper presented at American Sociological Association, San Francisco.

Figley, C. R., & Leventman, S. (1980). *Strangers at home: Vietnam veterans since the war.* New York: Praeger.

Fine, M., Rothbart, G., & Sudman, S. (1979). *On finding the needle in the haystack: Multiplicity sampling procedures.* Paper presented at American Association for Public Opinion Research meeting, Buck Hills.

Fischer, C. S., Jackson, R. M., Steuve, C. A., Gerson, K., Jones, L. M., & Baldassare, M. (1977). *Networks and places.* New York: Free Press.

Ford, C., & Spaulding, R. (1973). The Pueblo incident: A comparison of factors related to coping with extreme stress. *Archives of General Psychiatry, 29,* 340–343.

Frank, J. D. (1973). *Persuasion and healing.* Baltimore: Johns Hopkins University Press.

Frank, J. D. (1974). Psychotherapy: The restoration of morale. *American Journal of Psychiatry, 32,* 230–233.

Frazier, P., & Borgida, E. (September, 1985). Rape trauma syndrome evidence in court. *American Psychologist, 40,* (9).

Frye, J. S., & Stockton, R. A. (1982). Discriminant analysis of post-traumatic stress disorder among a group of Vietnam veterans. *American Journal of Psychiatry, 139,* 52–56.

Furlong, W. B. (1967, May 7). The re-entry problem of the Vietvets. *New York Times Magazine,* p. 23.

Futterman, S., & Pumpian-Mindlin, E. (1951). Traumatic war neuroses for five years later. *Journal of Psychiatry, 108,* 401.

Gates, T. (1970). *The report of the president's commission on all volunteer armed forces.* New York: MacMillan.

Gault, W. (1971). Some remarks on slaughter. *American Journal of Psychiatry, 128,* 450–454.

George, A. L. (1971). Primary groups, organization, and military performance. In R. W. Little (Ed.), *Handbook of military institutions* (pp. 293–319). Beverly Hills, CA: Sage.

Goodwin, D. W., Davis, D. H., & Robins, L. N. (1975). Drinking amid abundant illicit drugs: The Vietnam case. *Archives of General Psychiatry, 32* (2), 230–233.

Gore, S. (1978). The effect of social support on moderating the health consequences of unemployment. *Journal of Health and Social Behavior, 19,* 157–165.

Gore, S. (1981). Stress-buffering functions of social supports; An appraisal and clarification of research models. In B. S. Dohrenwend & B. P. Dohrenwend (Eds.), *Stressful life events and their contexts* (pp. 202–222). New York: Prodist.

Gottlieb, B. H. (1981). *Social networks and social support.* Beverly Hills, CA: Sage.

Gove, W. R. (1972). The relationship between sex roles, marital status, and mental illness. *Social Forces, 51,* 34–44.

Gove, W. R. (1973). Sex, marital status and mortality. *American Journal of Sociology, 79,* 45–67.

Grannovetter, M. (1973). The strength of weak ties. *American Journal of Sociology, 78,* 1360–1380.

Green, B., Grace, M., Lindy, J., & Titchener (1983). Levels of functional impairment following a civilian disaster: The Beverly Hills Supper Club fire. *Journal of Consulting and Clinical Psychiatry, 51* (4), 573–580.

Gregory, S. W. (1977). Toward an actuated description of cohesion and disintegration in the American army. *Armed Forces and Society, 3,* 463–473.

Grinker, R. R., & Spiegel, J. P. (1945). *Men under stress.* Philadelphia: Blakiston.

Gurin, G., Veroff, J., & Feld, S. (1960). *Americans view their mental health*. New York: Basic Books.

Haley, S. (1978). Treatment implications of post-combat stress response syndromes for mental health professionals. In C. Figley (Ed.), *Stress disorders among Vietnam veterans* (pp. 254–267). New York: Brunner/Mazel.

Hare, P. A. (1976). *Handbook of small group research*. New York: Free Press.

Harris, L. (1980). *Myths and realities: A study of attitudes toward Vietnam era veterans*. Washington, DC: Veterans Administration, Senate Committee.

Hayes, J. R. (1975). The dialectics of resistance: An analysis of the GI movement. *Journal of Social Issues, 31*, 125–139.

Helmer, J. (1974). *Bringing the war home: The American soldier before Vietnam and after*. New York: Free Press.

Helzer, J. E. (1983). Methodological issues in the interpretation of the consequences of extreme situations. In B. P. Dohrenwend & B. S. Dorhenwend (Eds.), *Stressful life events and their contexts*. New York: Neale Watson.

Helzer, J. E., Robins, L. N., Wish, E., & Hesselbrock, M. (1979). Depression in Vietnam veterans and civilian controls. *American Journal of Psychiatry, 136*, 526–529.

Helzer, J. E., Robins, L. N., Davis,. (1976). Depressive disorders in Vietnam returnees. *Journal of Nervous and Mental Disease, 163*, 177–185

Henderson, S. (1980). A development in social psychiatry: The systematic study of social bonds. *Journal of Nervous and Mental Disorders, 168*, 63–69.

Henderson, S., Byrne, D. G., & Duncan-Jones, P. (1981). *Neurosis and the social environment*. New York: Academic Press.

Hocking, F. (1970). Extreme environmental stress and its significance for psychopathology. *American Journal of Psychotherapy, 24*, 4–26.

Horowitz, M. (1976). *Stress response syndromes*. New York: Aronson.

Horowitz, M., & Solomon, G. (1978). Delayed stress response syndromes in Vietnam veterans. In C. Figley (Ed.), *Stress disorders among Vietnam veterans* (pp. 268–280). New York: Brunner/Mazel.

Horowitz, M. J., Wilner, N., & Alvarez, W. (1979). Impact of event scale: A measure of subjective stress. *Psychosomatic Medicine, 41*, 209–218.

Horowitz, M. J., Wilner, N., Kaltreider, N., & Alvarez, W. (1980). Signs and symptoms of posttraumatic stress disorder. *Archives of General Psychiatry, 37*, 209–218.

Houland, K. I., Lumsdaine, A. A., & Sheffield, F. D. (1949). *Experiments in mass communication. Studies in social psychology in World War II*. Volume III. Princeton: Princeton University Press.

Ingraham, L. H. (1974). The Nam and the world: A description of heroin use by the US army enlisted men serving in the Republic of South Vietnam. *Psychiatry, 37*, 114–128.

Jennings, M. K., & Markus, G. C. (1977). The effect of military service on political attitudes: A panel study. *American Political Science Review, 71*, 131–147.

Johns, J. H. (1983, April). *The changing nature of the American military and its impact on cohesion*. Paper presented to the Northeast Region Interuniversity Seminar on Armed Forces and Society.

Johnson, L. (1980). Scars of war: Alienation and estrangement among wounded Vietnam veterans. In C. R. Figley & S. Leventman (Eds.), *Strangers at home: Vietnam veterans since the war* (pp. 213–227). New York: Praeger.

Kadushin, C. (1966). The friends and supporters of psychotherapy On social circles in urban life. *American Sociological Review, 31*, 786–802.

Kadushin, C. (1969). *Why people go to psychiatrists*. New York: Atherton.

Kadushin, C. (1982). Social density and mental health. In P. Marsden & N. Lin (Eds.), *Social structure and network analysis* (pp.147–158). Beverly Hills, CA: Sage.

Kadushin, C. (1983a). Mental health and the interpersonal environment: A re-examination of some effects of social structure on mental health. *American Sociological Review, 48,* 188–198.

Kadushin, C. (1983b). Networking: No panacea. *Social Policy, 13,* 59–60.

Kadushin, C. G., Boulanger, G., & Martin, J. (1981). Long term stress reactions: Some causes, consequences, and naturally occurring support systems. In *Legacies of Vietnam: Comparative adjustment of veterans and their peers, a study prepared for the Veterans Administration* (pp. 475–706). Washington, DC: US Government Printing Office.

Kaplan, B. H., Cassell, J. C., & Gore, S. (1977). Social support and health. *Medical Care, 15,* 47–57.

Kaplan, H. B., Robbins, C., & Martin, S. S. (1983). Antecedents of psychological distress in young adults: Self-rejection, deprivation of social support, and life events. *Journal of Health and Social Behavior, 24,* 230–243.

Kardiner, A. (1969). Traumatic neuroses of war. In S. Arieti (Ed.), *American Handbook of Psychiatry.* New York: Basic Books.

Keane, T. & Fairbank, J. (1983). Survey analysis of combat-related stress disorders in Vietnam Veterans. *American Journal of Psychiatry, 140,* 348–350

Kessler, R. C., & Essex, M. (1982). Marital status and depression: The importance of coping resources. *Social Forces, 61,* 484–507.

Klonoff, H., McDougall, G., Clark, C., Kramer, P., & Horgan, J. (1976). The neuro-psychological, psychiatric and physical effects of prolonged and severe stress: 30 years later. *Journal of Nervous and Mental Disease, 163.*

Knox, D. (1984, June 24). A war from all sides [review of *Longtime Passing,* by Myra MacPherson]. *New York Times Book Review,* p. 20.

Kobasa, S., & Puccetti, M. (1983). Personality and social resources in stress resistance. *Journal of Personality and Social Psychology, 45* (4), 839–850.

Komarovsky, M. (1974). Patterns of self disclosure of male undergraduates. *Journal of Marriage and the Family, 36,* (4), 677–686.

Krystal, I. (1968). *Massive psychic trauma.* New York: IUP.

Lacoursiere, R. B., Godfrey, K. E., & Ruby, L. M. (1980). Traumatic neurosis in the etiology of alcoholism: Vietnam combat and other trauma. *American Journal of Psychiatry, 137,* 966–968.

LaGuardia, R. L., Smith, G., Francois, R., & Bachman, L. (1983). Incidence of delayed stress disorder among Vietnam era veterans: The effect of priming on response set. *American Journal of Orthopsychiatry, 53,* 18–26.

Lang, K. (1980). American military performance in Vietnam: Background and analysis. *Journal of Political and Military Sociology, 8,* 269–286.

LaRocco, J. M., House, J. S., & French, J. R. (1980). Social support, occupational stress, and health. *Journal of Health and Social Behavior, 21,* 202–208.

Laufer, R. S., Yager, T., Frey-Wouters, E., & Donnellan, J. (1981). *Legacies of Vietnam.* Vol. III Postwar trauma; Social and psychological problems of Vietnam veterans in the aftermath of the Vietnam war. Washington, DC: US Government Printing Office.

Lazarsfeld, P. (1949). "The American Soldier": A review. *Public Opinion Quarterly.*

Leavy, R. L. (1983). Social support and psychological disorder: A review. *Journal of Community Psychology, 11,* 1–.

Levy, C. J. (1973). *Spoils of war.* Boston: Houghton-Mifflin.

Lifton, R. J. (1973). *Home from the war.* New York: Simon & Schuster.

Lin, N., Simeone, R. S., Ensel, W. M., & Kuo, W. (1979). Social support, stressful life events, and illness: A model and an empirical test. *Journal of Health and Social Behavior, 20,* 108–119.

Lipkin, J. O., Blank, A. S., Parson, E. R., & Smith, J. (1982). Vietnam veterans and post-traumatic stress disorder. *Hospital and Community Psychiatry, 33* (11), 908–912.

Little, R. W. (1964). Buddy relations and combat performance. In M. Janovitz (Ed.), *The new military: Patterns of changing organization* (pp. 195–223). New York: Russell Sage.

Litwak, E. (1979). *Support networks and the disabled: The transition from the community to the institutional setting.* Paper presented at meeting of Gerontological Society, Washington, DC.

Litwak, E., & Szelenyi, I. (1969). Primary structures and their functions: Kin, neighbors, and friends. *American Sociological Review, 34,* 465-481.

Lowenthal, M. F., & Haven, C. (1968). Interaction and adaption: Intimacy as a critical variable. *American Sociological Review, 33,* 20-30.

Malloy, P. F., Fairbank, J. A., & Keane, T. M. (1983). Validation of a multimethod assessment of PTSD in Vietnam veterans. *Journal of Consulting and Clinical Psychiatry, 51* (4), 488-494.

Marin, P. (1981, Nov.). Living in moral pain. *Psychology Today,* pp. 68-69.

Marlowe, D. H. (1982). *Cohesion, anticipated breakdown, and endurance in battle: Considerations for severe and high intensity combat.* Washington, DC: Army Institute for Research.

Marshall, S. L. A. (1947). *Men against fire.* New York: Morrow.

Martin, J. L. (1981). *The effects of partner support and peer support on psychological demoralization: A comparative analysis of young adult men and their Vietnam veteran peers.* Unpublished doctoral dissertation, Graduate Center of CUNY.

Martin, R. (1983). *The professional army and military labor: The battle for internal control.* Paper presented at Eastern Sociological Society Annual Meeting, Boston.

McAllister, L., & Fischer, C. S. (1978). A procedure for surveying personal networks. *Sociological Methods and Research, 7,* 131-148.

McCoy, A. W. (1972). *The politics of heroin in Southeast Asia.* New York: Harper & Row.

McFarlane, A. H., Neale, K. A., Norman, G. R., Roy, R. G., & Streiner, D. L. (1981). Methodological issues in developing a scale to measure social support. *Schizophrenia Bulletin, 7,* 90-100.

Mechanic, D. (1978). Sex, illness, illness behavior and the use of health services. *Social Science and Medicine, 12,* 207-214.

Merbaum, M., & Hefez, A. (1976). Some personality characteristics of soldiers exposed to extreme war stress. *Journal of Consulting and Clinical Psychology, 44* (1), 1-6.

Merton, R. K., & Lazarsfeld, P. F., (Eds) (1950). *Continuities in social research: Studies in the scope and method of "The American Soldier".* Glencoe, IL: Free Press.

Michael, L. M. (1980). *An investigation of the substance use behavior of men of the Vietnam era generation.* Unpublished doctoral dissertation, Teachers College, Columbia University.

Moskos, Jr, C. C. (1970). *The American enlisted man: The rank and file in today's military.* New York: Russell Sage.

Moskos, Jr, C. C. (1975). The American combat soldier in Vietnam. *Journal of Social Issues, 31,* 25-37.

Murdock, E. C., (1967). *Patriotism limited: 1862-1865. The Civil War draft and the bounty system.* Kent, OH: Kent State University Press.

Murdock, E. C., (1971). *One million men: The Civil War draft in the North.* Worcester, MA: Hoffernan Press Inc.

Nace, E. P., O'Brien, C. O., Mintz, J. M., Ream, N., & Meyers, A. L. (1978). Adjustment among Vietnam veteran drug users two years post service. In C. R. Figley (Ed.), *Stress disorders among Vietnam veterans* (pp. 71-128). New York: Brunner/Mazel.

Nelson, P. D., & Berry, N. H. (1968). Cohesion in Maine recruit platoons. *Journal of Psychology, 68,* 63-71.

Nuckolls, K. B., Cassel, J., & Kaplan, H. B. (1972). Psychosocial assets, life crises and the prognosis of pregnancy. *American Journal of Epidemiology, 95,* 431-441.

Olstad, K. (1975). Brave new men: A basis for discussion. In J. W. Petras (Ed.), *Readings in male sexuality* (pp. 160-178). Port Washington, NY: Alfred.

Panzarella, R., Mantell, D., & Bridenbaugh, R. (1978). Psychiatric syndromes, self-concepts, and Vietnam veterans. In C. R. Figley (Ed.), *Stress disorders among Vietnam veterans* (pp. 148-172). New York: Brunner/Mazel.

Parsons, E. R. (1982). The reparation of the self: Clinical and theoretical dimensions in the treatment of Vietnam combat veterans. *Journal of Contemporary Psychotherapy, 14* (1), 4–56.

Penk, W. E., Robinowitz, R., Roberts, W. R., Patterson, E. T., Dolan, M. P., & Atkins, H. G. (1981). Adjustment differences among male substance abusers varying in degree of combat experience in Vietnam. *Journal of Consulting and Clinical Psychology, 49,* 426–437.

Phillips, S. L., & Fischer, C. S. (1981). Measuring social support networks in general populations. In B. S. Dohrenwend & B. P. Dorhenwend (Eds.), *Stressful life events and their contexts* (pp. 223–233). New York: Prodist.

Pilisuk, M. (1975). The legacy of the Vietnam veterans. *Journal of Social Issues, 31,* 3–12.

Pollock, J., White, D., & Gold, F. (1975). When soldiers return: Combat and political alienation among white Vietnam veterans. In D. Schwartz & S. Schwartz (Eds.), *New directions in political socialization* (pp. 317–333). New York: Free Press.

Polner, M. (1971). *No victory parades.* New York: Holt, Rinehart & Winston.

Postel, E. B. (1968). Marijuana use in Vietnam: A preliminary report. *USARV Medical Bulletin, PAM4D11,* 26–59.

Ricks, D., & Berry, J. (1970). Family and symptom patterns that precede schizophrenia. In M. Roff & D. F. Ricks (Eds.), *Life history research in psychopathology.* Minneapolis: University of Minnesota Press.

Rindskopf, D., Kadushin, C., & Boulanger, G. (1984). *Using latent class analysis to validate psychiatric diagnosis.* Unpublished manuscript.

Roberts, W., Penk, W., Robinowitz, W., Dolan, M., Gearing, M., & Patterson,E. (1982). Interpersonal problems of Vietnam combat veterans with symptoms of posttraumatic stress disorder. *Journal of Abnormal Psychology, 91,* 444–450.

Robins, L. N. (1970). Antecedents of character disorder. In *Life history research in psychopathology.* Minneapolis: University of Minnesota Press.

Robins, L. N. (1974). *The Vietnam drug user returns* (Special Action Office Monograph). Washington, DC: US Government Printing Office.

Robins, L. N. (1978). The interaction of setting and predisposition in explaining novel behavior: Drug initiations before, in, and after Vietnam. In D. Kandel (Ed.), *Longitudinal research on drug use* (pp. 179–196). Washington, DC: Hemisphere Publishing.

Robins, L. N., Helzer, J. D., Hesselbrock, M., & Wish, E. D. (1977). Vietnam veterans three years after Vietnam: How our study changed our view of heroin. In L. Brill & C. Winick (Eds.), *Yearbook of substance use and abuse* (pp. 213–230). New York: Human Sciences Press.

Robins, L. N., Helzer, J. E., & Davis, D. N. (1975). Narcotic use in Southeast Asia and afterward: An interview study of 898 Vietnam returnees. *Archives of General Psychiatry, 32,* 955–961.

Rohrbaugh, M., Eads, G., & Press, S. (1974). Effects of the Vietnam experience on subsequent drug use among servicemen. *International Journal of the Addictions, 9,* 25–40.

Role of VA reassessed in clash on major policy, (1977, April 14). *New York Times,* p. 1.

Rossi, P. W. (1966). Research strategies in measuring peer group influence. In T. M. Newcomb & E. K. Wilson (Eds.), *College peer groups* (pp. 190–214). Chicago: Aldine.

Rothbart, G., Sloan, L., & Joyce, K. (1981). *Legacies of Vietnam.* Vol. II Educational and work careers: Men in the Vietnam generation. Washington, DC: US Government Printing Office.

Sanders, C. R. (1973). Doper's Wonderland: Functional drug use by military personnel in Vietnam. *Journal of Drug Issues, 3,* 65–78.

Sarason, I. (1985). *Social support: Theory, research and applications.* The Hague.

Savage, P., & Gabriel, R. D. (1976). Cohesion and disintegration in the American army. *Armed Forces and Society, 2,* 340–376.

Schulman, N. (1972). Network analysis: A new addition to an old bag of tricks. *Acta Sociologica, 19,* 307–323.

Segal, D. R., & Segal, M. W. (1976). The impact of military service on trust in government, international attitudes, and social status. In (Ed.), *The social psychology of military service* (pp. 201-211). Beverly Hills,CA: Sage.

Senter, M. S. (1983). *Civil-military integration and civilian control: A test of Janowitz's model.* Unpublished manuscript.

Shatan, C. (1973). Soldiers in mourning: Vietnam veterans' self help groups. *American Journal of Orthopsychiatry, 42,* 300-301.

Shatan, C. (1978). Stress disorders among Vietnam veterans: The emotional context of combat continues. In C. R. Figley (Ed.), *Stress disorders among Vietnam veterans* (pp. 43-53). New York: Brunner/Mazel.

Shils, E. A. (1950). Primary groups in the America army. In R. K. Merton & R. F. Lazarsfeld (Eds.), *Continuities in social research: Studies in the scope and method of the American soldier* (pp. 16-39). Glencoe, IL: Free Press.

Shils, E. A., & Janowitz, M. (1948). Cohesion and disintegration in the Wehrmacht in World War II. *Public Opinion Quarterly, 12,* 280-315.

Shirom, A. (1976). On some correlates of combat performance. *Administrative Science Quarterly, 21,* 419-432.

Sierles, F. S., Chen, J. J., McFarland, R. E., & Taylor, M. A. (1983). Posttraumatic stress disorder and concurrent psychiatric illness: A preliminary report. *American Journal of Psychiatry, 140.*

Simmel, G. (1955). *Conflict & the web of group affiliations.* New York: Free Press.

Smith, J. R. (1981). *A review of 120 years of psychological literature on reaction to combat from the Civil War through the Vietnam War, 1860-1980.* Unpublished manuscript, Duke University

Smith, J. R. (1985). Rap groups and group therapy. In S. M. Sonnenberg, A. S. Blank Jr & J. Talbott (Eds.), *Psychiatric problems of Vietnam veterans.* Washington, DC: American Psychiatric Press.

Smith, R. B. (1971). Disaffection, delegitimation, and consequences aggregate trends for World War II, Korea, and Vietnam. In C. Moskos (Ed.), *Public opinion and the military establishment.* Beverly Hills, CA: Sage.

Social issues: Returning heroes get the cold shoulder (1971, July 31). *Business Week,* pp. 46-48.

Sosa, R., Kennel, J., Klaus, M., Robertson, S., & Arretia, J. (1980). The effect of a supportive companion on prenatal problems, length of perinatal labor, and mother-infant interaction. *The New England Journal of Medicine,303,* 597-600.

Special report: What Vietnam did to us. (1981, December 14). *Newsweek,* pp. 46-52.

Stanton, M. D. (1976). Drugs, Vietnam, and the Vietnam veteran: An overview. *American Journal of Drug and Alcohol Abuse, 3,* 557-510.

Steiner, M., & Neumann, M. (1978). Traumatic neuroses and social support in the Yom Kippur war returnees. *Military medicine, 142 (12),* 866-868.

Stouffer, S. (1950a). *Measurement and prediction. studies in social psychology in World War II.* Volume IV. Princeton: Princeton University Press.

Stouffer, S. (1950b). Some afterthoughts of a contributor to "The American Soldier." In Merton, R. K., & Lazarsfeld, P. F., *Continuities in Social Research: Studies in the scope and method of "The American Soldier"* (197-212). Glencoe, IL: Free Press.

Stouffer, S., Lumsdaine, A., Lumsdaine, M., Williams Jr, R., Smith, M., Janis, I., Star, S., & Cottrell, L. (1949). *The American soldier: Combat and its aftermath.* Princeton: Princeton University Press.

Stouffer, S., Suchman, E., DeVinney, L., Star, S., & Williams Jr, R. (1949). *The American soldier: Adjustment during army life.* Princeton: Princeton University Press.

Strange, R., & Brown, D. (1970). Home from the war: A study of psychiatric problems in Vietnam returnees. *American Journal of Psychiatry, 127,* 488-492.

Strayer, R., & Ellenhorn, L. (1975). Vietnam veterans: A study exploring adjustment patterns and attitudes. *Journal of Social Issues, 3,* 81–94.

Surrey, D. (1982). *Choice of conscience: Vietnam era military and draft evaders in Canada.* New York: Praeger Publications.

Swank, R. L. (1949). Combat exhaustion: A descriptive and statistic alanalysis of causes, symptoms and signs. *Journal of Nervous and Mental Disease, 109,* 475–508.

Symonds, M. (1980). The "second injury" to victims. *Evaluation and Change,* Special Issue, 36–38

Thoits, P. A. (1982). Conceptual, methodological and theoretical problems in studying social support as a buffer against life stress. *Journal of Health and Social Behavior, 23,* 145–158.

Tischler, G. L. (1969). Patterns of psychiatric attrition and of behavior in a combat zone. In P. Bourne (Ed.), *The psychology and physiology of stress.* New York: Academic Press

Turner, R. J., & Noh, S. (1983). Class and psychological vulnerability among women: The significance of social support and personal control. *Journal of Health and Social Behavior, 24,* 2–15.

Tziner, A., & Vardi, Y. (1982). Effects of command style and group cohesiveness on the performance effectiveness of self-selected tank crews. *Journal of Applied Psychology, 67,* 769–775.

U. S. Bureau of the Census (1975). *Statistical abstract of the United States 196th Annual Edition.* Washington, DC: US Government Printing Office.

U. S. 97th Congress, 1st Session House Committee (1981). *Legacies of Vietnam Comparative adjustment of veterans and their peers.* Washington, DC: US Government Printing Office.

Veroff, J., Douvan, E., & Kulka, R. A. (1981). *The inner American: A self-portrait from 1957–1976.* New York: Basic Books.

Veroff, J., Kulka, R. A., & Douvan, E. (1981). *Mental health in America: Patterns of help seeking from 1957–1976.* New York: Basic Books.

Weisaeth, L. (1983). *PTSD After an industrial disaster: Point prevalences, etiological and prognostic factors.* Vienna: Paper VII World Congress of Psychology.

Wellman, B. (1979). The community question: The intimate network of East Yorkers. *American Journal of Sociology, 84,* 1202–1231.

Wilbur, R. S. (1974). The battle against drug dependency within the military. *Journal of Drug Issues, 4,* 11–31.

Williams, C. (1983). The mental foxhole: The Vietnam veteran's search for meaning. *American Journal of Orthopsychiatry, 53,* 4–17.

Williams, T. (1980). *Post-traumatic stress disorders of the Vietnam veteran.* Cincinnati, OH: Disabled American Veterans.

Wittner, L. (1969). *Rebels against war: The American peace movement, 1941–1960.* New York: Columbia University Press.

Wolf, S., & Ripley, H. (1947). Reactions among allied POWs subjected to three years of imprisonment and torture by the Japanese. *American Journal of Psychiatry, 104,* 180–193.

Worthington, R. E. (1978). Demographic and pre-service variables as predictors of postmilitary service adjustment. In C. R. Figley (Ed.), *Stress disorders among Vietnam veterans* (pp. 173–187). New York: Brunner/Mazel.

Wortman, C. B. (1984). Social support and the cancer patient. In American Cancer Society, *Proceedings of the Working conference on methodology in behavior and psychosocial cancer research, April 21-23, 1983* (pp. 2217–2384). New York: Lippincott.

Yager, J. (1976). Postcombat violent behavior in psychiatrically maladjusting soldiers. *Archives of General Psychiatry, 33,* 1332–1335.

Zinberg, N. E. (1972). Heroin use in Vietnam and the United States. *Archives of General Psychiatry, 26,* 480–488.

Author Index

Numbers in *italics* denote pages with bibliographic information.

Subject Index